RELIGIOUS LIFE

The Challenge of Tomorrow

Edited by
Cassian J. Yuhaus, CP, HED

Preface by
Barbara Lawler Thomas, SCN

PAULIST PRESS
New York, NY ● Mahwah, NJ

255.04
Yuc

Library of Congress Cataloging-in-Publication Data

Religious life: the challenge of tomorrow / edited by Cassian J. Yuhaus; preface by Barbara Lawler Thomas.
    p. cm.
Includes bibliographical references.
ISBN 0-8091-3476-4
1. Monastic and religious life. 2. Sociology, Christian (Catholic) I. Yuhaus, Cassian J.
BX2435.R428   1994
255—dc20   94-1893
                                                                            CIP

Published by Paulist Press
997 Macarthur Boulevard
Mahwah, New Jersey 07430

Printed and bound in the
United States of America

Contents

DEDICATION

TO
THE OUTSTANDING SCHOLARS
MY DEAR FRIENDS
WHO
MADE THIS WORK POSSIBLE
AND
TO ALL WHO ARE CONCERNED
ABOUT
WHERE WE ARE GOING

Preface

Barbara Lawler Thomas, SCN

Many indications in this era of change serve as a keen reminder that at no time in the history of the life and mission of religious congregations has there been a clearer call to responsibility in shaping the nature of what we refer to today as The Future Religious Life. Fidelity to history, to tradition and to charism have consistently served as criteria for decision making in the past twenty-five years of renewal. For direction during this present time of even more rapid change, attentiveness to the signs of the times and to the social needs of the day is without question necessary for strategic planning for the future.

As women and men religious, our stories have been told over and over during this post-Vatican II period. Our past is consistently reenacted as we struggle to plan wisely for the future of our life and mission. The call, yet to be heeded by many, is one that goes far beyond providing for our own present and near-future needs. It is a challenge to serious corporate effort to ensure that in the future there will be that life which we call religious.

The model established for communities on the American frontier in the early 1800s was not necessarily designed as "a form of religious life." Without precedent on American soil, however, that same model has served church and society as such from its beginning. Seeds were planted; the soil was nurtured. Newness came to this primitive land. Sensitive to the needs of the community in their midst, women and men responded to the signs of their day. Theirs was a prophetic stance. Animated by the Spirit theirs was a virtual witness to the gospel of Jesus Christ.

Almost two hundred years later, within the context of the pages which follow, there is an explicit invitation to come and do likewise. The essays which follow are highly reflective of religious life as a challenge which invites us to go beyond the borders of the past twenty-five years of renewal, beyond what constitutes our reality as women and men religious today. The creative approach to this work, derived primarily from a shared experience on the occasion of the twenty-fifth Anniversary of the Passionist Institutes on Religious Life, bids us focus on the necessity of a shared vision, without which future religious life will hardly emerge.

1

The scholarship, as well as the experience and the gifts of the various presenters, testifies to a common spirit of hope, that hope which is rooted in faith and in a determination not to be gripped by fear, nor blocked by overwhelming obstacles. I personally share the hope of the editor that this publication, which marks the beginning of a dialogue, may be also the means of increased hope. Out of this hope the articulation of a shared vision may be born.

In spite of the demands on religious congregations during the post-Vatican renewal years, inspired creativity among women and men has flourished, especially among those specifically engaged in shared efforts to further the mission of the church. The contents of this publication witness to this gift. Feminist theological scholarship, which is becoming more dominant among women religious scholars, speaks to the gift of prophecy and witnesses to the gospel through the use of personal gifts for the good of all concerned.

The contributions of the authors embody challenge. Their willingness to share knowledge and scholarship, as well as personal sacred history, gives promise of movement toward a shared vision out of which may well rise a new model for the future. This we must believe.

Some years ago Bruggemann declared that the American church was so greatly enculturated to the ethos of consumerism that it had little power to believe or to act.[1] The implications of this bleak message can be very threatening to us even today. On the other hand, there are signs on the horizon which indicate that there are women and men among us who do believe and who do act. Pertinent data to this effect are evidenced in this volume.

Lest we tend to experience ourselves beyond Bruggemann's admonition, however, excerpts from meditations of Teilhard de Chardin may give us reason to pause as we reflect on our own personal experience:

How can it be
that "when I come down from the mountain"
and in spite of the glorious vision I still retain,
I find that I am so little better a person,
    so little at peace,
so incapable of expressing in my actions,
and thus adequately communicating to others,
    the wonderful unity that I feel encompassing me?

I began to think that most of our weaknesses
are due to the fact that our "belief" is too narrow,
and that we don't believe through to the end.
To stop believing a second too soon,

or not to believe enough,
is sufficient to ruin the whole structure
   of what we are building.[2]

The authors who speak to us today in this collection of essays do not suggest that the future religious life is ours to design, but rather that in response to our common call to prophetic witness, it is ours to build. It is ours to plant seeds for what is to come, to read the signs of our times and to ponder the word of God in a spirit of hope for what the future holds for our world. In a word: It is ours to listen, to be still, to maintain a discerning stance and to move toward that vision which will lead to prophetic witness by all who are called.

For some these words may be unsettling. There are those for whom envisioning the future is neither inviting nor possible. For many, however, it is both inviting and possible.

Yet, two questions remain: What precisely will strengthen our belief? What will enable us to act?

This compendium of essays, designed to serve as a witness to the value of shared experience and shared faith, may well lead to strengthened belief and a willingness to act in new ways for those courageous enough to *Come and See.*

Notes

1. Walter Bruggemann, *The Prophetic Imagination* (Philadelphia: Fortress Press, 1978), p. 11.

2. Blanche Gallagher, *Meditations with Teilhard de Chardin* (Santa Fe: Bear and Company, 1988), pp.72-73.

Introduction

Cassian J. Yuhaus, CP, HED

No one seriously concerned about religious life, in whatever position in church or society, can afford to bypass these powerful reflections on our situation. The richness, originality and challenge of these research papers prompt an immediate response of confidence in the vitality and future of religious life.

It may be helpful to know a bit about their origin.

Since the awful mandate to renewal given to all religious at the close of the council by the great Pope Paul VI in 1966 (cf. *Ecclesiae Sanctae*), I have made the study of religious life my central concern. My work at the Center for Applied Research in the Apostolate (CARA) of Washington, D.C. and at the Institute for World Concerns of Duquesne University found its full flowering in the Ministry for Religious, Research and Consultancy to which I now dedicate all my energies. I have been privileged to walk alongside religious on every continent in every kind of predicament as together we searched out our responses to the mandate of 1966.

Through the generous collaboration of my Passionist brothers and sisters, my involvement early on took a very specific form in the establishment of the International Institute for Religious to which more that 20,000 religious responded over the decades.

When the time came to celebrate our twenty-fifth, I wrote to a group of outstanding scholars and asked them quite simply if they would contribute a research paper. The parameters were as simply stated:

"I am requesting you to prepare a research paper on the theme of our Institute:

Religious Life Today
The Continuing Journey
Vision and Hope

"You would serve our purpose well if you could concentrate on two principal points: The Present Moment and the Future.

5

"The Present Moment: what it contains, how we came to be where we are and where we came from.

"The Future: Share with us your insights, your vision and your hope. Tell us what you see as inevitable, as optional. What are the cautions and the hazards that we need to be aware of? Perhaps you can give us some recommendations.

"The particular perspective of your analysis will be based on your expertise and your personal experience. Some perspectives come readily to mind:

The theology of religious life yesterday, today and tomorrow
Transformations in mission and ministry
The centrality of contemplation and community, both lost and found or
    rediscovered
Religious in church and world of yesterday, today and tomorrow
Mutual relations: hierarchy, clergy and religious, male and female
'The poor' as the determinant factor of the religious ideal yesterday, today
    and tomorrow
Issues of authority and obedience and charism
Justice ministry and the ecology in relationship to cloister and obedience

"The possibilities are quite without limit. You alone can decide what is most in accord with your expertise and your experience. I hope personal experience will flow into your presentation."

I remain deeply impressed and somewhat overwhelmed by the care and concern given to my request in the preparation of these responses. Each scholar fully understood and accepted the challenge.

There are many other scholars who were prevented from responding because of pressing commitments. I wish to acknowledge my gratitude to them as well: Fr. Carroll Stuhlmueller, CP, Sr. Anne Kelly, CSJ, Henri Nouen, Fr. Ron Carrignan, OMI, Sr. Miriam T. McGinnis, Fr. John Coleman, SJ, Sr. Barbara Lawler Thomas, SCN, Sr. Joan Delaney, MM, Fr. Don Senior, CP and Sr. Agnes Hughes, IHM. Perhaps a second volume may contain their responses and several others who expressed a keen interest in this work.

It should be noted that each response is complete in itself. This was purposefully done in order to allow each researcher full freedom to address the issues, present and future, as perceived from one's particular vantage point in research and experience. Nonetheless, they are not disjointed. Several dominant convictions emerge.

Among these, permit me to suggest the following: The first is the conviction about the vitality and vigor of religious life today. Despite severe stress and strain from within as well as outside the church, extremely troublesome issues, the religious life today presents itself in the eyes of our respondents as very much alive, determined and committed. But this is chastened somewhat as it is coupled with an equally strong conviction of the ending of an era. Religious life, as we have known it in its counter-reformation expression, is ended. Religious life shall endure. Past forms, styles and expressions, medieval in origins and apologetically defensive in spirit, are gone. New forms, new styles, new and appropriate contemporary expression are emerging and must emerge. If these papers testify to anything, they testify to the purification of religious life and its re-emergence in a pristine, evangelical purity, more awesome than we had imagined, fearless and unreliant on external signs of privilege, status or prestige, whether hierarchic or civic in origin.

It has already been suggested—in fact, some communities have already implemented the idea that any one of these research papers would serve as an excellent preparation for assemblies and chapters. A further value is seen in their use as a resource to leadership. Nonetheless, the original intent is the strongest: to provide a challenge and a stimulus to all religious, female and male, to the hierarchy and the laity to look without flinching into the reality of our situation and not to hesitate to let go of the past and walk with conviction and courage toward that new and different future we are being called to pursue energetically and which these papers illumine considerably.

It remains to me to thank my colleagues and associates who made this excellent study possible. In the first place, to each of our contributors without whom nothing would have happened. To my Passionist sisters and brothers who support me all the day long. To the thousands of participants in the International Institute for Religious and to those communities who enabled me to work alongside them in the "adventure in grace" and "journey of hope." Finally, to my secretaries, especially the late Mrs. Florence Worocelo who was taken from us suddenly in the midst of preparation of the manuscripts. And to Fr. Kevin Lynch and Paulist Press, ever so encouraging and patient with me.

Long before publication, advance sales have been significant. I apologize for my delay in finalizing this work. I am certain that no one will be disappointed in the least. Each of us shall be enriched and all of us convinced of the permanence, the solidity, the value of religious life to the church and world of tomorrow.

Contemporary Religious Life:
Death or Transformation?

Sandra M. Schneiders, IHM

I. Introduction

No one who attends carefully to the present experience of religious life in North America can be entirely sanguine about its present or its future. Despite the celebratory character of this gathering (and certainly the twenty-five year work of the Institute for Religious is something to celebrate) we are all aware of the signs of diminishment that mark contemporary religious life: aging membership, decline in recruitment, dwindling financial resources in the face of relentlessly rising costs, loss of institutions, if we attend only to the material problems. When these are compounded by ecclesiastical harassment of individual members in their ministries and of congregations in their legitimate exercise of self-determination and by intense struggles within congregations over self-understanding and identity, the picture can look bleak indeed.

Some people confront these distressing data with a panic that is barely held at bay by reactive rigidity. Others take refuge in a fatalistic resignation expressed in a fatigued hope that the congregation will at least die with dignity. Still others try not to think about the situation and to get on with the day-to-day business of life and ministry while secretly hoping that they will not be the ones who finally have to turn out the lights.

Nevertheless, in the face of such indisputable cause for concern, other factors which suggest a different line of reflection seem to be at work among large numbers of religious, especially women. In the past few years I have been increasingly struck by two features of contemporary religious life that have puzzled and intrigued me. My data are not scientific. They are gleaned, however, from experience with a large number of individual religious, often in the context of spiritual direction or renewal work, and with religious congregations and their leaders, usually in the context of community events such as assemblies, workshops, and reflection weekends.

9

As I articulated this puzzling experience for myself my reflection became a bit clearer and I hesitantly shared it with several groups of religious. I gave a very short presentation on the subject to the sisters of the diocese of Oakland, California during a Sisters' Day of Reflection in the fall of 1990 and was surprised at the depth of response it elicited. In 1991 I hinted at the same material in a ten-minute contribution to a videotape designed for use in my own congregation, and that same year I gave a fuller presentation to a group of religious from a number of congregations at Maria Center in St. Louis. On both occasions I was again surprised by the resonance the material evoked in the experience of the participants. In January of 1992 I developed the reflections into a more coherent presentation as part of a weekend seminar that I gave for several hundred religious in New Zealand. Congregational leaders and sisters overwhelmingly agreed that that presentation, among the four in the seminar, was the most useful for their individual and communal reflection. I mention this history by way of saying that, on the one hand, these reflections are based on my own experience rather than on anything that has been or perhaps can be established by objective research, but, on the other hand, they seem to resonate with the experience of many other religious in a variety of congregations here and abroad.

Consequently, when I was invited to participate in this Anniversary Institute I decided to try to put the reflections in publishable form, and that effort is what I offer you today in hopes that your reflections will confirm or correct, challenge and enrich my own.

II. Features of the Contemporary Experience of Religious Life

The two features of our recent experience as religious that have precipitated my reflections are the following: first, a paradox and second, a malaise. First, it seems extremely *paradoxical* that, on the one hand, religious congregations are exhibiting all of the sociological characteristics of declining institutions, and, on the other hand, they are not exhibiting the attitudes and behaviors that such decline usually precipitates.[1] Organizations predictably follow a life cycle of emergence, growth and expansion, decline, and demise, each phase characterized by typical observable traits. By any objective criteria most religious congregations are in the decline phase of the cycle and some are close to demise. The decline phase is manifested by diminishment in membership and material resources which decreases the group's effectiveness in accomplishing its goal. American women's religious congregations have declined from over 180,000 members in 1966 to 126,000 in the early 1990s. Today only one percent of sisters are under thirty years of age[2] while the median age in most congregations is over sixty. Congregations which once attracted fifty or sixty postulants a year now receive one or two. The financial and institutional dimensions of congregational life are commensurate with this decline in personnel.

The typical attitudes and behaviors of declining institutions are despair, cynicism, self-interest, protective maintenance strategies such as internal "turf battles," hardening of boundaries, restriction of resources to in-house projects, and identification with external sources of wealth and power.

However, based on the widespread sampling of congregational documents by the Leadership Conference of Women Religious (LCWR) Task Force on Religious Life in 1985[3] and on the paper, "Reflections Upon the Religious Life of U.S. Women Religious" prepared by LCWR for the Fifth Inter-American Conference on Religious Life in the same year,[4] these materially declining organizations exhibit the kinds of outwardly focused attitudes and behaviors that are characteristic of expanding organizations rather than declining ones. Religious congregations, especially of women, are overwhelmingly characterized by energetic and visionary planning for the future, a willingness to risk, permeability of boundaries and increasing inclusiveness, active identification with the poor and oppressed, internal unity, a high level of personal commitment of members, and the relative absence of survival anxiety. One could interpret this paradox as expressing a denial of reality on the part of religious. Or one could wonder, as I have heard many congregational leaders do, at the healthy attitudes and ongoing commitment, in the face of overwhelming odds, of women who are clear-eyed realists about the organizational facts.

The second feature of contemporary religious experience which has captured my attention and which seems, at least at one level, to contradict the evidence of hope and commitment just mentioned is the profound malaise, the pervasive sense of darkness that marks the day-to-day experience of many individual religious and even of congregations. Even as religious go on with life and ministry with a remarkable courage and commitment there is a darkness which is not gloom, pessimism, or self-pity. It can only be called suffering. But suffering, which is a part of every worthwhile life, is not an occasional episode in the life of many religious today. It seems to be almost a state of being, a dimension of everything experienced or undertaken.

A number of writers have, in recent years, attempted to analyze and suggest remedies for this malaise. Most have suggested that the negative features of contemporary first world culture have infiltrated and undermined the original religious vision and resulted in a loss of corporate focus with consequent energy diffusion and depression among the members. Mary Jo Leddy, for example, working from the standpoint of political philosophy, attributes the current malaise to a widespread surrender by religious to the decadent liberalism of the late twentieth century American empire with its hedonistic consumerism and destructive individualism and suggests that we experiment with radical pluralism in hopes that some small communities of shared vision will emerge to take up where morally exhausted large congregations have left off.[5]

Gerald Arbuckle, in a number of writings,[6] has used the theoretical framework of cultural anthropology to analyze the current malaise. He suggests that religious congregations, following the normal life cycle of institutions, have become distanced from their founding myths and are experiencing the resulting potentially creative social chaos. The refounding activity of individual prophetic figures supported by authority and followed by the rank and file is required to actualize that potential.

Joe Holland has suggested that religious life has run its course in the history of the church[7] and that it is time to resituate intense Christian life in the family and the work-place rather than in the non-biologically grounded contexts of parish and religious life.

The Vatican, of course, has attributed the malaise in religious life to what it perceives as widespread laxity or even infidelity of religious, especially American women, in regard to the so-called "essential elements" of religious life and proposes as a remedy a return to the totalitarian lifestyle of pre-conciliar convent life.[8]

The underlying presupposition of these and some other analyses is that the suffering in religious life today is an indication of something that is wrong, either morally or organizationally, with religious and/or religious life. The source of the flaw is modern culture or the relation of religious life to that culture. It is certainly a welcome sign of increased sophistication that contemporary analysts of religious life are taking more seriously the influence of culture on the experience of religious. And there is no doubt that religious today are susceptible to the same culturally generated problems and temptations that bedevil modern society as a whole.[9] Finally, it is certainly true that the anthropological patterns and sociological dynamics that affect groups in general also apply to that form of community that we call religious life.

But, this being said, my experience with religious has left me with a sense that these analyses, while insightful and useful at one level, have somehow not connected with the deepest experience of most religious. My suspicion is that the real cause of the current suffering in religious life, although precipitated by cultural change, is deeper than culture—that it is, in the final analysis, spiritual. I also suspect that it is not due primarily to personal infidelity or corporate mistakes even though it is very much concerned with purification. In a nutshell, the thesis I want to explore is that religious are experiencing, corporately as well as personally, something akin to or analogous to what John of the Cross called the "Dark Night," a dangerous and painful purificatory passage from a known and comfortable but somewhat immature stage of spirituality to a radically new experience of God. Perhaps the mystical tradition of the church can be a resource for understanding the current experience at a deeper level and finding some direction for living it faithfully.

III. THE "DARK NIGHT"

The Carmelite specialist in John of the Cross, Constance Fitzgerald, in a now justly famous article, suggested a few years ago that the category of the Dark Night of the Soul from the spiritual theology of the Spanish mystic might be useful for analyzing the current cultural experience of societal impasse in the face of the overwhelming problems and suffering of late modernity and especially the suffering of women in a patriarchal and sexist church.[10] Although she recognized that John was writing about the interior experience, particularly the prayer experience, of the enclosed individual contemplative, Fitzgerald contended that his description of the spiritual journey, especially of its purificatory dimension, was applicable beyond the narrow boundaries of the author's intent.[11] I am proposing that it might be helpful to examine the suffering among religious in the same light.

For some time I resisted this line of reflection not only because most of the religious with whom I have contact are not enclosed contemplatives but especially because I am suspicious of the tendency of religious people, when faced with the inevitable pain caused by our own shortcomings or the systemic injustice of the institutions in which we participate, to take refuge in pious victimhood. This temptation is perhaps especially dangerous for women who have been taught to deny, absorb, or capitalize on suffering instead of doing something about it. But I have been led by several factors to re-examine the possibility that spirituality rather than culture, or rather that the conjunction between spirituality and culture, is the locus of the current malaise in religious life.

First, contrary to what has been suggested by some analysts of religious life, it is not my experience that the majority of religious, especially religious women, have sold out to the materialism of contemporary liberal culture. If anything, religious women work harder and longer for less pay than anyone in the church with comparable qualifications. They are more often than not too responsible for their own good. They remain in ministerial positions that are patently abusive because of their commitment to God's people. Without any coercive pressure from superiors these religious not only make their annual retreat (sometimes at the price of vacation) but attend summer courses, prayer workshops, days of reflection, personal development seminars, and lectures. They are voracious readers of spiritual books, seek out spiritual direction despite high costs in time, money and travel, and spend semesters and even years in spiritual renewal programs. Religious participate conscientiously, often at the price of already scarce free time, in congregational tasks. In short, if my observations are at all accurate, religious women are at least as committed as they ever were to ministry, community, and their own spiritual lives. And the fact that these dimensions of their lives are no longer either provided for or enforced by authority means that they are acting out of personal conviction rather than routine or obligation.

Second, when religious give voice, often in the context of spiritual direction or faith sharing, to the pervasive suffering that I have observed, they tend to talk little about overwork, underpay, lack of job satisfaction and official recognition, or even clerical oppression. They talk about the inability to pray, the lost sense of God's presence, agonizing alienation from church and sacraments, fear of loss of faith, a sense of inauthenticity or shallowness in ministry because of the theological incoherence of their own positions on issues, their inarticulateness or even paralysis in the effort to share faith in community, soul fatigue.

In short, the suffering of religious who have survived the quarter century since Vatican II does not seem to be due, in the main, to serious infidelity, either individual or corporate. And it does tend to center in their religious experience rather than in external circumstances no matter how much the latter may exacerbate it. The Dark Night, as John of the Cross describes it, is the experience of purification that comes upon the person who has, for a long time, lived the interior life with fidelity and courage but who remains in need of purification not from gross sins of omission or commission, not from laxity or negligence, but from the roots of sinfulness to which the conscious mind does not have access and which are, therefore, not amenable to the direct action of the will. The apparent similarity between the character of the suffering that seems so widespread among religious today and the nature of the Dark Night as it is described in the classics of spirituality has led me to ask whether the two might be related in the current experience of religious.

Finally, there seems something significant in the fact that the Dark Night, which has always been considered the individual experience of particular people as they developed in the spiritual life, seems today to be a widespread and simultaneous experience of a whole group. That has led me to inquire into the relationship between the spiritual experience of religious and the ecclesial and societal situation of the American Catholic Church at the close of the modern period. For the sake of clarity I will discuss in succession what, in fact, has been chronologically overlapping, namely the effects of Vatican II and the effects of the death of modernity and the birth of the postmodern era. I will suggest, not as a theological proposition but as an heuristic hypothesis, that Vatican II worked upon religious something at least analogous to the active phase of what John of the Cross calls the Dark Night of the Senses while the interaction of Christian faith with the shattering of the modern mindset is causing something analogous to the passive phase of that Night and perhaps even the beginning of the Night of the Spirit.

IV. VATICAN II AND THE ACTIVE NIGHT

Basic to all that follows is the proposition that the central meaning and foundational impetus of religious life is, and always has been, the search for God. Religious life as a sociological phenomenon is essentially an organized lifestyle that facilitates the God-quest in a particular historical and cultural setting. For ministerial religious service of others is integral to that quest but does not exhaust it or substitute for it. Therefore, whatever threatens, undermines, or seems to invalidate this God-search is bound to cause profound unease and disorientation for the authentic religious. The events of our lifetime have touched that God-quest in very intimate ways. My hypothesis is that, however inarticulate many religious are on the subject, the root of the pervasive suffering among religious today is the impact on the God-quest itself of the radical ecclesial and societal upheaval we have been experiencing.

For most religious alive today the period of their religious life up to the 1960s was one of extraordinary stability. The organization of religious life seemed perfectly suited to its ends, namely, the perfection of the religious and the salvation of souls.[12] Faith was laid out in catechism-clear propositions which no one questioned, the liturgy was rich and invariable, authority structures were clear and effective, the status of religious in the society of the church and their role in its apostolic work were well-defined and unchallenged. Religious were the "good sisters," the professional religious elite of the church. Nowhere perhaps was this more true than here in the United States in the 1950s and 1960s, the period of the Sister Formation Movement, when women religious became not only a spiritual vanguard but some of the best educated and most professionally competent women in the world.[13]

Vatican II, in the space of a few years, occasioned the dismantling of this entire structure. Almost overnight, in historical perspective, the external overlay of religious life was stripped away, a stripping that religious themselves willingly undertook in the effort to renew their life according to the council's vision of a church newly in, with, and for the world after centuries of self-imposed exile and animosity. The council also changed every other sector of the church, clerical and lay, and these changes also had repercussions on religious life.

The ministerial explosion among the laity obscured the apostolate as a reason for being a religious, throwing them back on the question of ultimate motivation not only for entering but for staying. The positive re-evaluation of marriage as a vocation to holiness called into question the assumption that consecrated celibacy was a higher state of life. The privileged status of religious was symbolically surrendered by the abandonment of religious garb and titles, and the allure of mystery vanished with the opening up of cloistered dwellings, raising the question of religious identity. Financial security, freedom from responsibility within the authority structure of a total institution, and escape from sexual issues in the monosexual community disappeared within a few years as congregations diversified their ministries, divested themselves of institutional holdings and property, changed their procedures for deploying personnel, and emerged from the convent as fortress into the ordinariness of neighborhood life. All the "perks" of the life such as instant identity, job security, and the assurance of institutional backing whether one was right or wrong disappeared. In short, all the unrecognized enticements to religious life that had played some role in virtually every teenager's vocation came out into the open and demanded honest re-examination.

Some interpreted this almost overnight dismantling of a centuries-old lifestyle as blessed liberation. Others saw it as unmitigated disaster. But what it surely did was throw all religious back on the one thing necessary. If religious life could not be justified by ministry, provided no securities and no escapes, did not make one mysterious or special, was not a higher or more perfect form of life much less an assurance of salvation, there was only one reason for continuing, and some discovered that that was not the reason they had entered or stayed while others concluded it was not enough of a reason to continue. As many left and few entered, religious who stayed got in touch in a new way with the real meaning of religious vocation, the naked God-quest at the center of their hearts which made a mysteriously exclusive and total demand upon them and to which they could only respond by the gift of their whole lives in consecrated celibacy, voluntary poverty, community, and corporate mission. Those who continued to choose religious life had now to choose it in purified faith because it was largely devoid of compensatory packaging.

Interestingly enough, this stripping to essentials is exactly what the first phase of the Dark Night of the Senses is supposed to do. It strips away the false sweetness of the spiritual life by definitively detaching the person from everything, good as well as evil, which competes with God in one's life.[14] As John of the Cross says, the point is not that a person be actually deprived of all good things, but that one become detached from them, that they cease to be one's motivation or reward.[15] But for most people actual deprivation is necessary for detachment to be achieved, and this educative deprivation occurs through the surrender, willingly and finally, of everything that competes with the love of God by providing the satisfaction we yearn for.[16]

Religious deprived themselves in the years following Vatican II of all of the sociological and ecclesiastical comforts of religious life, a deprivation that cut much deeper than the relatively easy material mortifications of preconciliar convent life. The suffering of willing surrender of identity, status, power, a sense of societal worth, self-evident rightness, approval by ecclesiastical authority, spiritual superiority, all of which were at least ambiguous values, was deepened by the irretrievable loss of some very real goods. Scores, even hundreds of lifelong companions no longer walked with us. Institutions deeply entwined with our congregations' histories and our own vocations were closed. Cherished ministries were surrendered. Traditions and customs that nourished the corporate myth and helped sustain a coherent world slipped away. All of this was a stripping that left most religious very vulnerable even as they courageously ventured forth from the safe confines of the convent into new and dangerous missions in the fields of social justice, direct pastoral ministry, and even non-church related services.

V. POST-MODERNITY AND THE PASSIVE NIGHT

A. The Transition from the Active to the Passive Night

As John of the Cross says, the painful stripping of self that is undertaken in the active phase of the Night of the Senses cannot be compared to the suffering that characterizes the passive phase of this Night. But between the two phases there is a period of peace, a time in which the person is aware of being close to God, feels spiritually settled, enjoys an intense interior life, and willingly shares that life with others.[17]

Perhaps, if we can remember back that far, some of us will be able to see an analogy between John's description of these happy "beginners" (as he calls them), relatively free from carnal and spiritual attachments, basking in the maternal love of a generous God, and ourselves in the euphoria of the immediate years after the council. No task was too arduous, no risk too great, no meeting too long as we took up our new identity among the people of God. We poured ourselves into intensive community building, developed new prayer forms, made directed retreats, prepared beautiful liturgies, retrained for new ministries, marched for civil rights and peace, even went to jail to witness for justice. We gloried in our role of empowering the laity while bravely confronting the guardians of clerical turf. Like John's "beginners" we thought we had arrived at our true home. With our lay companions, in ecumenical solidarity, and strengthened by a personalized spirituality that was psychologically honest and prophetically engaged we anticipated long careers building the city of God where our tears would be turned into dancing.

B. The Need for Passive Purification

John of the Cross warns his readers, however, that the period of and security between the two phases of the Dark Night is relatively brief and he devotes six chapters to an embarrassingly detailed description of what he calls the "imperfections of beginners,"[18] that is, of those who have passed through the purification of the active Night. What John describes in these six chapters in terms of enclosed contemplatives is the deeply rooted and hydra-headed spiritual egoism that is too subtle to be recognized by the person herself or himself and which resists all one's efforts at self-purification, both through active detachment and through willing acceptance of life's misfortunes. There is a great deal we can do about our sins, our attachments, our selfishness, says John. But the roots of our sins lie far below the threshold of consciousness. It is not that we refuse to deal with these springs of evil; it is that we do not have access to them. Only God, through a purifying action that we cannot cause, escape, or control, can extirpate the very roots of alienation from self and God and bring the person finally into the fullness of the contemplative life.

Although John was talking about the interior life of individual contemplatives brought about primarily through and within their prayer experience, his teaching seems applicable in many ways also to the experience of ministerial religious because it is not really a description of a particular lifestyle but of the spiritual itinerary itself. The heuristic hypothesis I am proposing is that the cultural cataclysm that many analysts are beginning to call the transition from modernity to post-modernity is functioning in the lives of many religious in a way analogous to the purifying trials of the interior life that John describes apropos of the enclosed contemplative.

1. POST-MODERNITY

Historical periodization is tentative at best and ideologically distorted at worst. Women, people of color, the poor would probably not divide western history neatly into classical antiquity, the middle ages, and modern times. But many of our best cultural analysts, especially those who are sensitive to the voices of the marginalized, are coming to a consensus that at the close of the twentieth century we are standing on the cusp between the modern world which is dying and something new which is emerging if we do not destroy the planet or annihilate ourselves. A cultural transformation comparable in depth and significance to the sixteenth century transition from the medieval to the modern world is happening. But we are much clearer about what is dying than about what is being born. Modernity, that is, the worldview, including the ideology, the values, the political and economic systems, and the characteristic projects, which has been the self-evident reality structure, at least in the west, for the last four centuries is crumbling around us. To call what is aborning "post-modernity" is a bit like referring to the forthcoming blessed event as "the baby." It is not very precise but we have no cultural sonogram machine.

The word itself, post-modernity, does give us some important clues. Not only is this new era chronologically subsequent to modernity, but it is tensively related to it in a way that modernity was not related to the medieval period. Modernity involved, to a large extent, the repudiation of the medieval world view with its three-tiered universe, interventionist God, dogma-ruled intellectual life, and church-centered social order. The renaissance, the scientific revolution, the enlightenment, and the Protestant reformation which shaped the modern mind changed the most fundamental presuppositions about reality and ushered in a worldview that had to replace, because it could not absorb, the medieval vision.

This no doubt explains in part the violent opposition of the church to modernity, or what it eventually called the heresy of "modernism."[19] The medieval world was built by the church, explained by the church, and ruled by the church. In the modern world evidence, critical reason, pluralism, freedom of conscience, the autonomy of the individual, political diversity, and economic laissez-faire supplanted the world the church built, and the church resolutely resisted virtually every aspect of modernity right up to the opening of the Second Vatican Council. Of course, there were intellectual moderns in the church such as Loisy, George Tyrrell, and Teilhard de Chardin. But on the whole, the church managed to remain a medieval enclave in the midst of modernity preserving a papacy that was a sixteenth century divine right monarchy complete with titled nobility, liveried guards, sumptuous court ceremonies, inquisitions and symbolic executions of dissidents. It went on teaching a perennial philosophy which serenely ignored the developments in the physical and social sciences while denying the findings of the emerging human sciences such as psychology. It ran entire educational and social systems which enabled Catholics to live in a self-imposed ghetto from which non-Catholic "heretics" with their modern ideas were barred, and to propagate a theology that was internally coherent but increasingly out of touch with the moral, intellectual, and social experience even of its own members to say nothing of the rest of the world.

At Vatican II the church threw back the curtains and opened the windows on modernity. But what met its startled gaze was not the dewey freshness of a dawning era but the twilight of a dying age. We only momentarily mistook the pollution-laden air for heady drafts of pristine modernity because we had lived so long enclosed that we had forgotten what fresh air smells like. Modernity was almost over when the church decided to engage it.

No one had lived the medieval life of the church in the modern world as totally and as committedly as religious, especially religious women. Our peasant dress, pre-electric lights horaria, romantic ceremonies and feudal titles bore eloquent witness to our alienation from modernity. Nevertheless, and perhaps precisely because we were so schooled to thinking with the institutional church in all things, no group in the church embraced the conciliar agenda with such fervor as religious women. We not only opened the windows to peek out but rushed out into the street as eager to embrace the modern world as we had been faithful in cherishing the medieval one. What has actually happened is that religious are being challenged to help bury a modernity in which we never participated and to enter into post-modernity without having learned the modern lessons needed to function in this new era. Religious are deeply enmeshed in this complicated situation.

Cultural critics are beginning to discern two major and largely incompatible strands in the emerging post-modern *Zeitgeist*. One is deconstructive and involves a repudiation of any worldview or unified vision of reality resulting in a nihilistic embrace of total relativism and a value-neutral absolute pluralism which despairs of any ultimate meaning. The other strand is constructive. Although it sees with increasing clarity the dead-ends to which the premises of modernity have led, constructive post-modernism does not envision a total repudiation or replacement of modernity but an integration of its genuine values (and there are some such as the ideal of liberty and equality and the intellectual honesty of critical thought) into a higher synthesis. In my view, deconstructive post-modernism is little more than a counsel of despair in the face of truly overwhelming contemporary challenges. But the constructive post-modernism, which is not a romantic or a sullen anti-modernism but a vision of an alternative world, seems our last best hope if we are to keep the human enterprise going.

Even a thumbnail sketch of a post-modern vision is well beyond the scope of this paper.[20] But for the purposes of this presentation I will try to give a sense of what is emerging by discussing three salient characteristics of modernity, the challenge to them of the emerging post-modern sensibility, and the effects of this clash of worldviews on the religious imagination and spirituality of people just emerging from the theological middle ages, namely Catholics in general but religious in particular. What I will be trying to suggest is that the interaction between a culture in transition and an ecclesial experience that is "out of synch" with either pole of the transition has generated a spiritual situation in which the God-quest of religious is seriously threatened and that the effect is an experience that has some interesting analogies with what John of the Cross described as the passive phase of the Dark Night of the Senses.

2. MODERNITY AND POST-MODERNITY IN CONFLICT

The modern worldview which was born of the scientific revolution and developed through the enlightenment into the technological age has numerous defining characteristics, but three that underlie the others are pervasive rationalism, hierarchical dualism, and the myth of progress.

Rationalism, the boundless confidence in the capacity of the human mind to know everything by means of the so-called scientific method, is fundamental to the modern worldview. It has resulted in the repudiation of mystery as a meaningful category, the objectification of all reality, the justification of whatever destruction is necessary to extract the secrets of nature, a radically secular view of public reality within which there is no place for the religious, the reduction of reality to what can be scientifically investigated, in short, all the forms of materialistic positivism that have fragmented and impoverished our experience and alienated us from God, nature, one another, and ourselves.

A second feature of modernity is a pervasive *hierarchical dualism.* In the modern frame of reference all reality in every sphere is divided into two parts with one part being superior to and dominant over the other. Thus, mind over matter, objective over subjective, intellect over emotion, the demonstrative over intuitive, prose over poetry, God over humanity, humanity over nature, white over colored, clergy over lay, master over slave, European over Asian, rich over poor, light over darkness, adult over child, speech over silence, power over weakness, and on and on. Basic to this entire dualistic scheme is the fundamental dualism, male over female, thought to reflect the hierarchy of creator over creation which grounds its necessity, absoluteness, and immutability. Out of this schema has come an ideology of rape. Domination and subordination is the primary mode of all relationship.

The third feature of modernity is the *myth of progress* according to which change is always improvement and whatever is new is better. Progress is regarded as inevitable and therefore beyond moral evaluation. Whatever can be done must be done and therefore should be done. The ultimate symbol of the destructive tyranny of this myth over the modern mind is the deliberate creation of a bomb which could end life on earth.

The negative results of modernity are becoming ever more evident. Ecological disasters multiply, armed conflict is global, the abuse and exploitation of women and children is epidemic, our enormously inflated economy is out of control, we face reproductive chaos, the information glut causes growing confusion and paralysis, and cynical despair is pervasive.

What cultural critics are calling constructive post-modernism is the emerging worldview of those who have begun to realize that modernity has run its course. To continue to operate on the premises of modernity is cosmocidal. We need to re-envision the whole world order, reimagine the whole human enterprise if we are to survive, much less flourish. Against the reductionistic rationalism of positivistic science a new science and especially a new cosmology is emerging. The universe in this view is not a free-standing, objective, purely material substance which we have a right and a duty to dominate and exploit for our immediate ends but an infinite, complex process in which everything is related to everything else and nothing is standing still. It does not belong to us but we to it and it has been entrusted to our stewardship for generations yet unborn. This intricate whole is mysterious and beautiful and lovable. Reverence, care, and cooperation—even repentance—are the proper attitudes with which to approach this universe whose secrets we must ask for with appropriate humility and awe. And this tiny blue-green planet earth, a mere speck in the universe, is not a strip mine or a dump. It is our mother—raped, bleeding, and near to death—and the absolutely necessary condition of our life. We do not have much time in which to repent of the violent rationalism of the modern era.

Against the hierarchical dualism of modernity the post-modern worldview is characterized by its embrace of the feminist critique of patriarchy with its implied repudiation of hierarchical dualism in every sphere and its appeal for egalitarian mutuality in relationships and inclusive community not only among humans but of humans within nature and of creation with God.

And against the runaway myth of progress constructive post-modernism is, among other things, re-evaluating native patterns of life which affirm a reverence for reality that sets limits to human projects and calls for responsibly envisioning the results of our actions, not just for ourselves and future generations but for the whole of reality. It is beginning to ask qualitative rather than purely quantitative questions about what we are capable of doing. There may be many things we can do that we ought not to do and change can be regressive as well as progressive.

The attitudes and insights emerging as integral to constructive post-modernism are frequently in conflict with official church theology which is still a medieval pre-critical deductive dogmatism with a thin veneer of modern terminology not yet dry on its surface. But this is the theology upon which contemporary religious founded their spirituality. Increasingly, it is a theology which is incredible to, and therefore completely non-functional for, many religious who, after the briefest exposure to modern critical thought, are already caught up in the post-critical agenda of a new era.

These religious know, even when they are unable to articulate it, that there is no absolute, unchanging truth available to humans, that all human knowledge is perspectival and limited and therefore relative, and thus that human infallibility is a contradiction in terms. They are learning that all reality is evolutionary, dynamic, interconnected and thus that everything is to some degree indeterminate and ultimately mysterious with ourselves the most mysterious of all. Claims about unchanging natures and non-discussable moral absolutes derived from them are increasingly unintelligible. They know that feminism is not a first world aberration threatening the family and making women aspire to functions beyond their nature but the *sine qua non* of a truly human approach to relationships; that hierarchy is at best terminally dysfunctional and at worst a systemic sin. The list could be extended, but the point is that most religious who have been active in the church since the council are living with a transformed consciousness, an increasingly postmodern worldview, which has little foundation in an organized theology because the medieval theology which they learned well in pre-conciliar days and even the minimally modern theology they have caught up on since the council have been rendered almost useless by the clash between modern and post-modern rationalities.

3. EFFECT ON SPIRITUALITY OF THIS CONFLICT

The effect of being enmeshed in the generalized incoherence of a cultural transition which renders one's functional theology inoperable is spiritual disorientation. Without attempting even to list the areas in which this disorientation is appearing, I will give a few typical examples.

God is a major problem for many religious, especially for those who really pray, who actually seek to reach God in some experiential way. The God of official, i.e. medieval, theology is non-credible. Modern explorations into outer space have made a God "up there" or "out there" inconceivable. Modern depth psychology makes a God "within" difficult to imagine and generates a healthy suspicion about the role of our own projections in our God-images. But post-modern sensibilities have exacerbated the situation well beyond the modern God-problem. How can a post-modern mind encompass a God who is totally transcendent, outside the universe, omniscient, omnipotent, immutable, perfect, unaffected by our actions, absolute in "his" moral judgments which admit of no exceptions, and who exercises unaccountable and absolute power over all? And even if one could imagine such a God, could one relate to him? Is he not the very epitome of the modern nightmare: hyper-rational, dominating, non-relational?

Feminism, furthermore, has made an all-male, indeed triply male, God both incredible and repugnant to many women while increasing appreciation of the great world religions and of the religions of native peoples has made the absolutist and exclusivist claims of Christian theology sound arrogant if not imperialistic.

The God-problem is not ameliorated for many post-moderns by an appeal to *Jesus* as the Christ. Modern, and especially post-modern, cosmology makes a resurrected human being hard to conceive. Questions about where and how Jesus exists lead ineluctably toward the question of whether he exists. Is Jesus finally just a man, a singular historical example of what it means to live as a God-centered human, but one who has died and is available to us only as an example from the past? What can resurrection mean except that the community continues to believe in Jesus' message? Is prayer to Jesus realistic or just a projection of a celibate need for intimacy?

The problems are compounded when one gets to the *church*. Can the real God of all creation really be tied in some special or exclusive way to one narrow strand of human history that is only a few thousand years old? Can a patriarchal power structure which not only legitimates but sacralizes structures of domination really be a, much less the, privileged mediation of salvation? And if there are no clear answers to these questions, is it honest to propagate this church, at least in its institutional form?

The *liturgy and sacraments* present almost insuperable problems for many religious. Not only are there massive theoretical questions about what is really going on once a medieval theology of transubstantiation, real presence, and quasi-substantial sin-acts have foundered on post-substantialist post-modern premises, but the galling experience of sacralized male domination which comes to ritual expression in sacramental dependence is so enraging for many women that they simply cannot participate on a regular basis.

These questions are not the theoretical fantasies of underemployed academics. They dominate the consciousness of many religious, especially of those who pray. The effect of the constant nagging presence of these insoluble conundrums is profound darkness that enshrouds the very heart of religious life, namely, the God-search that is its *raison d'être*. Many religious, if my observations are at all accurate, are experiencing a serious crisis of faith which is affecting every area of their lives. They deal daily with the question of why they are in ministry given their personal uncertainty about the very existence, much less the character of God. They struggle over representing an institution they are not even sure should exist. They agonize over trying to build authentic community with people they suspect could hardly guess how profoundly alienated they are and who would be shocked if they could. They sit in prayer wondering if there is anyone, anything even, there in the darkness. They wonder how they can participate even once more in a liturgy, in sacraments which seem to be either the primitive private magic of semi-educated functionaries or the violent rituals of male power.

Even allowing such questions to formulate themselves is terrifying, or, worse, perversely seductive. The struggle is exhausting; the rage is overpowering; the darkness is impenetrable. The ultimate question struggling for expression is "What is the meaning of religious life in the absence of God?"

VI. INSTRUCTION FROM THE MYSTICAL TRADITION

If the description above is at all true to the actual experience of religious who are trying to live a post-modern spirituality in a dying modern culture with the resources of a medieval theology and spiritual formation, there is perhaps something to be learned from the mystical tradition. Although the Dark Night bears upon several areas of spiritual experience, for the sake of limits and concentration I am going to deal with only one, namely, the purification of the God-image. I will use John of the Cross' systematic presentation of the Dark Night to pursue my hypothesis, namely, that the darkness which pervades the experience of so many religious today may have more to do with the journey from a kind of collective arrested spiritual development that characterized pre-conciliar religious life to the spiritual maturity required for participation in a new age than it does with cultural contamination.

John, in *The Dark Night,* Book I, discusses the passive phase of what he calls the purification of the senses or what we might view as the purification that takes place in the sphere where a person interacts with this world. For ministerial religious this is a primary sphere of their spirituality. John divides his reflections into a consideration of why this experience of purification is necessary, a description of what the person experiences, signs for discerning whether a person who is submerged in darkness and suffering is actually undergoing the purification that leads to contemplation or is simply disintegrating psychologically, and what a person can do not only to survive this experience but to cooperate with God's inner work. I will follow John's pattern drawing an analogy between what he has to say about the experience of contemplatives in prayer and what many religious seem to be experiencing today in their active lives.

A. *Purpose of the Dark Night*

John of the Cross, as we noted above, devotes a long section of Book I to describing the inner, unrecognized, and inaccessible roots of sinfulness that remain in the person who has successfully traversed the active night of detachment and grounding in virtue, a process most religious began in the uniform discipline of pre-conciliar convent spirituality and largely completed in the self-stripping that the conciliar renewal brought about. But something remains unfinished in the spiritual project. Basic to all of what John calls the "imperfections of beginners" that remain to be dealt with is the inadequacy of their God-concept. John says, "They still think of God and speak of [God] as little children, and their knowledge and experience of [God] is like that of little children.... The reason is that they have not reached perfection, which is union of the soul with God."[21]

As we have said, the modern science of psychology, especially Freudianism, has made the same point more brutally and perhaps more convincingly. It has made us aware of the powerful role that projection of need plays in the construction of the God-image. It is not sin in the usual sense of the word but the deeply rooted and unhealthy compulsions of the ego, the fear of death, the alienation of authority and responsibility, the tyranny of the persona with its denials and shoulds, the need for immediate gratification, and so on which have functioned in our construction of a God of the gaps who meets our needs and solves our problems. This "God" fulfills our intimacy needs without making us face sexuality realistically. He tells us what to do without ambiguity and rewards our self-alienating submission with immortality. He protects us from harm and injustice and keeps our religious persona intact. He makes us special by calling us to a higher life. In short, he is a God made in our image and according to our needs. Furthermore, this God is also one who could be imaged easily and theologically explained with the tools of medieval theology. The theology of our youth connived with our lack of psychological sophistication to keep us spiritually immature.

The assault of modern psychology and science on this comfortable God-image has been aggravated by post-modern views of reality which have undermined the theological explanations of God that enabled us to think coherently about divine reality while making the classical attributes of God not only incredible but repellent. In other words, cultural developments may be playing the role of stripping us of any capacity to think God and therefore to relate to God. At one level this can be explained as a purely historical development: medieval psychology, theology, and cosmology have been replaced by new ways of thinking. But perhaps the deeper explanation is that only an assault which could get past the tight defenses of a need-dominated spirituality is capable of radically undermining the immature, ego-compulsed substitute for God that must be surrendered if we are ever to know, to encounter, the Holy Mystery who has no name. However this takes place in a Carmelite monastery, perhaps the way it takes place for a contemporary active minister is in her or his engagement with the thought forms of post-modernity. While we lived in an impregnable medieval enclave we did not have to take seriously what we now cannot avoid. We cannot have one mentality and sensibility for everyday life and another for prayer. What will not wash, imaginatively or intellectually, from nine to five in the office will not function at six in the chapel either.

The purpose of the Dark Night, however it is precipitated, is the destruction of all that impedes the full union of the person with the real God. The ultimate source of this purifying action is the contemplative inflow of God into the person. The real God, ultimately mysterious and totally foreign to our projections, cannot coexist with the God of our immature imagination. It is hard to imagine a more effective assault on the false God-image than that which we have been undergoing since our emergence from pre-conciliar convent life.

B. Description

John of the Cross describes the experience of this Dark Night in words that are strangely relevant to contemporary experience as I have heard many religious articulate it. He says that in the midst of this purificatory fire the mind is plunged into darkness; the will is dry; the memory is empty; the affections are in anguish.[22] God has disappeared from the horizon of experience. The heart of the religious project, the God-quest, seems pointless, futile, indeed impossible. The inner life becomes a war zone; one feels impure and weak and vaguely sinful without being able to point to anything concrete whose correction would make one feel more whole. Friends, spiritual directors, fellow religious seem distant and unreliable or even uninteresting. Reading is no help and prayer is utterly barren. There is deep inner fatigue, discouragement, a sense of worthlessness and hypocrisy in ministry. Sometimes passions long quiet surge up uncontrollably. Just getting up in the morning seems more than one can manage.[23]

C. Discernment

This description, as has been pointed out often enough, sounds a lot like classic burnout, or psychological depression.[24] The modern tendency is to seek counseling, take a sabbatical, or go on vacation. And indeed all of these can be useful approaches. But John of the Cross cautions that one cannot "cure" the Dark Night. It must cure us. Consequently, even though psychological disturbance may be part of the experience and require appropriate professional care, it is important to be able to recognize the spiritual experience of purification so that we do not short-circuit the work of God.

John of the Cross offers three signs[25] that, when they occur together, indicate that the person experiencing this searing darkness is not simply disintegrating psychologically, but is actually undergoing the purifying action of the Spirit. Although it seems that people seldom can recognize these signs in themselves, partly because they are rightly aware of the part their own brokenness plays in their misery,[26] they often unwittingly express them to a spiritual director. The first sign is the darkness itself, the person's inability to find joy or satisfaction in anything. When the darkness is really the work of contemplation there is little inclination to compensate for the spiritual pain by sensual excess. The person knows somehow that there is no substitute for what has been lost.

But, and this is the second sign and one I see very often in religious, the person has a persistent concern about God, a kind of nostalgia for God. Such people long for God and suffer from God's absence. They are constantly searching for something, anything that will assure them that God exists or offer hope that they may someday once again glimpse God's face. Often what they most want from a spiritual director is just the experience that someone who seems credible to them still believes in God, even communes with God. And they are sure that it is their own tepidity or mistakes or lack of sincerity that is responsible for their abandonment. If only they could get it right, find the right form of prayer or the right schedule or the right book, the darkness would lift.

The third sign is the powerlessness of the person, despite deep desire and sometimes furious effort, to bring God back. The person simply cannot pray, and the harder one tries, the more impotent one is.

Often what the person cannot see, the gradually emerging fruits of the purifying suffering, is very evident to those around them.[27] The perseverance itself, the dogged day-to-day fidelity in the midst of total darkness and without inner support, is evidence enough that something positive is afoot. A new kind of humility and lack of affectation born of true self-knowledge lends a certain grace to their presence. Since they are nothing and have nothing there is no sense pretending anymore. Their solidarity with the "little ones," the poor, is no longer tinged with condescension or aloofness for they are the poor. Their fidelity to people and to the truth becomes uncomplicated by the power agendas and self-protectiveness of former times when the defense of the persona was of paramount importance. They seem to have just enough strength to suffer what has to be suffered for justice's sake and they are unwilling to burden others with their pain or to cause anyone else to share their doubts. They are not arrogant but they also can no longer be intimidated by power. Because they have nothing left to lose they cannot be bought. They hope against hope, not in brave speeches but simply by not walking away despite all the evidence that there is no reason to stay. The gift of wisdom is beginning to infuse all their actions. They are a kind of incarnation of Peter's "Lord, to whom can I go; you have the words of eternal life" (cf. Jn

6:68). As John of the Cross says, the transformation is taking place even though the person himself or herself cannot see or feel it.

It seems to me that the paradox with which this paper began bears many of the marks of this transformation. Religious who see their congregations diminishing, their works threatened, who are themselves suffering from violent sexism in society and church, whose ministerial efforts are frustrated again and again by the power structure in which they do not share, who find liturgy abusive and prayer empty are nevertheless steadfast in planning and hoping for a future they cannot imagine they will see. They are faithful in ministry and in prayer. They are not cynical or self-pitying. Their energies are turned outward even as the dark fire of the Spirit painfully consumes the inner dross.

D. Negotiating the Passage of the Dark Night

The passage through the Dark Night, spiritual authors warn, is perilous, and many people do not make it. Two serious temptations are characteristic of this passage. The first is to try to turn back toward the now outworn spirituality of one's former experience, an effort that cannot succeed. The second temptation, and by far the most dangerous, is to give up. Today giving up can easily take the form of a vocational or career change. If one cannot pray, if ministry seems rootless and hypocritical, if one cannot even believe in God, one might as well put one's efforts into something that has at least some human merit like an intimate relationship, raising a family, or becoming a secular professional in the helping fields. My suspicion is that some of the departures from religious life in the last few years have been the despairing surrender of people who could find no help anywhere in the midst of the Dark Night.[28]

What is to be done by the person in this situation? What help can be offered? John of the Cross was talking to enclosed contemplatives and his advice bears mainly on their prayer. He tries to assure them that they should persevere in prayer but without trying to force any thoughts or acts. They should simply rest quietly, even though they feel they are wasting time, because the silent work of God that is going on within can only be hindered by mental or affective busyness.[29] This advice is certainly applicable to the contemporary individual who is furiously trying to make prayer "work" when the time for this activity is over. But I am concerned also with the Dark Night as a corporate experience of ministerial religious. What can we—as congregations and communities, as leaders and spiritual directors—do to cooperate with this purificatory process? Let me make a few very tentative suggestions in light of the present situation which is very different from that of the sixteenth century.

First, we can explore, openly and courageously, the possibility that the problems we are struggling with have a deeper cause and purpose than we have been prepared to imagine and we can mobilize the resources of the tradition of spirituality to help us at least understand, and help others to understand, what might be going on.

Second, I think we need to undertake a serious, corporate theological re-education of ourselves. The theology which undergirded our spirituality in the past cannot be resuscitated and intelligent people cannot live a spirituality which is theologically bootless. We are, to a large extent, running on theological empty. It is not just people who are going to teach theology or run catechetical programs who need a broad and deep exposure to contemporary theology. It is every religious for whom the medieval theological synthesis does not and cannot function. Contemporary theology has made major advances in rethinking the God question, revitalizing christology, regrounding the sacraments in human experience, struggling with the anomalies raised by the encounter with the world religions, integrating the feminist critique into mainstream theology, interfacing moral theology and the contemporary human sciences. If we are convinced that every religious needs at least basic knowledge of psychology if she is going to have enough self-knowledge to deal with her own development, we should also be convinced that every religious needs a workable theological framework if she is to deal with the God-question today.

Third, in the vast array of reading material available to us today we have a resource that John of the Cross and his contemporaries could not dream of. There is readable, non-technical but very sound material available on post-modernism, psychology, contemporary philosophy, models of God and church, revelation, biblical interpretation, and almost every other dimension of the current crises facing us as individuals and as a society. Serious reading ought to be as much a part of the discipline of contemporary religious life as daily prayer.

Fourth, and suggested much more hesitantly, I think that if we could find a way to facilitate among us a faith-sharing that allowed us to speak of our negative experience, of our spiritual suffering, we could do much for each other. We tell our stories (somewhat expurgated), share our moments of insight, discuss issues and even values. But do we dare, even in very carefully selected groups, surface the deep issues of God, eucharist, Jesus, praying, believing? Would it be worth the risk to get to the bedrock level of faith with one another?

Fifth, we might try diversifying our prayer repertoire. The eastern religions in particular have developed methods for concentration and attention that are non-rational, non-discursive and that might be of more help in the effort to be silent and receptive than traditional western forms. Zen and Yoga, Centering Prayer, awareness exercises have all proven helpful to some people.[30]

Finally, something that most religious have always intuitively known and that seems a matter of conviction with most religious I talk to: perseverance in prayer no matter what happens or does not happen. This can be almost impossibly difficult when God seems totally absent, even non-existent over long stretches of time. But the feeble desire, the barely felt hope, even the wish against all hope that there is a God is prayer, and that prayer needs the nourishment of time and place and effort the way a match in a gale needs a protecting hand.

VII. CONCLUSION

If it is true that religious, not only individually in many cases, but corporately, experience a profound purification that touches not only our institutional holdings, our numerical and financial strength, our high status and privileged self-image but even more intimately our God-image, and the God-quest which is the very ground and reason for our life, then the passage through this crisis cannot be accomplished, ultimately, on any other than spiritual grounds.

If the preceding analysis has any validity the stakes are very high. Our entire culture is involved in a deep crisis, the crisis of transition from modernity to post-modernity on which our physical survival depends, but also a crisis of transition from the human-centered spirituality which banished God to his heaven and left the world to us to a genuinely theocentric spirituality on which our spiritual survival depends. If religious, who may be in the vanguard of this transition precisely because they are, as it were, obsessed with God, can lead the way through this darkness, they may be in a position to make a contribution to post-modernity far more important than the contribution of schools and hospitals in the modern period.

The future of religious life, from many points of view, looks quite bleak. This is especially true according to the criteria of well-being that modernity has taught us to use: quantity, numbers, money, power, leverage, status. But scripture offers another vision to our struggling hope. In the book of Deuteronomy God says, "For you are a people holy to Yahweh your God; Yahweh your God has chosen you to be a people for God's own possession.... It was not because you were more in number than any other people that Yahweh loved you and chose you, for you are the least of all peoples; but it is because Yahweh loves you and is keeping the promise sworn to your forebears.... Know therefore that Yahweh your God is God, the faithful God who keeps covenant and steadfast love with those who love God in return" (cf. Dt 7:6-9).

Notes

1. Patricia Wittberg in "Outward Orientation in Declining Organizations: Reflections on the LCWR Document," *Claiming Our Truth: Reflections on Identity by United States Women Religious,* ed. by Nadine Foley (Washington, D.C.: Leadership Conference of Women Religious, 1988), 89-105 documents this paradox and suggests that the outward focus of declining congregations may be dysfunctional for organizational survival. I find her sociological description and analysis very clarifying but I am suggesting in this paper another kind of explanation of the phenomenon and a different response to it.

2. For statistics, see Marie Augusta Neal, *Catholic Sisters in Transition: From the 1960's to the 1980's* (Wilmington: Michael Glazier, 1984), pp. 18-22 as brought up to date by Lora Ann Quiñonez and Mary Daniel Turner, *The Transformation of American Catholic Sisters* (Philadelphia: Temple University Press, 1992), p. 141 and Wittberg, "Outward Orientation," pp. 89-90.

3. Anne Munley, "An Exploratory Content Analysis of Major Themes Present in Selected Documents of United States Women Religious," in *Claiming Our Truth,* pp. 184-191.

4. Available in *Claiming our Truth,* pp. 173-181.

5. See Mary Jo Leddy, *Reweaving Religious Life: Beyond the Liberal Model* (Mystic: Twenty-Third Publications, 1990).

6. See, e.g., Gerald A. Arbuckle, *Out of Chaos: Refounding Religious Congregations* (New York/Mahwah: Paulist, 1988).

7. See Joe Holland, "Family, Work, and Culture: A Postmodern Recovery of Holiness," *Sacred Interconnections: Postmodern Spirituality, Political Economy, and Art,* ed. David Ray Griffin (Albany: State University of New York, 1990), 103-122.

8. See the document "Essential Elements in Church Teaching on Religious Life," available in *Origins* 13 (July 7, 1983), 133-142.

For a very good sociological analysis of pre-conciliar religious community life as that of a "total institution" see Patricia Wittberg, *Creating a Future for Religious Life: A Sociological Perspective* (New York/Mahwah: Paulist, 1991), pp. 11-35.

9. For a very insightful analysis of the cultural malaise of late modernity, see Albert Borgmann, *Crossing the Postmodern Divide* (Chicago/London: University of Chicago, 1992), esp. pp. 20-47.

For a theological appraisal see Douglas C. Bowman, *Beyond the Modern Mind: The Spiritual and Ethical Challenge of the Environmental Crisis* (New York: Pilgrim, 1990), esp. pp. 7-23.

For an attempt to draw out the implications for spirituality of the collapse of modernity, see David Ray Griffin, "Introduction: Postmodern Spirituality and

Society," *Spirituality and Society: Postmodern Visions,* ed. David Ray Griffin (Albany: State University of New York, 1988), 1-31.

10. Constance Fitzgerald, "Impasse and Dark Night," *Women's Spirituality: Resources for Christian Development,* ed. Joann Wolski Conn (New York/Mahwah: Paulist, 1986), 287-311. (This article first appeared in 1984 and is reprinted in the Conn volume with permission of the original publisher, Harper & Row.)

11. The legitimacy of the move from the original intention of an author to a current meaning of a text which has been resituated in a later context is the subject of textual hermeneutics. Very useful on this subject is the work of Paul Ricoeur, esp. his *Interpretation Theory: Discourse and the Surplus of Meaning* (Fort Worth: Texas Christian University, 1976). I have developed a theory of hermeneutical actualization of biblical texts which would be applicable also to texts from the history of spirituality. See Sandra M. Schneiders, *The Revelatory Text: Interpreting the New Testament as Sacred Scripture* (San Francisco: Harper, 1991), esp. pp. 138-150.

12. Although this formulation, which was somehow embedded in virtually all constitutions as the primary and secondary end of the Institute, is unacceptable to most congregations today because it is dualistic, other-worldly, and disembodied, it did express in the language of an earlier time the focus of religious life as the search for God.

13. For a brief history of the effect of the Sister Formation Movement on American sisters see Elizabeth Kolmer, *Religious Women in the United States: A Survey of the Influential Literature from 1950 to 1983* (Wilmington: Michael Glazier, 1984), pp. 19-31 and Quiñonez and Turner, *Transformation,* pp. 3-30.

14. See John of the Cross, *The Ascent of Mount Carmel,* Bk. I, chs. 2-13 (available in *The Collected Works of St. John of the Cross,* tr. Kieran Kavanaugh and Otilio Rodriguez (Washington, D.C.: Institute of Carmelite Publications, 1979).

15. See *The Ascent,* Bk. I, ch. 3, parag. 4.

16. See *The Ascent,* Bk. I, ch. 4.

17. See *The Dark Night,* Bk. I, ch. 1, parags. 2-3.

18. See *The Dark Night,* Bk. I, chs. 2-7.

19. Although the term "modernism" can be traced back only to about 1905 and its formal condemnation by Pius X in the encyclical *Pascendi Dominici Gregis* to 1907, the official church's resistance to the enlightenment and its implications for theology reaches back through the pontificates of Leo XIII and Pius IX. For a good description of the modernist controversy and its effects on the church see Gabriel Daly, "Modernism," *The New Dictionary of Theology,* eds. Joseph A. Komonchak, Mary Collins, and Dermot A. Lane (Wilmington: Michael Glazier, 1987), 668-670.

20. See the references in note 8 for some clarifying presentations of post-modernism.

21. *The Dark Night,* Bk. II, ch. 3, parag. 3. Although John is here speaking of "proficients" (those who have passed through the purification of the Night of the Senses) at the beginning of the Night of the Spirit what he says is true *a fortiori* of "beginners."

22. *The Dark Night,* Bk. I, ch. 9, esp. parag. 7.

23. See *The Dark Night,* Bk. I, ch. 14.

24. One of the best explanations of the distinction between psychological disintegration and the psychic manifestations of spiritual growth is Roberto Assagioli, "Self-Realization and Psychological Disturbance," in *Psychosynthesis: A Manual of Principles and Techniques* (New York: Penguin, 1965), 35-59.

25. Actually, John of the Cross gives two complementary presentations of the signs: *The Ascent*, Bk. II, ch. 13, parags. 2-4 and *The Dark Night*, Bk. I, ch. 9, parags. 2-8.

26. Fitzgerald in "Impasse," p. 297 writes: "The most confusing and damnable part of the dark night is the suspicion and fear that much of the darkness is of one's own making. Since dark night is a limit experience, and since it does expose human fragility, brokenness, neurotic dependence, and lack of integration, it is understandable that it undermines a person's self-esteem and activates anxious self-analysis."

27. See *The Dark Night*, Bk. I, chs. 12-13.

28. John of the Cross describes the plight of those who have "no one to understand" them in *The Dark Night*, Bk. I, ch. 10, parag. 2.

29. *The Dark Night*, Bk. I, ch. 10.

30. The writings of the Indian Jesuit Anthony de Mello, such as *Sadhana: A Way to God, Christian Exercises in Eastern Form* (St. Louis: The Institute of Jesuit Sources, 1978), have proven helpful to many.

Living the Vision: The Present Moment and Future Prospects for Religious Life

Barbara Fiand, SND de N

Every once in a while, I believe, God reaches out to us in a very special way and somehow makes us feel very concretely that we are resurrection people. When Cassian Yuhaus first called me this past spring and asked me to take time to prepare a reflection concerning religious life to be shared with you on this very special occasion, I was in the middle of a new course at the seminary and immersed in a heavy speaking schedule. My summer looked extremely crowded and the only reason I accepted his invitation was that, aside from the fact that I considered this a very exciting celebration, he also was extremely persuasive and so very kind that I could not find it in me to decline. I did, however, put the project of getting ready for this event on the back burner, so to speak.

Now things on back burners have a tendency to simmer quietly. Eventually, however, they bubble up, and that is what happened in this case quite unexpectedly. I experienced what I would call one of those special resurrection moments. It happened on Holy Saturday of this year's Holy Week during the liturgy's proclamation of the gospel. You will recall that the reading for that night tells of women who went to the tomb of Jesus to anoint his body. As they arrived, however, they did not find Jesus. They were met, instead, by two angels who asked them this startling question: *"Why do you seek the living among the dead?"* Here it was where I experienced a special breakthrough where, for a moment, my attention drifted away from the rest of the proclamation and I was struck by the incredible challenge of that question, as well as by its relevance for religious life today.

Why do we so often seek the living among the dead? There is no doubt that religious life today is in crisis. We, along with the culture that in many respects birthed our mode of living the evangelical counsels, are experiencing a monumental paradigm collapse. Nothing seems any longer what it was. Entire structures appear to be imploding before our very eyes and the word is out, though it is at times vehemently rejected, that we can't go back home again to the way it was, no matter how much we loved it.

Now students of culture and of social consciousness[1] assure us that when

35

paradigms collapse the only worthwhile and creative thing to do is to start from point zero. They suggest that all attempts to rearrange matters: to rectify old views and fit them into a newly emerging vision so that no one will feel hurt, so that tradition will not be violated, and all will remain orderly, only serve to distort things and to de-energize, if not destroy creativity. When paradigms collapse, the only creative thing to do is to let go, so that free space is created for the new to emerge.

This is extremely difficult since, among other things, not all of us are aware of the death of our primary paradigms at the same time and, therefore, we keep holding on; we keep looking through outdated lenses. Our vision becomes blurred, but somehow we keep plodding along and keep thinking that if only we strained our eyes a bit more things might get back into focus. We lack "releasement," but somehow we think that not letting go is "being faithful to our founders," that holding on is "walking in their footsteps." We keep looking for the living among the dead and, as a consequence, the resurrection escapes us.

The words of Carl Jung come to mind: "No one can make history who is not willing to risk everything for it, to carry the experiment with his [her] own life through to the bitter end, and to declare that his/her life is not a continuation of the past, but a new beginning."[2] This, I believe, is what it means to be "resurrection people." This is also what it means, in the truest sense, to be faithful. Faithfulness, more than anything else, revolves around creativity, around depth listening that blossoms into hope-filled spontaneity. Being faithful to our founders is, therefore, being true to the life-giving approach that they brought to their here and now. They saw a situation of need and responded to it radically. Loyalty to that kind of tradition means, first and foremost, seizing the present moment and responding to it in creative obedience to the now. It does not mean obsession with what appears to me to be an ever more debilitating past. It does not mean holding on to the good ideas of our founders without checking for their relevance today. It does not mean looking for the living among the dead.

"No one," Jung tells us, "can make history who is not willing to risk everything for it." History, however, and with it its cultural expression and authenticity, is directly proportionate to the development of consciousness on the part of individual persons shaping that history. The opening up of awareness—human transcendence—directly influences cultural depth and transformation, and it is here where I see the relevance for religious in the years to come. It is here where I see unbelievable need and, therefore, limitless opportunity. It is here where I see call.

In a work entitled "Problems of Modern Psychotherapy," and written just two years after his previously quoted observation, Jung has this to say about western culture: "Our civilization is still young, and young civilizations need all the arts of the animal-tamer to make the defiant barbarian and the savage in us more or less tractable. But at a higher cultural level we forgo compulsion and turn to self-development."[3] It is my contention that the time to take ownership of this "higher cultural level" has dawned upon us and that we will not succeed in shaping any tomorrows for ourselves personally or institutionally, and above all and most importantly for our culture and ultimately for our globe, unless each one of us accepts this challenge in our individualized and communal lives, and in this way enables our civilization to embrace it as well. What does this mean?

Religious are not new to pioneering, to creating the new where others could not or would not. The virgin territory, however, into which we are asked to venture at this crisis point in western civilization is not, as I see it, geographic as much as it is psychic. It will not demand the conversion of swamps and forests into arable land to provide for our boarding schools and hospitals. It will ask, instead, for personal conversion, for inner transformation. A transformative future, I believe, does not require that we work hard at changing other people's lives. It demands first and foremost our own transformation and the subsequent witnessing to a new way of seeing, of interacting, of holding ourselves in relationship with others, with God, with the universe. It asks for a new ethos, a new way of dwelling on earth.

Perhaps a bit of specificity will help us get a handle on what is required here. It is a well known fact that all changes in a person's or an institution's life grow of necessity out of a change in this person's or institution's vision of reality. Our vision, however, depends on our consciousness which, in turn, is radically connected to the consciousness of the culture in which we find ourselves. Unless we, therefore, understand at least somewhat the momentum of awareness in human culture, we will find it difficult to understand the *why* of the shifts in vision that are asked of us, and of the need for change.

Religious life, as we said already, finds itself today, along with the culture in which we live, in the pain and confusion of radical change, of disintegration, of disorientation, of "lostness," of the dark night, of crisis. We are in a major turning point of our own journey, and being a religious today can, therefore, be extremely difficult and disconcerting. It is important during this time, however, to remember that, although crises are not pleasant experiences in anybody's life, and cultural crises are generally wrought with turmoil and confusion, we ought not over-emphasize the pain of this moment and should attempt to understand our era in history, rather, as a holy opportunity; as a cosmic groaning, if you will, for redemption; as clearly part of the gospel event of dying and rising.

I believe that if we cannot get ourselves to see this, we will miss a precious opportunity for new birth. In crisis, my friends, is our refounding. Karen Schwarz says it well when in *Review for Religious* she points out that

"New paradigms emerge out of old truths and are the result of a gradual letting go of traditional assumptions, prejudices and ways of thought...we do not know where we are going...a deep faith and a lot of listening will mark our way forward."⁴

The word crisis comes to us from the Greeks and means "turning point." Philosophers as well as psychologists and spiritual writers assure us that everything aware of itself experiences crises—moments of transition—in its own consciousness. Crises of consciousness are, therefore, not unhealthy, but are, in fact, signs of normality and health even though experiencing them can be extremely unpleasant.⁵ Furthermore, just as individuals are ontologically designated toward expansion of consciousness and go through specific developmental phases of awareness, so do groups of individuals and, in fact, entire cultures. As their phases of awareness climax, i.e. reach their inherent perfection, they begin to disintegrate. Yet in this very disintegration lie the seeds for the breakthrough into a still deeper level of awareness. The disintegration, therefore, is the painful but necessary part of the turning point of growth. We generally identify the term "crisis" with this painful aspect. Thus we tend to miss the fact that crises are creative moments of tremendous import that carry within them also great excitement and joy.

Simply put, we might say that every ontological crisis or turning point in maturation has six parts to it:

1. There is the reaching of perfection or climax in one particular level of awareness. This is understandably accompanied by a sense of well-being and accomplishment, of "having arrived."

2. The period of fulfillment is generally followed, however, by an overall feeling of boredom, of "is this all there is?" which is accompanied by disenchantment and disintegration.

3. Next comes a period of lostness, the desert experience of the "dark night." One does not know where to turn. Sometimes individuals, institutions, and even cultures make a lot of noise during this time. I call it the phenomenon of "whistling in the dark as one walks past the cemetery." A lot of activity tends to make us forget momentarily the experience of desolation with which we seem to be afflicted. As congregations, we hold strategic meetings, make all sorts of plans, make numerous declarations about new beginnings. Individuals may talk much, laugh loudly and bluster. They may also drown their crisis in work. Psychologists call this "being in denial."

4. The desert, if endured and suffered through, however, eventually gives way to a new vision. It will do this, of course, only in its own time. Vision is gift. It isn't something we strategize or plan for. It isn't deserved or earned. It is the dawn after the darkness. It comes when it will and as it will: sometimes gently, sometimes exuberantly. It is pure grace—like the bridegroom in the middle of the night.

5. There follows a period of experimentation and exploration with the new vision. Sometimes it is extreme. Always it is exciting and energizing.

6. Finally, after enough experimentation and celebration has taken place, a general integration of the new level with previous levels of awareness takes place.

Now, although individuals, institutions, and civilizations all pass through ontological levels of awareness and the crises that accompany them, they obviously do not all pass through them simultaneously. Furthermore, whereas individuals are called to pass through these levels in their particular lifetimes, institutions and certainly civilizations can take centuries if not millennia to do the same. It can be readily surmised, therefore, that when individuals are more advanced than the cultures or institutions in which they live, they can experience a great deal of suffering. They are also often called to prophetic witness, to social transformation, to martyrdom. It is my sense that the difficulty and pain we find ourselves in today is as acute as it is because of the intersection of crises. The following graph on page 40 may help to clarify what, upon first reflection, may appear unduly complicated.

Elsewhere I have drawn a parallel between the levels of human consciousness as discussed by Bernard J. Boelen in his book *Personal Maturity* (column 1) and Beatrice Bruteau's theory of the evolution of cultural consciousness from the "paleo feminine," through the "masculine," into the "participatory" (column 2). I have also suggested that parallels can be drawn in the evolution of religion from animism and magic, through the systematization of the mystery and a general deductive approach to theology, to induction, experience, and an overall praxis oriented religious consciousness that draws away from dualism to wholeness (column 3).[6] Similar evolutionary patterns are discussed by Richard Tarnas in his book *The Passion of the Western Mind* (Crown/Harmony, 1990). An even bolder approach is posited by Genia Pauli Haddon in her book *Body Metaphors: Releasing the God Feminine in Us All* (Crossroad, 1988).

PERSONAL MATURATION

As the graph indicates, we can identify at least three levels of human maturation. Within these Bernard Boelen sees four ontological crises marking distinct shifts in awareness during which disintegration of previous perspectives and ultimately their reintegration on a higher plane occurs.

The first level can best be understood as biological. It is ours during our sojourn in our mother's womb and remains with us even after the birth crisis during the period of coenesthesis and general at-oneness with our mother. It is the level of dependence—a state of undifferentiated cosmic unity where

LEVELS OF CONSCIOUSNESS

	1 **Human Consciousness**	**2** **Cultural Consciousness**	**3** **Religious Consciousness**	**4** **Institutional Consciousness**
Mid-life Crisis IV	PERSONAL LEVEL Self Interdependence Wholeness	HOLISTIC LEVEL Union in Diversity Inclusion Coniunctio Participation	EXPERIENTIAL LEVEL Unity in Diversity Accepting Polarities/Paradox The Whole/Mystical Union Induction/Praxis	INCLUSIVE LEVEL Diversity in Membership Society of Equals Communion Hospitality/Welcome of Others
Negative Adolescence Crisis III	FUNCTIONAL LEVEL Ego Emergence Opposition to Significant Other	MASCULINE CONSCIOUSNESS Separation from the Whole Emergence of the Hero	DUALISM Idealism/Materialism Systematization of Mystery	CASTE SYSTEM Exclusion, Hierarchism Bureaucracy
Autonomy Crisis II	Independence Uniqueness	Abstraction, Objectification Isolation/Focus	Speculative Theology Theory: Intellectual Assent	Functionalism Institutional Involvement
Birth Crisis I	BIOLOGICAL LEVEL Coenesthesis Symbiotic union Dependence	PALEO FEMININE LEVEL Herd Mentality Tribal Unity Ostracization Meant Death	MYSTERY RELIGIONS Animism Magic	CLAN Blind Obedience Total Group Identification Group Norms/Lack of Self

the general sense of my existence arises from the sum of my bodily impressions. Recent research in fetal psychology, especially by such pioneers as Stanislav Grof and Frank Lake, identify this rather forgotten period of our existence as tremendously influential for subsequent psychic development.[7]

The second level might best be identified as the level of functionality and of independence. It happens upon us during the period of *ego*-emergence (often known as the "terrible two's" and identified by Boelen as the crisis of autonomy). It is marked by a general stance of over-againstness and a need for separation and the acquiring of an individual identity. One recognizes oneself in one's difference from others and takes an individualistic stance vis-à-vis life and one's surroundings. Mutuality and sharing are not yet recognized as viable and commendable modes of interaction. The functional level, especially in its later phases, is marked by competition and ambition. Its values are in the calculable, in what can be measured and compared. It is the level of the rational, during which we are moved toward higher and higher abstraction even as we experience an ever growing alienation from our own embodiment. Its institutional parallel can probably best be understood by the term "bureaucracy"—so well described by Patricia Wittberg in her book, *Creating a Future for Religious Life,* and still a powerful mode of official interaction in religious congregations at present.[8]

The functional period climaxes for the individual during the objectifying phase of negative adolescence and ultimately gives way to the third level of consciousness marked by interdependence and an acceptance and, in fact, craving for the interpersonal. The third level is by far the longest and contains within itself numerous sub-levels. In Jungian terms, the entire second journey of life is experienced on this level. There we encounter the wider horizons of the self, and our ego as locus of activity, functionality, and primary identity yields center stage to the deeper dimensions of human existence.

Once again, it is important to emphasize that no level yields readily to the next. There is, especially during the more mature crises of human growth, confusion, pain, disorientation, alienation, the experience of desolation, of "sickness unto death," and intense resistance. But the pain is necessary pain to facilitate the letting go and to stimulate the process of conversion. And often when the night is darkest and all hope seems to have dissipated, the moment of insight breaks through. There comes, as pure gift, a gentle breeze—revelation dawns and light appears at the end of the tunnel.

But with conversion comes the mandate to embrace the gift, to surrender to the new, to cease seeking for the living among the dead, and to let one's life be transformed. The conversion of authentic maturation presents one with insights that affect one's entire way of being. There is marked change in one's disposition, one's value orientation, one's actions. Insight moves toward radical depth.

It is clear, of course, that this insight is not something we choose or effect on our own, but rather something to which we are summoned and in the face of which even our response, although it is free, takes on the form of surrender-as-gift, rather than planned execution. Individually and culturally as well as institutionally this call can always be shunned and one can fixate then wherever one finds oneself. This choice is, however, not effected without great loss of personal and cultural as well as institutional integrity. It is the betrayal of one's birthright and, within the Christian context, of one's baptism into the Christ event and the Christification of the cosmos for which all of us were created.

CULTURAL MATURATION

As will be noticed, the second column outlined on the graph identifies the movements of our culture. It is, as I already mentioned, also divided into three levels. We will recall Jung's observation, that our culture is still very young and that we still seem to need a great deal of time for the taming of the barbarian within. It is my hope, of course, that most of us at this point of our development do at least recognize the barbarian and, therefore, no longer project the shadow within upon our neighbor or other nations and cultures. Watching the news and monitoring our nation's international activities frequently discourages me, however, in the hope that is true for western adults generally. Jung's suggestion to forgo compulsion and turn to the development of the self seems to be going largely unheeded. And it is here, precisely because of this general apathy, that I believe we as religious need to risk all and put our lives on the line for the shaping of history.

It would seem to me that as a culture our developmental level overall is probably somewhere in the negative phases of the functional or what Bruteau calls the "masculine" level. Though our national and international rhetoric often would have us believe differently, the confrontational style still seems to be our predominant mode of operation: we build weapons to threaten others into peace while our inner cities fester in poverty, degradation, and violence. Bigger is still better for most of us, and having or "making" it takes precedence on almost all counts over *being*. Our foreign aid is largely in arms, and even if we work toward development, it is frequently in the giving of things to raise others' standard of living for our economic advantage—not in the nurturance and empowerment of their own cultures. There is a general boredom or *ennui* about life among many of our young people, and despair among the old. Psychologists tell us that we live in the age of alienation. We seem to find ourselves, therefore, in a general atmosphere of upheaval. What used to be is no longer. Old values appear to have perished. Our heroes have died and, with them, much hope and enthusiasm.

In order to get a more accurate picture of cultural development, it is helpful to parallel it more specifically with Boelen's individual progression from dependence through independence to interdependence. What Boelen identifies as the biological level, Bruteau, with reference to our culture, sees as the paleo feminine era. It came to an end somewhere around 3000 BCE after it had held us within its womb for what is estimated to have been over twenty thousand years. The paleo feminine era was marked by tribal unity and an almost symbiotic bonding with the clan. Nature enveloped the early human with its overpowering presence. Religion was animistic and tribal; ostracization spelled annihilation.

Just as each individual's infant phase is marked by universal at-one-ness with his or her surroundings, so for the paleo feminine consciousness there is cosmic unity, almost total absorption. Though its primary influence disappeared with the advent of the second level of consciousness, it cannot be denied that vestiges of it remain even to this day. The intense group identification and stress on blind obedience in religious congregations prior to Vatican II, for example, which so frequently resulted in thwarted ego development and regression to childishness and moral irresponsibility, situates this lifestyle quite readily on the clan level of consciousness paralleling the paleo feminine.

It is clear that the mode of consciousness of ancient culture imposed severe limitations on progress and individual maturation. Though the paleo feminine had its in-built securities, during its dominance freedom as an essential human dimension had not adequately evolved yet. There emerged, therefore, in due time among the peoples of the tribes those willing to "risk everything for the sake of history"; those who would steal fire from the gods; those who, as the Greeks would tell us, destroyed the domain of Mother Earth and erected their kingdom in the heavens. They were later called the heroes, for they brought consciousness out of the enslavement by the herd into individual awareness. They claimed for humans their power to reason and, as the centuries moved on, they developed it.

As I mentioned already, Bruteau calls the level of consciousness earned for the human race by these heroes the "masculine" form of consciousness. Like the functional level of Boelen, it developed because of its propensity to separate, to objectify, to take apart and analyze, to put over-against. It stressed diversification, abstraction, and independence as the way of salvation from the herd, the tribe. Its strength lay in its capacity to focus, to set apart, to confront, to subdue, to over-power for the sake of progress. It established itself in claiming "difference from" rather than "union with."

Few of us will find it difficult to recognize the mode of consciousness described here as that of our age. Few also would want to argue that in our time its implosion, because of its waning relevance in our quest for meaning, seems imminent. Fixation here can, of course, also be possible and, with fixation, invariably regression to the barbaric and self-destructive. If it is true that individuals who do not allow themselves to be moved through the ontological crises never reach fullness of personhood and thus betray themselves as well as their history, then it is equally true that cultures that fear to embrace higher forms of awareness and of interrelationship than the ones in which they find themselves and to which they have become accustomed also betray themselves.

PARTICIPATORY CONSCIOUSNESS

Bruteau offers a third form of consciousness. It parallels Boelen's "personal" level. She insists that it cannot authentically arise through rebellion or the overthrow of an old oppressive order. Rather it must emerge through conversion, through a genuine revolution of consciousness that transcends the dualistic and divisive modes of perceiving reality and, taking up within itself the lessons learned during previous levels of awareness, aims at wholeness without absorption. In "participatory" consciousness, as she calls it, inclusion rather than exclusion will be viewed as strength. Interdependence—the union of levels one (dependence) and two (independence) on a higher plain—will be valued. In this new paradigm the stress will be placed on unity in diversity rather than either conformity (as in the clan phase of awareness) or individualism (as in our collapsing paradigm of today). It will, as you can see, be a gathering together of both the functional or masculine and the paleo-feminine modes of awareness and will effect a moving of both into a deeper mode. Instead of over-againstness and confrontation as well as competition, this deeper form of consciousness, to which we as individuals and as cultures are called in the building up of our history, values mutual affirmation and trust. One does not find one's identity in comparing oneself negatively with the other; one rather sees oneself as loved, as good, and, therefore, knows the other as loved and as good also.

If we surrender to this call to conversion, our task will be to empower one another individually and, ultimately, internationally as well, rather than to yield to the temptation of overpowering and dominating. If we surrender to this form of perception, we will no longer experience the need to "preserve ourselves," to maintain a defensive posture. Our stance, rather, will ever more become one of self-possession; hence we can lose ourselves. From ego-enhancement we will be moved to embrace the mystery that we are. Just as ego-consciousness—along with its ability to abstract, isolate, deduce, control—was necessary at one time in the evolution of human beings from the herd instinct to rational thought, so, we will now see, the time has come to allow humanity not only to honor its head achievements— its strength—but to embrace its heart—its vulnerability, as well—and to seek creativity there.

It is clear, of course, that we are not talking here about returning to the primitive form of emotionalism and superstition that characterized the time before the emergence of reason. We are rather pointing toward a synthetic gathering together, a movement from isolation to incorporation, a conversion of consciousness that takes up the rational and discursive contributions of the previous levels into itself and converts them into a deeper, more truly human form of awareness out of which authentic human relating can then flow. Many of the transformative elements envisioned by the Leadership Conference of Women Religious and the Conference of Major Superiors of Men in 1989 speak to this mode of relating.

Nevertheless, the skeptics among us might easily see this vision as a dream of impossible magnitude. This, of course, is not so. What we are describing here is a way of seeing modeled for us some two thousand years ago by a carpenter preacher in Palestine. He was, it is true, crucified for it by the functional forms of consciousness prevalent at that time. But he was raised up!

My friends, we live in the fullness of time, in the fullness of his resurrection. The vision is already here. The revolution has already claimed its first hero. He dwells now in our midst and calls us to conversion. It is for us to claim our heritage. And it is here where I see the future of religious life today.

Because of our vision statements and chapter acts, because of the ideals we set forth in many of our documents, it would be too easy to delude ourselves into thinking, however, that indeed the vision is already realized in our midst. This, no doubt, is one of the reasons why so many of us are puzzled by the seeming lack of interest in our life together and the lack of response to our attempts at gaining new membership. But for us, as for all Christians of good will, the reign of God is here and also not yet. Our future, then, lies in striving for what is not yet. It seems that proposals about what religious might do, what works and causes they might involve themselves in, are not difficult to find. Our own documents abound with objectives and plans. It is more difficult to find it within ourselves, to reflect on, and to abide in the question as to what we might be, what we are called to strive for inwardly; to allow for conversion to touch our inner attitudes, our way of being.

There is, of course, a certain complexity and a need for a great deal of honest discernment in what I am claiming here. Perhaps a point by point identification of my position will make the task a bit easier:

First, it is clear that religious, like all other human beings, are called to depth maturation or holiness, and that the third level of consciousness ought, therefore, to be their quest, as it is for any other maturing person.

Second, it cannot be ignored that religious, like all other persons in their culture, are also affected by their culture—are the products of their culture—no matter how much they would see themselves and their lifestyle as almost automatically counter-cultural.

Third, religious institutions, as well, are culturally influenced. What Patricia Wittberg SC so eloquently describes as the bureaucracy of our communal lives and the tendency to move toward associative models of interrelationship speaks accurately to our preoccupation with functionality and its effectiveness, as well as to our need for independence.

Our concern for our survival, our endless drawing up of objectives, our actuarial studies, persistent fears about retirement funds, five year plans, various mission statements, and stacks of paper sent out annually and faithfully filled out and returned to headquarters for still another self-study of one kind or another all manifest what seems to me a feverish holding on to what is slipping from our grasp. It reminds me of the whistling in the dark I mentioned earlier. It comes with an inability to face death, and thus to ready oneself for a new, but also perhaps radically different life.

Fourth, hard as it may be to face, religious life as predominantly institutional is dying. Our convents and our schools are closing. Our hospitals are largely lay administered. The good works for which we have been founded are being performed by numerous other wonderful people. The boundaries between the sacred and the profane are disappearing, and those who came to join us because they still see relevance in our life are calling us to radical gospel living.

Fifth, to live the gospel today requires third level values. In the third and fourth columns of the diagram, I have attempted to outline the development of consciousness through which religious institutions are progressing. Much of this outline is explained in detail in my book, *Where Two or Three Are Gathered,* and does not necessitate repeating here. Suffice it to say that I see us in a variety of places within the three levels. As I mentioned already, the transformative elements articulated in 1989 clearly speak to the vision of level three. So also do the voices of many among us working among the disenfranchised of our culture. In many respects, however, our words and our lifestyle and policies do not connect, and how we relate to each other, as well as to those interested in bonding with us, lacks much of the relational justice that we proclaim for the world beyond our institutions.

Honoring diversity of culture and inclusivity in our membership cannot be achieved by the year 2010 unless behavior and the vision that induces it opens up today. The clan values, still pervasive among us, and the cast-like nitpicking concerning who belongs and who has not yet done all that is required for full membership, who may attend certain meetings, and who is not invited, what kind of ring, or cross, or veil who can wear and when (all in the name of tradition and of honoring our heritage), need to be addressed candidly. Their relevance for today needs to be questioned, and the hidden and often unconscious motivation for the perpetuation of such issues needs to be explored.

It is my experience that leadership here is often sadly lacking. We can so easily reject the call to inner transformation by pointing out that religious ought to be dealing with bigger things than worrying about the regressive behavior in their own midst. But the sad fact remains that unless our life together empowers us through justice and love, our modeling of it in our ministry will eventually appear hollow as well. The need to address the injustice in others can easily become compulsive if it is not balanced by the awareness of personal sin and an earnest attempt to address the latter. Jung's warning that "at a higher cultural level we forgo compulsion and turn to self-development" can be dismissed as a luxury that we cannot afford in a world of injustice, oppression, and cruelty only at our own peril.

Often the resistance to examining our mode of living together comes from a fear that if we finally address community life, we will be forced to return to pre-Vatican II models of co-habitation, to what Sandra Schneiders identifies so accurately as the primary family model of group living that reduces all of us to infantilism and invariably brings about psychological regression.[9] It is my suggestion, however, that the unexamined life exposes us to many more serious dangers. To begin with, there is a certain irresponsibility in drifting into various and sundry living arrangements. We are what we are today as ministers, as professionals, because we consciously chose to diversify and to educate ourselves accordingly. Our life together does not deserve less. Trends in communal lifestyles are worth taking seriously only to the extent to which they are backed by vision and purpose. Religious embracing the holistic level of consciousness cannot afford being objects of fate tossed about by fads.

Second, and perhaps even more insidiously, there is in the unexamined life a tendency (sometimes quite unrecognized) to fixate in previous modes of consciousness even as one is proclaiming the rhetoric of liberation. Old clan values have a tendency to invade even the most advanced attitudes when critical self-awareness is absent:

(a) Shared prayer, as beautiful as it sounds, can be terribly oppressive especially if everyone is "expected" to be there.

(b) Consensus decision making, as I have explored elsewhere,[10] far from honoring each member's uniqueness (level 3), can serve instead to tyrannize the group and thwart all honest discernment.

(c) At the local community level, decisions made in common for the sake of shared authority can reduce community life to the ridiculous and, in resisting all discernment of gifts, often lowers our expectations to mediocrity.

Witnessing to the third level of consciousness, to which, I believe, we are called in this age of cultural crisis, demands that we examine our life together and explore the unhealthy patterns of fixation and regression still festering there. This, without question, demands great personal and communal courage and a genuine return to the holiness of our founders, as well as the pioneering spirit of our forefathers and foremothers. Our journey in this regard, as I pointed out already, will be primarily psychic, and will open us up both to our collective strength as well as to our darkness. This can indeed be frightening. I do not believe, however, that we have any choice if we are to remain true to our call to wholeness.

Great holiness demands great sacrifice. "No one can make history who is not willing to risk everything." This is the tradition passed on to us by our founders. It asks us to liberate hitherto unknown, because unconscious, energies and to trust that the Spirit of God, once more as always, will move over the chaos of our lives and make all things new.

Notes

1. Joel Arthur Barker, *The Business of Paradigms,* Discovering the Future Series (Burnsville: Charthouse International Learning Corporation, 1990), video cassette presentation.

2. C.G. Jung, *Psychological Reflections,* ed. Jolande Jacobi & R.F.C. Hull (Princeton: Princeton University Press, 1978), p. 147.

3. Ibid., pp. 147-148.

4. Karen Schwarz, "Alternate Forms of Membership in Religious Congregations," *Review for Religious,* Vol. 50, No. 4, p. 562.

5. Bernard J. Boelen, *Personal Maturity* (New York: Seabury, 1979). The entire book deals with the essential necessity as well as the health of ontological crises in human maturation.

6. Barbara Fiand, *Where Two or Three Are Gathered* (New York: Crossroad, 1992), ch. 1.

7. A well-written account summarizing the findings of both of these scholars in this area can be found in June Singer's *Love's Energies* (Boston: Sigo Press, 1990), chs. 11-12.

8. Patricia Wittberg S.C., *Creating a Future for Religious Life* (New York: Paulist Press, 1991), ch. 3.

9. Sandra Schneiders, *New Wineskins* (New York: Paulist Press, 1986), p. 147.

10. Barbara Fiand, *Where Two or Three Are Gathered* (New York: Crossroad, 1992), p. 52.

A Discerning Approach to Contemporary Religious Life: Reading the Signs

Benjamin Tonna, STD

Religious life can be approached as a tradition which developed to recapture the radical experience of the first disciples "who ate and drank with him after he rose from the dead" (Acts 10:41). That experience proved foundational for the church.

The church, of course, is more than an experience. It is also a mystery. As soon as that mystery is "lived out," however, it generates the experience of discipleship. And when John Paul II states that religious life is "at the very heart of the ecclesial mystery,"[1] the implication is that this life is also an experience in which the heart of that mystery is "lived out." It is the objective church in the process of being subjectively experienced by women and men religious.

When that experience is systematically handed on as a tradition, it acquires a social dimension. It becomes an institution which makes accessible to Christians of different times and places those conditions in which it has been and can still be "lived out." Because it happens in the church and because it facilitates the experience of "being church," it is a fully fledged ecclesial tradition.

That tradition has not been of one piece. It has not simply reproduced the precise conditions which accompanied discipleship and the church in the first place. As it was handed on, it took on broad new patterns which were not there in the beginning.

Padberg identifies the major forms which it has picked up in the course of its passage through history: *seclusion* (from about 250 A.D., in the east, in groups of disciples of hermits); *community* (with the monastic movement which began in the sixth century); *urban, mobile and lay* dimensions (with the mendicants of the twelfth century); *clerical and apostolic* patterns (fifteenth century) and *centralization* (nineteenth and twentieth centuries). Vatican II reviewed its foundations and, in Padberg's words,

50

The quantity and especially the quality of that change can be evoked by simply recalling ten words or phrases from Vatican II: Aggiornamento, Collegiality, Dialogue, People of God, Liturgy, Religious Liberty, Inculturation, Gaudium et Spes, Ecumenism and Revelation.[2]

The convergence of these ten traits with the characteristics of the current experience of "being church" points to the centrality of the religious life tradition in the "lived out" ecclesial mystery.

My Proposal

The period covered by that change coincides with the twenty-five years of the International Institute for Religious which we are celebrating with this meeting. My proposal, in this paper, is to focus on the experience of that period, as lived and recorded by those directly involved in it. My hope is that the exercise will yield fresh insight on the present moment and on the future prospects of the religious life tradition.

I approach that experience with an act of faith. The same Lord who was present at its beginnings is still with it today. Insofar as it is an experience *with him* it is not just the project of women and men religious. It is also his project. Consequently, with them, he must have had—and he must still have—plans for the ongoing joint enterprise. And he must be working on them.

I will strive to "live out" this act of faith by discerning. Humbly, I will try to catch any visible signs of the invisible work of the Spirit of the Lord on the religious life tradition, as the Spirit provides those committed to it with fresh experiences of "living out" the very mystery of the church.

My discernment exercise will be personal and communal: I will do the discerning *on my own* but I will be working on the experience of *the many* involved in contemporary religious life.

I do not expect or pretend to "see" the plans of the Spirit. But I do hope to make contact with them as I began to see signs of the active presence which the Lord has promised his church: "Know that I am with you always, until the end of the world" (Mt 28:20).

My discernment will be based on my "living out" the mysteries of the incarnation and redemption. "The Word became flesh and made his dwelling among us" (Jn 1:14) means that he made his all aspects of the human condition, except sin. Consequently, any dimension of that condition has the potential of becoming a carrier of signs of his active presence, a *locus theologicus*, a place from which God can speak. And since the whole purpose of the incarnation was redemption, I can expect to find signs of his activated plans of salvation in any one of its dimensions. Indeed, I hope to encounter a multitude of them in that particular human condition which is religious life.

I will structure my discerning approach in seven steps: *Frame, Hope, Watch, Probe, Test, Map and Go!* In the first step, I will focus the religious life experience which I will be scrutinizing for signs. This will provide boundaries for the discernment exercise. In the second step, I will take a contemplative look at the reality they contain. In the third, Watch, step, I will assemble and organize available information about it, and in the fourth, Probe, step, I will examine it for any recurring patterns. The fifth, Test, step will check emerging patterns against those which characterize salvation history. I will then spell out the options for behavior which flow from the patterns which pass that test. This will be the Map step. In the final—Go!—step, I will choose an option and act on it.

The steps are really seven moments of a discernment cycle and they tend to overlap and to reinforce one another. Indeed, the last one loops back to the first to make discernment an ongoing process.

1. THE FRAME STEP: PARAMETERS FOR DISCERNMENT

My discernment will be concerned with religious life as it has been lived by those involved in it during the last twenty-five years. The context will be global but the area on which I will discern will be confined to the experience of the 160,000 women and men religious in the United States and the 160,100 in Latin America, as this has been recorded and examined by the Third National Assembly of the Leadership Conference of Women Religious (LCWR) and the Conference of Major Superiors of Men (CMSM) held in Louisville, Kentucky, August 19-23, 1989 and the IX General Assembly of the Confederation of Latin American Religious (CLAR) held in Cuautitlan, Mexico in February 1991.

As context, I will keep in mind the global statistics of the period. There were 1,293,466 priests, sisters, brothers and novices in the world in 1973 and 1,053,022 in 1988, according to Vatican sources. This means a drop of 13% in sheer numbers for the fifteen year period. The corresponding shifts, in percentages, were, for women 14%, for men 11% and for brothers 19%. There was a dramatic increase of 44% for novices.[3]

A more significant context for the exercise, however, is that provided by the *sensus ecclesiae* or the "feeling" of the universal church about it. In the words of Shaun McCarty S.T., the current mood is one of an earnest search for meaning:

The crisis facing religious (mainly in the United States and in Western Europe) is marked by a decrease in vocations, an increase in median age, and a growing complexity of ministerial needs...many are experiencing either sadness, fear, anger, helplessness, hopelessness, or some combination of the above!...Religious life is in transition.... I would suggest enlarging one's perspectives so as to face the future with hope.... It is also my contention that, though painful, crisis bears potential for growth. "Crisis" literally means being presented with a situation demanding decision. The word for discernment in Greek is diakrisis, that is, a sorting out. It is that sorting out that I would like to address. As all Christians, religious have a responsibility to discern the signs of the times in the process of making decisions for the future in a spirit of hope for the coming of the kingdom. So the question is: what help is available in reading the signs of the times that are pertinent to what has always been a changing shape of religious life?[4]

A significant indicator of this searching stance is the choice of the religious life and its mission in the church and the world as the topic of the IX Synod of Bishops, scheduled for 1994.

2. THE HOPE STEP: DISCERNING BY CONTEMPLATING AND HOPING

The experience of contemporary women and men religious can be approached in a contemplative stance. I can look at it with those inner eyes of faith which alert me to the stirrings of salvation history as this unfolds within it. I believe that, lodged deep within religious life, there are *semina Verbi* that is, those *seeds of the Word* which Vatican II in *Ad Gentes*, indicated as present in cultures.[5]

My faith in the mysteries of the incarnation and the redemption assures me that the visible, historical Jesus of Nazareth lives on as the invisible risen Christ; that he acts through a visible church, his mystical body, the *sacramentum mundi*—or *sign for the world*; that he acts through his seeds, generously sown by his Spirit, in the cultures humanity lives by.

Surely then, if these *semina Verbi* can be found in all cultures, I can expect them to be present and operative in the specific culture constituted by religious life. Like all cultures, this is a way of life, a "lived out" experience. Again, I do not expect to see those seeds. But I can establish contact with them by contemplating their presence there. Indeed, I can hope to see the shoots they must send to the surface of the soil of their cultures as they germinate and grow.

From my "cloud of unknowing" I therefore contemplate the hidden seeds, hoping that signs of their vibrant life will penetrate my darkness to become the visible signs of the times I seek in order to move closer to the invisible seeds of the Word.

My faith, here, merges with my hope. In Kerstien's words:

> The basis and centre of Christian faith is the message of Jesus and its promises, and Jesus being raised by God. But these two things, the message and the resurrection, are not really themselves in their entirety without the return of Jesus, without the resurrection of all flesh (1 Cor 15), without the new heaven and the new earth (Rev 21:22). Hence faith in the resurrection of Jesus means hope in the universal consummation which is promised and prefigured by his resurrection.... In hope, the believer pierces the gap which has been opened up by the cross and resurrection of Jesus. Faith and hope are two inseparable moments of the one act of which (initial) love is the integrating centre.[6]

This hope, inspired by the incarnation and the redemption, offers me new opportunities for knowledge and action.

In knowledge terms, it makes me more sensitive to movement from the hidden seed of the Word which has been sown in the experience of women and men religious. Because I know that the seeds are there, I tend to be very attentive and I am likely to catch a host of small signs—which would then converge to constitute a major sign.

In action terms, the same hope moves me to respond existentially to these signs. By raising my consciousness of the presence of the loving and saving Lord, it pulls me toward him, as the beloved is attracted by her lover in the Song of Songs. It motivates me to search for the visible signs of the invisible lover. It enables me to experience, in these signs, his coming—through the *semina Verbi*. It will be in this experience that I will make contact with his power—and so be empowered to act and build the future.

Hope also offers new knowledge about the nature of action on that future. In its light, I contemplate the future of religious life not as something already "made" by the Lord but as a reality which has to be built jointly, as in the original project of the first church experience, by him and by those involved in it. That future will be the outcome of history. God, of course, remains the Lord of history. But this history has to be made by people, because

> we can only speak of history when the specifically human intervenes: freedom, responsibility, decision, possible failure in the individual and inter-subjective spheres. Freedom is the key to the new, to the coming of what never was before. History is played out between the freedom of God, the ground of all, and the freedom of man. Christian hope fixes

its gaze on the futurity which this play of freedoms makes possible and not on the predetermined goal of a development. Hope looks to history that is to come. God gives salvation in such a way that it has also to be achieved by man. Hence man goes towards the future which he hopes for from God by advancing towards his inner-worldly future.... Hope does not render effort superfluous but demands it.[7]

There is a very practical side to the hope which the contemplative stance inspires: the future of religious life does not only depend on the renewal and refounding effort of women and men religious but also on their freely and enthusiastically joining a major partner in the common project which it is— and has always been.

3. THE WATCH STEP: DISCERNING BY WATCHING FOR TRENDS

In the third moment of my discernment exercise, this same hope inspires me to heed the call of the gospel to "be on the watch!" (Lk 21:36) and to carefully observe all that is happening to religious life. The knowledge and action insights which it provides move me to scrutinize each aspect of the religious life experience as a possible *locus theologicus*, a carrier of signs of the salvific power of the seeds of his Word.

As I take in the information, however, I realize that I can hardly digest it in its raw form. Its chaotic volume overwhelms me. I have to find some way to make it manageable.

The convergence principle helps me do just that. It processes the data in the same way scrutineers manage the returns of complex elections: they are usually more interested in the persons on whom the votes cast tend to converge than in each single vote. With the principle, I begin to seek the points where the various items of the data about the religious life tradition tend to converge. Once I see these points, I can link them together and patterns begin to emerge to help me make sense of the information.

In my case, I am interested in the specific patterns which indicate how the religious life tradition is moving in history. Quite often, such patterns emerge as trends—those familiar data processing categories which reveal how a past is moving into a present and how a present is proceeding toward a future. Trends are patterns of time and time is the stuff of history.

Since I am focusing on the way in which the seeds of the Word may be driving religious life, trends stand a good chance of carrying signs of the energy which emanates from those seeds to give it direction. If the invisible seeds tend to move that reality forward, visible trends tend to record that motion.

The application of the convergence principle helps me watch with a purpose: if some experience happens regularly and consistently, then that experience is probably connected to a trend.

Trends in the U.S.

The LCWR-CMSM and CLAR assemblies took pains to process the information before them in the same way.

In the case of the LCWR-CMSM, Stephen Tutas S.M., the outgoing president of the CMSM, could derive, from the data, ten trends which, with the Assembly, he called transformative elements:

A gathering of leaders of the estimated 130,000 women religious and 30,000 men religious in the service of Church in the USA and beyond...[reflected] on the future of the world and the Church and the response of religious to these anticipated change.... Looking forward to the year 2010 means that we are dealing with four five year plans. Only a great belief in the value of religious life and the power of the Spirit at work among us enables religious to accept the mission as messengers of hope in the Church today. The assembly statement was a commitment: "we will nourish these transformative elements for religious life in the future." They were ten in number, arranged in the order of priorities. The first three are these:

1. **Prophetic witness:** Being converted by the example of Jesus and the values of the gospel, religious in the year 2010 will serve a prophetic role in church and in society. Living this prophetic witness will include critiquing societal and ecclesial values and structures, calling for systemic change and being converted by the marginalized with whom we serve.

2. **Contemplative attitude toward life:** Religious in the year 2010 will have a contemplative attitude toward life. They will be attentive to and motivated by the presence of the sacred in their own inner journeys, in the lives of others, and throughout creation. Recognizing contemplation as a way of life for the whole church, they will see themselves and their communities as centers of spirituality and the experience of God.

3. **Poor and marginalized persons as the focus for ministry:** Religious in 2010 will be investing their resources in direct service

with and advocacy for structural change on behalf of the poor. They will minister where others will not go. Their own listening to and learning from the poor and marginalized will shape all aspects of their lives.

The other transformative elements, without commentary, are:

4. Spirituality of wholeness and global interconnectedness

5. Charism and mission as sources of identity

6. Change of the locus of power

7. Living with less

8. Broad based, inclusive communities

9. Understanding ourselves as church

10. Developing interdependence among people of diverse cultures[8]

Trends in Latin America

In the case of CLAR, a survey of the federations of women and men religious in Latin America conducted before the 1991 assembly provided the gathering with a report which included a list of trends.[9]

Among these, the option for the poor emerged as crucial to the understanding of the major transformation of religious life currently in progress in Latin America. That option was being activated as an "insertion" in the local cultures of poverty. It was a dynamic experience, in *crescendo*, of "living for the poor, living with the poor, living like the poor, giving life for the poor (martyrdom)."[10]

Historically, insertion developed from the experience of implementing the option, in the 1960s and 1970s, on sociological, political, ethical and psychological grounds and the subsequent discussions and tensions of the 1980s. One side in the debate had made the point that the option was being imposed. In the 1990s the activation of the option had developed spiritual and theological roots. The very sensitivity to the poor which it had originally produced was now being experienced as a gift of the Spirit, indeed, as the fruit of this gift.

This shift was identified by the CLAR report as the basic, current trend of the religious life tradition in Latin America. The very experience of God and the silent and compassionate contemplation of his presence in the poor were highlighted as elements which were moving religious life to the new spiritual and theological commitment expressed by the concept of *insertion*, in which

> Religious life encounters impoverished peoples with distinct cultures—whether indigenous, afro-american, rural or suburban. We are rather far from a true dialogue with these cultures. We are also far from taking seriously the "seeds of the Word" sown in them. And yet this constitutes the only possibility of inculturating the Gospel. Insertion, however, and the experience of its praxis have put religious life on the road of inculturation—the slow and patient process which opens doors to cultures.[11]

The current thrust was moving from solidarity with and support for the poor to insertion among them. All local federations agreed on this point:

> All reports found in the sequela Christi, in the teaching of the Church, and in discernment lived in the light of the Word of God, the deepest roots of all this transformation.[12]

This foundational transformative trend, in turn, was being expressed in specific *trends*, all identified by the CLAR report, *toward*:

1. *A new spirituality:* with the accent on a new experience of God and a new prayer stance which motivate and promote the changes suggested by the signs of the times: there is more contemplation, more silence (with and from the people, especially in times of duress), more participation in the liturgy and in sacramental life.

2. *More quality community life:* "we are not women and men religious because we take the vows but we take the vows because we are women and men religious, who form a new family in the name of the Lord."[13]

3. *A new approach to charism:* the option for the poor is throwing more light on particular charisms.

4. *A deeper consciousness of the prophetic mission* of religious life: the option for the poor, the proclamation of the good news, the rediscovery of the political dimensions of the gospel and the insertion in local cultures are all connected and, together, constitute the mandate of religious.

5. *More intercongregational relationships.*

6. *More sharing of charism with the laity.*

7. *More integration of religious life in the mission of the church.*

8. *More communal and personal witness* to the presence of the kingdom.

9. *More presence of women* in the life of society, the church and religious life itself.

10. *More local vocations.*

11. *More attention to root new recruits in their cultures,* more contact of recruits with the local people and the local churches during the formative period.

12. *More insertion in the local churches,* notwithstanding current tensions and problems.

The final declaration of the Assembly confirmed the trends:

It is consoling to see that we, the 160,000 men and women religious who live and struggle in our extensive territory, not only have a sense of being faithful followers of Christ but that—as the Holy Father wrote recently—"our presence is a huge potential in terms of individuals and communities" [29-9-90]. So that this crisis situation might be converted into a time of grace, a genuine *kairos* for the men and women religious of the continent, we have lived these days in an intense climate of spiritual discernment.... Among the positive features, we would like to mention the growing awareness that the preferential option for the poor is a gift of the Spirit to the Church...we want to live and work on behalf of the poor; we want to live and work in favor of the poor; and some of us do it with them, and some like them. It is in this way that life lived among the poor is a very significant way of expressing our commitment to the poor. We recognize that this same option, with the encouragement of the Church's magisterium, has led to the rise of a new spirituality of consecrated life which is eminently Christocentric, incarnate, prophetic and contemplative, based on and inspired by the Word of God, read and prayed over with the poor, and in the light of the sad real life circumstances of the poor. The witness in martyrdom of many of our colleagues is the fruit of this spirituality.... We note that in many communities there is greater concern for the individual person and his or her life, the growing practice of communitarian discernment and an awareness of shared responsibility, solidarity, and interpersonal relations.... We value the growing intercongregationality which is happening with no loss of identity to the individual congregations and which is helping overcome clannishness and contributes to better identification of the charism proper to each.... We rejoice that in many places women's personal dignity is being appreciated, as is their ability to put their talents at the service of society and the Church; that the emergence of women as new subjects in society and the Church is being recognized.... We note a series of efforts towards shaping the formation of young religious and to work with the ongoing formation of older religious, in terms of a model which is both personalized and personalizing, which promotes freedom and participation based on activity and following a communitarian plan which is drawn up, implemented and evaluated regularly.[14]

Common Trends

The convergence principle can be used to find the points on which both LCWR-CMSM and CLAR assemblies merged. Cultures may differ but the good seeds sown in them come from the same source. Any convergence in the two sets of trends may point to a common call from the Word to all those involved in contemporary religious life.

A first confluence of the trends can be found in the issues addressed. Both prioritize spirituality, the option for the poor, prophecy, community and witness.

Within each of these issues, further convergencies can be identified.

Both the U.S. and Latin America prioritized contemplation, with the latter highlighting new experiences of God.

While the U.S. put the option for the poor as third priority, Latin America placed it first. The experience of the option as insertion by the latter in a context of massive poverty explains the difference of emphasis.

Almost inversely, prophecy is placed first by the U.S. and fourth by Latin America.

Community is prioritized in both situations but given different expressions. U.S. religious are more sensitive to its structural dimensions, as evidenced by the trend toward changes in authority and toward broad-based, inclusive communities (U.S. trends: 6 and 8). The Latin Americans stress what is actually happening in communities: communal discernment, affirmation of the self, freedom, participation (L.A. trends: 5.2 and 7). Both groups tend to understand community in more ecclesial terms (U.S. trend: 9, L.A. trends 7 and 13).

4. THE PROBE STEP: DISCERNING BY PROBING FOR VALUES

Of the many possible origins of trends, values have long been singled out as meriting special attention because of their primary role in moving the human condition. In this step, I apply the convergence principle to learn more about the values which drive the trends of contemporary religious life.

Values are what people consider as worth striving for. They are ideas and ideals held by individuals and groups about what is desirable, proper, good and, by implication, preferable. The very word *value,* when used as a verb, highlights their propensity to prioritize: when I value a thing, I put it before other things. This makes values powerful sources of human initiative. They have been called "attitudes about attitudes" in the sense that they bring order to the attitudes which move human behavior and, in a way, operate as pockets of energy, lodged deep in the human condition, driving people to enhance their lives by ensuring order in their behavior. They can even be considered as "spirits," a term which, in the Bible, also means energy. This raises the probability of their becoming a *locus theologicus* or carriers of signs of the seed of the Word.

Can the values which move the trends of contemporary religious life be identified? They can be approached through the behavior they generate. Brian P. Hall, in *Genesis Effect*, describes how specific behavior can point to specific values. He compiled a list of common human values and used it to clarify the values behind particular human situations.[15]

I used his list to clarify which particular values could have generated the trends identified by the Watch step. Between them, its one hundred and twenty-five values cover most human situations. The list is structured, assigning to each value a fixed position on one of its eight stages of a human growth track. The practical implication is that each value on it provides information on the point of arrival, on the journey of life, indicated by the behavior generated by that same value. In this sense, the list can be used to "measure" values.

The list served as an instrument in an exercise which involved my going through each trend to confront it with the list and thus find out which cluster of values could be working on it.

The *option for the poor* trend, for example, readily suggested such values on Hall's list as *presence, detachment, empathy, simplicity, new order, mission* and *justice*.

The exercise generated as many as fifty-seven values. I trimmed this number by using the techniques which Hall recommends—removing the values which appeared only sporadically in the trends and prioritizing the others according to their frequency.

Hall also suggests reordering the final list in developmental clusters. Values high on his scale are put on what he calls a *future* cluster, those on its low end on a *foundation* cluster and those in between on the critical *focus* cluster. Within each cluster, the values are chained in goal-means combinations. A coherent system emerges and illustrates how values interface to help people develop. When I applied this procedure, connections began to appear.

The cluster of future values consisted of *truth with interdependence, ecority with justice/world order, transcendence.* This means that people in religious life in the U.S. and Latin America were looking forward to full authenticity, in word and deed, and that they were moving toward that situation by seeking to work and to be together, both as individuals and in communities.

The second link in the chain meant that they were envisaging a future in which they would be addressing ecological issues by adopting and developing a global and comprehensive approach. *Ecority*, in fact, is a word created by Hall from *ecology, responsibility* and *authority*.

The two combinations of goals means values would lead to the "going beyond" (transcending) their current limits, in consciousness and in experiences, including the consciousness and experience of God.

This chain of future values describes the long term prospects suggested by the values which drive the identified trends. It constitutes a vision which can pull women and men religious forward.

Such a vision, however, has to be grounded in the present in order to generate this forward motion. This happens through a chain of foundation values formed by three links—*self-preservation with safety, security with tradition* and *self-worth.*

The first link concentrates on present reality by facing the issue of the very survival of religious life, vis-à-vis the writing on its statistical walls. The response is being sought in the safety nets of new vocations, renewed community life and improved relations with society.

The outcome would be security, a value which highlights the inclination to keep a vigilant eye on the doors through which destructive forces could enter. Here the means value of tradition is mobilized by a preference to reinforce those patterns of religious life which have worked in the past.

The linkage of security with tradition generates the critical value of self-worth. Women and men religious tend to see their foundations in terms of their getting in touch with their talents and gifts and sharing them with others in a situation of mutual respect.

In terms of actual energy, it is the focus cluster which merits careful consideration. It includes the values which move people to adopt priorities and to really work for what they consider as worth striving for. The values driving the trends, here, were identified as *worship with loyalty, wholeness with congruence, service with adaptability, presence with collaboration, contemplation with communal discernment.*

The first link in the chain means that women and men religious currently prioritize the attitude of rendering to God the respect which is due by taking very seriously strict adherence to their beliefs and to rites.

The link develops the value of wholeness which here means an inclination to develop the full potential of their lives harmoniously through the means value of congruence, which, in its turn, moves them to seek, above all, to experience and express feelings and thoughts in such a way as to give others the image that they are "of one piece."

Service is the normal outcome of such a combination of values. It is the attitude of positively contributing to other people's needs. It is ensured by the means goal of adaptability which always implies a readiness to adjust to circumstances. This leads to the key link of presence and collaboration.

Presence is "being with" others and is the value behind the option for the poor. It develops quickly when combined with the means value of collaboration or "working with" others. The linkage leads to contemplation.

Contemplation as a value means the disposition to see things through. It observes reality in breadth and depth, including the reality of other people. It flows into and depends on communal discernment, the inclination to take communal realities seriously and to try to understand them.

In real life, it is the whole complex of the three clusters which provides the motivation for the religious life experience. Future values constitute its promised land—worth striving for but still far off. Foundation values are the actual equipment for the journey toward it. Focus values are really the marching orders for today: they provide the stimulus to act and to move in specific directions.

5. THE TEST STEP: DISCERNING BY TESTING THE SPIRITS

"Do not trust every spirit but put every spirit to a test to see if they belong to God, because many false prophets have appeared in the world. This is how you can recognize God's spirit: every spirit that acknowledges Jesus Christ come in the flesh belongs to God" (1 Jn 4:1-2).

With these words John, the good disciple, indicates what discernment is all about: the process of deciding whether a specific human reality can be taken as a sign of a divine initiative. Can the "spirits" represented by the human values identified in the fourth step be signs of the active presence of the *semina Verbi* lodged in religious life? The application of John's unique criterion can supply the answer.

The test is the alignment or otherwise of these values with the values which "acknowledge Jesus." These would be the values contained in the gospel which Jesus preached. To identify them, I analyzed the core content of the preaching of Jesus, which was the kingdom of God. The concept brings to a head and, in a way, encapsulates salvation, with its basic plan and its ongoing history. When I pray "Your kingdom come!" I am actually praying for the activation of its plans in our days, for the seeds of the Word to come to fruition.

The liturgy, on the feast of Christ the King, thanks God for the coming of this kingdom, describing it in explicit value terms: "a kingdom of truth and life, a kingdom of holiness and grace, a kingdom of justice, love and peace"

(Preface of Christ the King). Here the church is actually experiencing and celebrating the life which the coming of the kingdom generates. The seven values put me on the track of the other values which drive this new gospel life.

The kingdom which Christ preached can be approached as a complex of attitudes which God, in his great gift of Christ, adopts toward, and reveals to, humanity. They are attitudes of salvation, covenant, love, communion and new life. Once they are accepted in faith, they inspire in people a complex of corresponding prioritizing attitudes which can be called kingdom values: acceptance of Christ promotes discipleship, salvation brings freedom, love generates love, communion begets holiness and the new life experiences heaven.

The key attitude, because of the priority it gives to Christ, is that of discipleship. It is built on faith, proceeds in hope, expresses itself in love. It involves growth. Discipleship becomes the new life of those who accept and expect the coming kingdom. This happened in the first experience of becoming church and of religious life. It is the experience of this life which the liturgy has been celebrating for two thousand years.

The analysis of the biblical and theological foundations of the kingdom concept from the perspective of the human attitudes it tends to prioritize helped me draw up the list in Figure 1. When I had identified its values I staggered them along Hall's development track to make it more readily comparable to his list of human values. The outcome was a list of the values of a *coming* kingdom of God. I call it a list of Christian values because it consists of "spirits who acknowledge Christ." But it can also be considered as a list of gospel values.

I used the list to apply John's criterion and test the "spirits" of religious life today. Taking the human values of the fourth step as these "spirits," I simply asked, for each of them: How does it compare with the Christian values which belong to the same stage of human growth?

Signs of the Future

I began by checking the values of the future cluster. These point in the direction of the vision which inspires and moves people to act. I found that, with the exception of ecority, the goal values of the Probe step aligned squarely with the values of the last two stages of the kingdom list. The means values were also in line: interdependence reflected union and could be combined with truth to lead to transcendence. By dropping ecority and rearranging the chain, I ended with a modified Christian cluster: *truth with union leading to transcendence.*

Figure 1: Christian Values

I: CHRIST AS HEALER		II: CHRIST AS MASTER	
1-A	1-B	2-A	2-B
Goal Values			
Fear of God	Happiness	Call/Vocation	Chosen/Elect
Healing	New Life	Grace	Salvation
Redemption	Stability	Liberation	Worship
Means Values			
Forgiveness	Faith	Brotherhood	Discipleship
Prayer	Patience	Community	Conversion
Power	Praise	Fidelity	Church
Refuge	Temperance	Fortitude	Love
Survival	Tradition	Hope	Prudence
Trust		Mercy	Victory
		Providence	

III: CHRIST AS FRIEND		IV: CHRIST AS LORD	
3-A	3-B	4-A	4-B
Goal Values			
Equality	Dignity	Contemplation	Glory
Freedom	Fulfillment	Holiness	Interdependence
Growth	Justice	Judgment	Transcendence
Justification	Presence	Resurrection	
Wholeness	Truth		
Means Values			
Dialogue	Charity	Intimacy	Communion
Friendship	Discernment	Renewal	Heaven
Generosity	Meaning	Simplicity	Universality
Participation	Mission	Union	
Reconciliation	Peace		
Search	Poverty		
Service	Unity		
Sharing			
Witness			

The implication is that the values identified can be taken into serious consideration as possible signs that the seeds of the Word are calling women and men religious in the Americas toward a vision of a future where reality, including the ultimate reality of God *(transcendence)*, is experienced through a sharper and deeper discovery of *truth*, realized through the coming together *(union)* of hitherto unconnected parts of their social and individual lives.

This may seem abstract and vague. But visions are like that. The cluster, however, does give an idea of the promised land of the coming kingdom, which can inspire women and men religious to risk the trajectory toward it.

Foundation Signs

Such a journey, however, demands a sound launching pad. This is provided by the foundation cluster. When confronted with the kingdom values of the first stages, it stood the test well.

Its goal values of self-preservation, security and self-worth showed congruence with the Christian values of healing, stability and call. For the corresponding means values, safety aligned well with refuge. In kingdom terms, the value chain becomes: *healing with refuge* leads to *stability* which, when linked *with tradition* generates *the call*.

This means that the same women and men religious can confidently undertake the journey toward the promised land when they give priority attention to *healing* existing cracks in the foundations of their religious life tradition by taking the necessary correcting precautions *(refuge)*, relying on the valid *traditions* which worked in the past, in such a way as to *stabilize* their response to the *call*.

Focus Signs

Focus values propel people from the launching pad of the foundation cluster toward the future. Can the values of the focus chain be pointing to energy released from the kingdom values of the hidden seed? If so, they can effectively move religious life forward to its future.

The first three—worship with loyalty, leading to wholeness—directly connect to the kingdom values of worship, obedience and wholeness.

The second link in the chain—wholeness with congruence, moving toward service—is difficult to align but service can be integrated in the value of presence.

The third group—now wholeness, congruence, leading to presence—fits in well with the gospel values of wholeness with witness, leading to presence.

The last values—presence with discernment, leading to contemplation—are directly reflected in the sixth stage of the kingdom list.

The modified focus list thus becomes: the link *wholeness with witness* leads to *presence* which, when coupled with *discernment* moves people to *contemplation.*

The implications, for religious life, are far-reaching. They throw precious light on the power—which may be emanating from the hidden seeds—to motivate women and men religious to call them to their future. They may constitute a complex of signs with the message that there will be growing awareness, among them, of their potential *wholeness* and of the skills needed to harness it in *witness* to the active *presence* of the incarnate and saving Lord of history; *contemplation,* by them, of the same Lord, in tandem with individual and communal *discernment,* will provide focus for their lives.

6. The Map Step: Discerning by Defining the Options

Action-Oriented Discernment

The conclusions of the fifth step point to three sets of values as possible signs of the seeds of the Word in the specific culture of contemporary religious life. They were derived from what, up to this point, has been a predominantly interior exercise. This sixth step moves closer to the seeds of the Word to tap their energy. It prepares for action. It seeks to indicate which specific behavior responds best to the call of the signs which may be coming from that Word. It "makes" the decision to act by mapping out available options so that, in the next and final step, discerners can "take" it.

To spell out the options, the procedure adopted by the Probe step has to be reversed. Instead of deriving values from behavior, I here have to imagine the behavior which best fits the value system identified by the Test step.

The exercise harnesses the energy released by the second moment of the discernment cycle: the same hope which pulled me in the direction of the seeds of the Word will now help me look the future in the face and actually build it by establishing contact with the power which emanates from the Word.

The options will be presented in terms of the models of religious life currently in use. That will help me place behavior in the frame of specific world views. Different scenarios emerge as people strive to translate values into behavior. Women and men religious are no exception and CLAR offers three frames of reference which I will use as world views: the classical, modern and solidarity models of religious life:

> The various models of religious life correspond to the various ecclesial models.... There is a traditional and conservative model, a modern liberal model and a third liberating and solidarity with the poor model. The latter corresponds to the solidarity model of a Church in search of the poor.[16]

The Classical Model

A VISION

The values of the future cluster tend to pull people toward the distant future. They usually present them with a vision of what they can ultimately be. For religious, they constitute an ideal which inspires their commitment to the long journey of discipleship.

In the classical model they seek and find meaning in ways of perceiving the *truth* of their call from God. The truth of their response will be experienced in behavior which translates the value of *union* into authentic relationships with God, with themselves, with the church and with society. The two values of truth and union will offer them new experiences of *transcendence*.

Within their communities, their behavior will be geared to facilitate the church experience by respecting the conditions for group and faith development which have worked in the past. The traditional vows, as codified by the church, will be lived as an expression of the *truth* of their total commitment to Christ (chastity) and of their radical and institutionalized ties to him (poverty and obedience).

Their lifestyle will condition their witness and ministry. In their search for *transcendence*, they will have recaptured the behavior patterns once connected with the seclusion dimension of early religious life. With their severely reduced numbers, this will make them less visible and will largely confine their witness and ministry to church circles, with the accent on the liturgy and on the works of mercy.

This vision of religious life recalls the golden age of monasticism.

A LAUNCHING PAD

Movement toward it, however, depends on the way religious will translate the values of the foundation cluster. In the classical model, they will tend to fall back on the characteristic historical patterns of the early church and of the founding members of their communities, in an effort to reinforce the foundations. This will be their way of living out the values of *healing* and *refuge*. Women and men religious will primarily understand themselves as called and on mission. But the call and the mission will be perceived as coming from the past to commission them to live out and hand on these early church and congregational behavior patterns in new and changing cultures.

The values of *stability with tradition* will lead them to prioritize behavior which will ensure for their community life continuity and consolidation rather than change and experiment. Valid traditions from the past will be respected. Past and present members of their communities will provide them with appropriate models for behavior. More specifically, the *refuge* value will help them rely more on the traditional ways of living the vows in their efforts to recapture the spirit of the gospel and to *heal* any deviations in lifestyles.

Their witness will derive directly from this stance and will be primarily directed at their own communities, in a holding operation. Their ministry will follow this pattern by concentrating on activities undertaken for and within the institutionalized church rather than directly in or for the world.

A FOCUS

It is the focus cluster, however, which best projects the future of religious life. Its values constitute current priorities and so are bound to powerfully influence future behavior.

The value of *wholeness* can thus be expected to lead to behavior which responds to the current and persistent call of church authorities to religious to radically "be what they are." The values of *presence* and *discernment* will inspire behavior and generate enough energy to help them adapt and move with the times. In particular, these values will raise their consciousness of the Lord's presence in human relationships. Through discernment they will move more confidently to *contemplation* of his activity in the unfolding of these relationships in day-to-day life. They will, however, tend to structure their contemplative stance on the models of the past, preferring those which linked it closely with solitude.

Women and men religious will strive to live up to the ideals profiled by renewal chapters and constitutions for their community lives. They will tend to "go by these books." These will help them appropriate the spirit of the vows as this is expressed by the charism of their community and applied by the same community to contemporary situations.

Presence to others will be given priority. It will be diffuse, rather than concentrated on the poor or on a particular category. They will deliberately behave as witnesses and consider that as their way of being present in a local church. This will primarily involve them in the traditional diocesan ministries.

The Modern Model

The same clusters of values will inspire different patterns of behavior when they are lived in the different world view of the modern model.

A VISION

For the future value cluster, behavior will be characterized by a massive mediation of cultures. Religious will primarily perceive their call to the followership of Christ in terms of the type of relationships operative in these cultures. The *truth* of the call will be seen in cultural terms and so will the personal meaning which it provides. The value of truth will inspire a cultural reading of this call and the existential, honest and radical response to it. It will also guide the practice of the vows.

It will be the value of *union*, however, which will shape their relationships with others. It will be lived as an acceptance of the positive side of cultural realities. It will color their experience of God and thus move them to *transcendence*. It will guide them, to build, in their local communities, in the light of the experience, an environment which will help them connect, through dialogue, to the people who share the same cultures.

Dialogue will also guide their day-to-day witness and ministry. The world will be heard and simultaneously addressed in the truth of an interactive relationship with what is going on in it. Dialogue, inspired by their union with God, will develop their interdependence with people, as Sally A. Kelly has pointed out:

> ...the central challenge is to a life of interdependence. In other words, the ideal of the "rugged individual" has no place in active religious life. Since many of us have cultivated this ideal in order to survive the past two decades in religious life, the challenge to live interdependently is one that strikes at the heart of our hard won "freedom." On the other hand interdependent living and dependent living are not synonymous. Interdependency demands that we take responsibility for our own lives and at the same time realize that we are part of an intricate web of relationships.[17]

Because of their concern with cultural reality, the witness and ministry of religious will not be confined to any particular category of people or to the poor. Preference will be given to the collective dimensions of society and they will be more visible on the media and on large-scale structures than in local communities.

A LAUNCHING PAD

The foundation cluster of values, in the modern model, will channel a high level of the energy of religious to refounding by repairing *(healing)* the cracks in the religious life tradition. This will mean their taking *refuge* in behavior which looks for remedies in the experience of prophetic contemporary women and men religious. They will also strive to give it *stability* by linking with traditions which have worked in the past. They will be the renewers of their orders, responsible for their passage into the future.

The vows will be interpreted and lived in a framework based on the beatitudes. Their witness and ministry will tend to highlight the collective rather than the personal approach to people.

A FOCUS

The values of the focus cluster will inspire women and men religious to seek and find personal integration and *wholeness* in behavior which enhances their awareness of their own potential and of the skills needed to develop it. They will understand their call as a personal invitation from Christ to fulfill this potential in an ever growing *union*, through discipleship, with him. Religious life will be understood as a support system for their response to this call. But they will progressively feel less dependent on its facilities and more on discernment.

Their consecration will inspire behavior which spells out their *presence* to him in *contemplative* prayer and to his people as his *witnesses* through the vows.

Community life will provide the first structure of this witness. Through it, religious will be very present to one another and intensely involved in the issues of the wider community. Their ministry will prioritize the inculturation of gospel values and will be marked by prophecy. *Discernment* will lead to the constant contemplation of the Lord at work on history through cultures.

The Solidarity Model

A VISION

Women and men religious will become very sensitive to the Lord as he calls them forth to join him and "dwell with him" in the grass roots and frontiers of humanity. His presence will first be sought here. They will seek to be present to him here, where they will experience the *truth* of his incarnation and find meaning in their lives. Fulfillment will be sought in an authentic relationship with the poor, with the Lord in and through these poor *(transcendence)*. Their consecration in religious life will be expressed by their radical commitment to search and meet him, existentially, in them.

This *union* with him will be further expressed in quality community life. It will be developed through the sharpening of their interpersonal skills. Reality—including that revealed by faith—will be experienced as interdependence—within their communities, between communities, with the poor.

The vows will be understood in a new light, as their way of responding to the first beatitude—"blessed be the poor." The poor, in turn, will be understood as the marginalized or "the last frontier."

Their witness to the world at large will emerge from this special relationship to the poor. It will also be based on their specific ministry to defend, support, educate and build the poor.

A LAUNCHING PAD

In their search for stable foundations, religious will find *refuge* in the local communities where Christians and people spend their lives. For them, these will constitute the church. The church, after all, is where Christians are. *Healing* for the present predicament of the religious life tradition will be sought in this refuge. They will expect to hear the Lord calling them forth through these people. They will attract recruits to religious life from these grassroots communities. In their endeavor to insert themselves fully in their culture, following the example of the incarnate Word, they will find *stability*. The very *traditions* of the popular religiosity of the people will be mobilized for witness and ministry. The vows will be interpreted and lived in ways which will enhance their witness to radical dedication to the Lord and to his people.

A FOCUS

They will seek to live the value of *wholeness* in a corporate dimension. Religious will only feel whole when they belong to and integrate with the poor. In this way, their *presence* to the poor will bring meaning to their lives: the more faithfully they respond to the call of the Lord present among the poor, the more present they will become to their very selves.

This presence, with *discernment*, will lead them to new experiences of God in "on site" *contemplation*, as they seek him in the people with whom they live. This will integrate contemplation better in their daily life. It will also give meaning to community living, as the search for God becomes more corporate.

Their witness to Christ will be expressed in this presence: together, and with the poor, they continue his "dwelling among us." The vows will be lived in the same spirit as "total attention to him." Their ministry will be focus on bringing the good news of the Lord's saving presence and power to the local people.

7. THE GO! STEP: DISCERNMENT IN ACTION

The choice of an option from the series generated by the sixth step constitutes the main challenge of the seventh and final step of the discernment cycle.

In this particular exercise I decided for the solidarity option. My reasons were based on the church and congruence principles of discernment.

The church principle checks for compatibility of the matter under scrutiny with the major sign for the world—the *sacramentum mundi* which is the church. When applied to this option, it clears it as more in line than the others with the ecclesiology of Vatican II, especially as this has been lived, during the last decades, by Christians in Latin America.

Religious life, by nature, is a church tradition, and the more it reflects the *sensus ecclesiae* the more existentially authentic it will be. As a tradition, it has always assured the church of its prophetic dimension. The solidarity option reflects this prophetic trait, both in its innovative attention to the poor and in its radical return to the sources of the beatitudes. It is also closer to the experience of discipleship in the early church.

The congruence principle looks beyond the borders of the church and checks for alignment of the signs of the times with what faith reveals about the patterns of salvation. It is John's test of the spirits. When applied to the three sets of available options, it points to the solidarity model as more in line than the other two with a dynamic view of an ongoing salvation through an ongoing incarnation.

My discernment exercise here prompts me to contemplate and act on a particular future of religious life which will be:

—a witness to the active presence of the Lord in history and to the possibility of freely accepting and living out his incarnational and salvific projects;

—a prophetic voice for his message to humanity expressed in solidarity with the first fruits of his salvation—the poor;

—a model for the church as its advance guard on its salvation journey through history;

—a movement of discovering, interpreting, acting on the signs of the times through discernment on the seeds of the Word in cultures.

The Loop

The choice and activation of an option, however, does not exhaust the agenda of the last step of the discernment cycle.

The action which discernment inspires is never based on the certitude that the decision which initiated it was right. Because it ultimately derives from the faith of discerners, it "believes without seeing."

Consequently, it has to be kept under scrutiny for signs of its validity or otherwise. In this way, the whole cycle of discernment loops back to start again with the first step—with a different frame of reference.

The focus of the Frame step will no longer be the religious life of the Americas. It will become the experience of implementing the solidarity option. As action on it will gather momentum, it can be expected to generate signs. And these will make possible the application of the confirmation principle of discernment. This principle works on the residual area of uncertainty which discernment has to live with. It scrutinizes the experience which the implementation of the option produces for signs which confirm or reject it. It was used by CLAR when its report pointed to the witness or martyrdom of women and men religious who had adopted the option for the poor as their inspiration. Theirs was a witness both to Christ's call which comes from the poor and to that form of response to that call which the option constitutes.

I can expect that something will happen, as I go into action, which will reduce or remove the area of my uncertainty. My hope that such signs will be forthcoming leads me to be on the watch for them, ready to probe and test them.

As my discernment becomes an ongoing process, I realize that this ongoing trait makes it a condition for discipleship. The only way to be able to follow Christ radically is to keep in conscious touch with his plans all the time. Good disciples have to take very seriously his "I call you friends since I have made known to you all that I heard from my Father" (Jn 15:15) and be prepared to let him share with them his ongoing plans.

I also realize that in contemporary religious life this condition is receiving more attention. As religious convene, in assemblies, chapters, meetings or institutes like ours, to seek commitment to the *sequela Christi*, they invariably go into discernment. They speak of it, they learn its skills, they reap its fruits as it knits them closer together, sharpens their mission goals, focuses their prophecy. I also realize that they are sharing the discovery. By promoting it within their ranks, they are promoting it within the church. Thanks to them, Christians are becoming more aware that, with discipleship, discernment belongs to them, too.

Something wonderful seems to be happening in the contemporary church. A trait of "being church" is being developed by religious and being shared with the whole church. This has happened before: the Franciscans practiced the poverty trait and became its witnesses and prophets. With Vatican II and with the experience of this last quarter of a century, that trait has been accepted as "the common condition" of Christians. Contemporary women and men in religious life may be doing the same thing with discernment. It may take them less than seven centuries to do so, given the present momentum and the information revolution.

In this, once again in its bimillennial history, religious life is proving that it belongs to the heart of the living church. It is its vanguard, opening the way for the future, this time through discernment.

Notes

1. John Paul II, *Letter to the Bishops of the United States on Religious Life*, 2/22/89, par. 2.

2. J.W. Padberg, S.J., "Understanding a Tradition of Religious Life," in *Religious Life*, edited by Gerald A. Arbuckle, S.M. and David Fleming, S.J. (Middlegreen: St Paul Publications, 1990), pp. 3-19.

3. "Pontifical Work for Vocations," 10/20/90, in *Regno Documenti*, p. 698f.

4. S. McCarty, S.T., "Enlarging Perspectives for the Future of Religious Life," *Review for Religious* 49:1, (1990), p. 15.

5. Vatican II, *Ad Gentes* (1965), nn. 11 and 15.

6. F. Kerstiens, "Hope," *Sacramentum Mundi* 3 (London: Burns and Oates, 1969), p. 63.

7. Ibid., p. 65.

8. S. Tutas, S.M., "The Third National LCWR-CMSM Assembly," *Review for Religious* 49:2 (1990), pp. 181-182.

9. "Current Trends in Religious Life in Latin America," *Boletino CLAR* 29 (1/1/91).

10. Ibid., n. 12.

11. Ibid., n. 17.

12. Ibid., n. 20.

13. Ibid., n. 29.

14. "Final Message from the IX Assembly of CLAR," in *Catholic International* 2 (1991), p. 530.

15. B. P. Hall, *The Genesis Effect* (New York: Paulist Press, 1986).

16. "Current Trends in Religious Life in Latin America," *Boletino CLAR* 29 (1/1/91), nn. 102-11.

17. S.A. Kenel, "Challenges Facing Active Religious Today," *Review for Religious* 49:1 (1990), p. 13.

An Amazing Journey:
A Road of Twists and Turns

Joan Chittister, O.S.B.

"If we stay on the road we are on," a Chinese proverb teaches tellingly, "we shall surely get where we are going." The warning is an important one at any time for any one. For the religious orders and congregations of the church, however, the wisdom may be most important of all because the roads taken by religious orders and congregations, at least in centuries past, have been instrumental in forging direction for the entire church. When religious became concerned for the poor, the poor became an agenda item for the church. When religious orders became concerned for the education of young women, the education of women became a priority of the church. When religious attended to the care of orphans and the elderly, the powerless and defenseless became a matter of concern for the entire church. The state of religious life is, then, subject matter for the entire people of God whom religious have dedicated themselves to serve.

Clearly, the role and nature of religious life is not a private matter. Accountability is owed the entire church. And the church owes accountability back. What was once a direction cast in stone has become since Vatican II a challenge made of mercury, seemingly erratic and fast-moving, perhaps, but necessarily impelling. The road that religious life takes in this era, too, will affect the church for decades to come. The possibilities are legion.

Religious life has taken directions in the last twenty-five years that are both promising and problematic. The question is, which is which? Of the changes that have taken place in religious life, what is misdirection and what is seed of things to come? To understand the distinctions, it is necessary to understand the situations that spawned them.

In the first place, the new worlds of the eighteenth and nineteenth centuries were ripe for religious development. Whole populations left Europe for the United States to gain economic security or political freedom or religious refuge. People pulled up roots in one country and left for another country either to gain something or to get away from something. At the same time, they also wanted to keep many things the same. They made great efforts to maintain their cultures, their identities and their religious practices or beliefs.

Group after group came, bringing both their customs and their church with them. Religious orders founded in Europe came to the United States with hordes of other emigrants. They followed these ethnic populations at the request of bishops or on the vision of far-seeing foundresses. Once here, they built the church of the United States and provided both the catechesis and the services the stability new groups needed to make their reorientation possible. So great was the need and so total the response that over six hundred new religious orders formed to meet the needs of one nationality after another. The emphasis everywhere was on providing the institutions necessary to preserve the faith community in a Protestant world and on giving the education it would take to enable Catholics to become inserted into Protestant societies.

Catholic orphanages, Catholic hospitals and Catholic schools became commonplace. The Catholic cocoon became a world within a world, a world unto itself. In this environment religious orders grew rapidly. There was, it seemed, no end to the widow's oil.

By 1962, the opening of Vatican II, religious life, at least for women, was characterized by several qualities which, in the long run, made progress certain but change inevitable. Personal invisibility, centralized authority, religious ritual and pervasive discipline became the glue that built new worlds and held congregations together in pioneer times but which weighed heavily on the membership as well. To enter pre-Vatican II religious life was to take on a kind of time-capsule in which people too often lost touch with life, with issues of personal growth and with their own needs.

At the same time, the personal sacrifice and rigidly defined obedience of the period made achievements commonplace that might otherwise have been impossible. In military fashion, objectives were set, commands were given, and results were achieved with sometimes great cost to the individuals involved. With nuns to spare, religious congregations built up a network of schools and social service agencies at the lowest possible cost and the highest possible quality. In less than one hundred years this network would challenge the best periods of church history for scope and public effectiveness.

Thanks to the committed service of religious orders, the smallest of villages and parishes were able to provide free education and low cost medical care, rivaling even the best of the publicly funded state schools of the country. As a result, by 1990 there were 821 Catholic hospitals and dispensaries, 742 special care homes, 876 child welfare centers and nurseries, 1,666 protective institutions, 1,771 special care facilities and over 2,500 grade schools, high schools and colleges in the United States, almost all of them either founded or staffed by religious congregations.

This social service network of the Roman Catholic Church in the United

States was built in large part on the backs of nuns who worked for nothing but the God of love and the love of God. Religious communities were the servants of a ghetto church under siege. As long as pioneer works abounded and the Catholic ghetto grew and public support continued, religious orders thrived. A theology of transcendence justified the giving of lives for the saving of souls and the rewards of a life to come.

Religious life in this mold allowed for the concentration of resources on the works of the time. To enter a teaching order or a nursing order or a missionary order was to be a teacher, a nurse or a missionary. Members went where they were sent to do what they were told to do. It was sacrifice of self that was sanctifying. Personal agendas were not to interfere with the work of the order. Personalism and individualism were not the order of the day. Institutionalism was.

In this era, too, the interface between secular life and religious life, between women religious and the society around them, was strong and clear. The servant was worthy of her hire. When religious came into an area, the people they served would serve them as well. They provided convents and labor and transportation and medical care and even food from their own tables for the tables of the nuns. It was an economically sound arrangement. The nuns gave professional service in the Catholic key; the people gave life support service; the church gave salvation to both.

Finally, religious witness at this time was distinct and focused on the Catholic community. There was no doubt about the value of religious life in the Catholic community. The church's theology of vocations affirmed its essential value and the Catholic population at large esteemed what defined and developed it. Religious life was the higher state of life, theology said, and religious stood, garbed and remote, in the middle of the Christian community, an eternal sign of the transcendent, the other-worldly, the life to come, and gave their lives for God and the church. It was a strong social bond, a necessary theological linkage, an indispensable part of an immigrant Catholic world.

But there were counterpoints to the situation, as successful as it seemed. Respect for authority decreased when authority, in its commitment to discipline, efficiency and productivity, became more defined as arbitrary rather than either visionary or caring. Charisms got swamped in institutionalism. Specific works consumed the identity of the congregation to such a point that the basic reason for the existence of each order became blurred and dim. An assembly of interchangeable parts, distinguishable more by uniform than by purpose or spirit, lost spirit and energy.

In 1960, however, with the election of John F. Kennedy as the first Roman Catholic president of the United States, the emergence of

Catholicism as a mainstream social force signaled a head-on collision between a theology of commitment and a theology of cult. Catholicism had come out of its cave into public favor. With the advent of Vatican II and the Constitution on the Church in the Modern World the church no longer proclaimed itself at war with the world. The church now saw itself as leaven as well as light. The effect of these new emphases in ecclesiology on the nature and structures of religious life can never be underestimated. More than that, those concepts, along with changes in the society around them, marked the end of an era.

Psychology began to stress the concept of personal development, personalism became the order of the day, mobility and technology brought people into contact with other peoples and other norms, consensus became the basis of group relationships, the liturgical renewal emphasized participation above ritual, the women's movement touched every facet of society, men's roles as well as women's. Religious life, too, would never again be quite the same. Gone was the social climate that understood invisibility, and supported centralized authority, and assumed rigid obedience and took the subservience of women for granted. Every institution in society began the long, hard process of wrenching renewal.

By the mid-1960s, at the apparent peak of their success, religious orders experienced a cataclysmic exodus. Over 25% of the professed religious of the church, most of them younger and newer members, left religious life. What had been the norm and nature of religious life was now questionable. What had worked in the past was now self-defeating. What had been idealized and idolized in the society before it now became suspect.

What is to be made of such a situation? What has happened to religious life as a result? What does it mean for the future of religious life? In fact, given this social climate, this theology and these circumstances, should there be any future for religious life at all? The answers are not as clear as the questions.

A basic principle of social psychology, an historical verity, a sad commentary on organizational leadership, is the social truism that organizations can die long before they cease to exist. In this case it is often difficult to determine whether what we are looking at is slow death or new life.

The fact is that religious life at present is much a product of the past: a blend of the reactionary, the prophetic and the profane, each in tension with the other. Institutionalism has given way to individualism. Authoritarianism has disappeared in the wake of collegiality. The theology of transcendence has been superseded by the theology of transformation. Cultic ritual has been foresworn for spirituality. A sense of congregational purpose has fallen victim to a commitment to personal development. Congregational works have disappeared in favor of individual ministries. The result of it all is a mixture of public confusion, personal agony and a pitched battle for resurrection. There is a strong streak of each dimension in all of them.

INDIVIDUALISM. The unnamed, unknown, ubiquitous and universal "good sister" is, for the most part, relegated to a long-lost past. In her place now is a highly autonomous and clearly self-defined woman religious who has a separate personality, separate gifts, and very separate needs. She stands alone. She has a mind, a conscience, and responsibility for herself and her choices. She is not an interchangeable part and she is not, by any means, a child. She expects to be asked and she expects to be heard. She expects to have her own credentials honored and she expects to be treated as an adult who makes moral choices and personal decisions.

Out of this new sense of self has emerged a corps of strong women, dedicated to mission and able to make clear and competent responses.

It is a situation in which we may all take justifiable pride but it also has serious pitfalls.

In the first place, the linkage between congregational presence and personal impact has become obscure. People engage individual sisters now, not the community or congregation to which they belong. As a result, the promise of continuity dims, the public consciousness of a stream of witnesses declines and the identification of the congregation as congregation with the needs of the times is at best hypothetical. The image of a phalanx of institutions standing as bulwarks against poverty or oppression in the society is diminished at the same time that the value of the individual religious is heightened. Worse, the image of religious life itself rises and falls on the work and personality and spiritual depth of individual members who may or may not best represent the character and quality of the entire congregation. Religious life becomes the various religious women and men that the world sees one at a time rather than the nature of the order or congregation itself.

Where, in a pre-Vatican church, institutionalism often consumed the character of individual religious, individual religious now consume the character of their entire orders. It is a heavy burden for any one person to carry. In those cases where the religious is a prophetic and pastoral presence, the order may well be credited beyond its merit. In other cases where the individual religious is marginal or indifferent, the whole order may be judged unfairly as a result.

COLLEGIALITY AND SUBSIDIARITY. The commitment of the church at Vatican II that decisions should be made at the lowest possible level by the largest possible group of people affected by them fits extremely well with the independent American character and its democratic culture. Americans expect to be consulted about things. American children are taught to express their opinions in pre-school and spend their lives from then on in independence training. The unfinished task for Americans, then, is not normally autonomy. What Americans need to learn is interdependence, that decisions made out of the context of the group, good as they may be at one level, may also be destructive at another. For religious, of course, the question becomes the relationship of authority figures to individual members.

Authoritarianism, a poor synonym for obedience, works its will on others for the sake of the productiveness of the group or the exercise of power itself. Obedience is a joint listening by the authority figure and the religious to the signals of the Holy Spirit around them: to the needs of the person herself, to the circumstances of the congregation, to the people in society whose needs are not being met, to the very purpose of the congregation itself. It is a decision made by two people together with the whole church in mind. To make a decision without weighing each of these elements in the balance and then to call it religious is to diminish the whole concept of religious obedience. On the one hand, obedience is not an exercise made of hoops and called holy. On the other hand, it is also not an excursion into adolescent rebellion.

Until balance is brought to the concept of obedience, congregations will be a loose aggregation of individuals with private agendas or a faceless corps of bodies without souls. Neither possibility is attractive and both plague religious life yet. Where congregations are weak, critics call for a return to "obedience." The real issue, however, may not be so much the lack of obedience as it is the lack of purpose in the group. With nothing to commit themselves to, religious commit themselves to themselves.

Authority and subsidiarity have both been out of control in contemporary society. A misuse of authority has reduced religious life to a condition of non-being masquerading as sanctification. In its name, women have been reduced to a state of mindless subservience. Personal gifts have gone untapped. Personal needs have been ignored.

But selfishness practiced in the name of subsidiarity has not always done much better. Under its aegis, communities have become vehicles for individual development, true, but they have not always been able to sustain the impact of the congregation itself as members moved from one personal arena to another. What is needed if religious life is to remain a force in contemporary society is a strong, clear blend of personal choices made in the context of the charism of the community itself. For the community as community to be effective, people must know what charisms are walking into the room anytime one of their members is present, in any work, anywhere.

Self-centeredness is not what took Jesus to the cross, but without the cross there would have been no resurrection for any of us. The question for this time is for what are religious, both as individuals and as groups, willing to give their lives in a world where people die daily on crosses not of their own choosing.

TRANSCENDENCE. Congregations across the country find themselves the inheritors of one theology of religious life and the creators of another one. The problem is that the two theologies are struggling to live in peaceful coexistence. Some members, schooled well in earlier forms of religious commitment, believe that religious life is to be a haven from the world, an anteroom to heaven, a crucible of personal pieties meant to enable human beings to transcend the world in anticipation of union with God in another life. Others in the same congregation stress the incarnational aspects of religious life. They see themselves as meant to be immersed in the world in order to be a transforming presence there. They signal the goodness of life and the commonness of the endeavor by living as Christians among Christians. They wear the clothes of the day and live in the apartments of the working class and move through society as everybody's sister and nobody's property.

Both are engaging concepts. Both come out of high motivation and respected theology. But the two are very difficult to meld in one common schedule or prayer form or lifestyle. One withdraws from society by being different from it; the other blends into society and so is largely invisible to it. As a result, the congregation itself becomes largely invisible to the very society it is trying to transform. They do good but largely uncoordinated works. They live life at its simplest materially and at its highest ethically and at its deepest socially but the impact of the congregation as congregation is at best obscure. The world simply cannot see the congregation as congregation anymore. Holders of the new theology have moved to its margins and the visible core is passive in a period when great new witness is needed.

It is a time of lost opportunities and diminished impact.

SPIRITUALITY. As much as institutions, common life and uniform garb characterized the religious life of pre-Vatican II, so did the practice of common prayer. Some communities prayed together literally for hours every day and kept up a full professional schedule at the same time. The problem was that the prayer life of most religious was centered in ritual and rote. Prayer was formal and structured into separate and set segments. It was more recitation than reflection, more quantity than quality, more a collection of traditional formulas than a sharing of faith experiences or a response to the realities of the time. With the advent of Vatican II and the renewal of religious life, common prayer was one of the first elements to be critiqued and found wanting. While monastic communities grappled with the temptation to use prayer as an escape from the needs of the time, in apostolic communities, common prayer was in large part abandoned in favor of personal prayer. More than that, work commonly became the prayer and the spirituality of the sister who now lived alone and worked alone and prayed alone. Ministry became the spiritual life. The people she worked with became the avenue of the face of God.

The value of the new situation lay in the fact that it released spiritual energy in every member of the congregation in whole new ways. Prayer became a conscious starting place for the pursuit of full personal development. Retreat centers emerged to meet the needs of spiritually starved religious. Desert days and houses of prayer became part of the warp and woof of apostolic life. Scripture study and shared prayer groups became givens. A whole new style of prayer life grew up in religious communities. Rote had become a thing of the past. A prayer-wheel mentality, the notion that the more prayers said the better, was no longer enough to satisfy the soul.

On the other hand, the problem with that situation lay in the fact that the religious found little daily distance now from the burdens of the immediate. "Come apart and rest awhile" became a lost gospel. Constantly poured out and little renewed, religious life became an unending routine of tasks. Worst of all, perhaps, the spirituality of the congregation and its sense of itself as a spiritual center began to dim both for religious themselves and for the people around them.

CHARISMS. Prior to Vatican II, the charism of the congregation was seldom discussed. It was, however, taken for granted. What was even more taken for granted was that individual gifts would be dedicated to maintaining the charism, or at least the works of the congregation itself. With the advent of Vatican II, a strange dichotomy appeared. The charism of the order was never more discussed, defined and debated than it was during the period of the chapters of renewal mandated to every order for the sake of rewriting its constitutions. At the same time, nothing, perhaps, operated less in the development of the order itself than did the idea of charism. Swept by the winds of personal development and confused about the difference between institutional ministries and individual gifts, groups opted almost universally for the value of individual ministries.

In the first place, traditional ministries—large schools and small hospitals—were financially vulnerable. Shrinking populations of students, the high cost of lay teachers to orders that no longer had the personnel to meet staffing needs themselves, the financial implications of a growing number of state requirements, the economic needs of the congregations themselves and obvious new social needs all collaborated to encourage the movement of religious out of institutional ministries into works on their own. It was a heady and exciting moment.

If, in the long run, anything enables religious congregations to make the transition from one era to another, this movement into new and individual ministries may well be it. "Bridge-builders," members who stayed in the community but who began to work in new arenas outside of it, supplied the contacts and experiences in new fields that congregations needed to begin to take up new roles in society. Transition in ministry for a congregation became an individual endeavor. As one religious after another began to work in areas outside of the congregation's institutional commitments, the congregation itself took on a new identity. Unfortunately, it is also true that the move of religious out of congregational apostolates has, in some cases at least, deprived the congregation of much of an identity at all. Everybody is clear about what the particular sister whom they know does; few know what the community itself is about.

This loss of institutional presence in society is more than a change of form. It is a change of impact as well. It is a change of social presence. It is a loss of charism, of that gift of the Holy Spirit that is given to an order for the building up of the kingdom of God on earth. But when charism goes, sincere people both inside the order and out of it begin to question why the order exists at all. What can possibly be done in a religious community that cannot be done by similarly committed people outside of it? The question is a serious one. On it, in fact, may hang the future of religious life.

PURPOSE AND MEANING. Prior to Vatican II, it was very clear what various religious congregations were about: they saved their own souls and the souls of others by teaching and nursing and caring for children. They formed the catechetical bulwark of the Catholic community in a Protestant world. They served the church. With Vatican II, the emphasis changed greatly.

The Catholic community had become integrated into mainstream society. Catholic ghettos were, for all practical purposes, a thing of the past. As Catholics moved into public works, the siege mentality of the church disappeared. The ecumenical movement brought acceptance and dignity to Catholics at all levels of society where only exclusion and rejection had often been before that. For religious, the new social climate was like stepping out into fresh air and sunlight. Suddenly, there was less and less reason to be different. Incarnational theology, the attempt to recognize the presence of goodness and of God in the here and now, the acceptance of life as it is—instead of the need to escape this life on behalf of a world to come, or, more likely, a world to be avoided here—became the tenor of the church in general and religious life in particular. Even the eucharist had taken on forms that were common and pedestrian. Religious life was sure to do the same.

The social encyclicals of the church, the new wave of liberation theology in the South American church, the waging of a violent and senseless war in Vietnam, the race riots of the 1960s and the sudden global consciousness of massive poverty and the concentration of capital led individual religious to make brave and inspired choices. One by one they went into new kinds of ghettos and new kinds of works for the poor. They worked with new groups of people. They lived with new kinds of communities. They wore new kinds of clothes. They became more intent on systemic change on behalf of the poor than they were on maintaining the Catholic system itself. They became the gadflies of society, goading it to new levels of conscience and new kinds of commitment.

But not all. Congregational change was not nearly so neat. In the heart of every community there were at least two other kinds of responses to the changes. Some members of the community, often the greater preponderance of the group, were intent on preserving what had been for years the works and glories of the institution. Another group wanted change but not for any overarching reason other than the achievement of their own personal interests or convenience. People who may have left religious life had it failed to change were—with the adaptations in lifestyle—able to stay. What they were not able to do was to recommit to any new or overriding purpose. The congregation had become a feathered nest, a warm refuge, a retreat from responsibility for them, while religious whose commitment was unwavering were left to negotiate the twists and turns of change, to rebuild the theology of religious life and, at the same time, to try to sweep the passive and comfortable along on the tide of renewal whether they cared about going or not.

Congregations themselves, aware of their rising median ages, began to focus considerable energies on the creation of retirement funds that would take members comfortably to their graves. The motives were good but the effects were often lethal.

Religious communities settled down. They began to move cautiously and carefully. Gone was the sense of pioneer risk that had brought them to the heights of success. They had lost a sense of congregational purpose. The question "Why stay?" had become the question "Why come?"

THE WOMEN'S MOVEMENT. Underlying the entire process of religious renewal, largely unseen and usually unnoted, was the surging consciousness of women that they had long been denied their share of the gospel, either its rights or its responsibilities. Like all the other factors of the period, the impact of this new awareness had both positive and negative effects on the ongoing development of religious life. The interesting thing, perhaps, is that in this case the two consequences derived from one and the same realization: the traditional dependence of the women of the church on the approval, affirmation and acceptance of the men of the church was demeaning to both of them. Women religious struck out on their own to open ministries outside the pale of their dioceses, to write constitutions far unlike the documents that had defined their lives before Vatican II, and, most important of all, to create new forms of the spiritual and communal life.

Permission of the pastor or the bishop or even the Vatican became of secondary concern to women who had once failed to move at all without the confirmation of the male church. As a result, women religious began to branch out into highly untraditional services: to chaplaincies in public hospitals, to women's centers under public auspices, to theology programs and to spiritual direction programs and to the operation of retreat centers—all of them in times past almost exclusively the province of priests. They became canonists and pastoral administrators and civic social service directors. They opened peace and justice centers, they went to jail in opposition to public policies, they became advocates of the poor and public critics of the systems of both government and church. They spoke out for the ordination of women and they rallied against the wars of the state. They began to identify with a whole new generation of the poor and oppressed. They became goads at the heart of both church and state.

At the same time, this new sensibility to the diminished role and oppression of women, to their disbarment from the decision-making centers of the church as well as from the sacraments, alienated many sisters from the church—and the church from them as well. Nevertheless, the new energy of the women's movement and the clear consciousness of the sinful effects of sexism have led women religious to open whole new areas of ministry and presence in the world.

The present, then, is a miscellany of opposites. In each of them, the past is clearly in tension with the future. Yet, it is out of these unresolved shards that the future must come if there is to be any future at all. The question, how? Communities are spent physically, limited financially, overburdened by empty facilities or declining ministries, and, for the most part, professionally unprepared to take on new works.

Dag Hammarskjöld wrote once: "When the morning freshness has been replaced by the weariness of mid-day; when the leg muscles quiver under the strain; when the climb seems useless and suddenly nothing will go quite as you will, it is precisely then that you must not hesitate."

Never have the words been truer. The fact is that most of religious life did not start with large numbers of people or great reserves of money or public and ecclesiastical approbation or even understanding. Religious life started from a small number of people with a vision so impelling that nothing less than its completion would satisfy them. If religious life has a problem in the present period, it is not that it lacks money or people. The problem is that it lacks vision. It lacks commitment to something so great that the very thirst for it drives it past all obstacles with a kind of glowing certainty that both inspires and attracts.

In the light of the present situation, a constellation of five elements will be necessary to bring religious life to new purpose and meaning. Without consensus, corporate commitment, social relevance, spiritual energy and prophetic action, the religious life of the future can hardly be a powerful presence, a leading light, a clear road in the world to come. Rather than carriers of the charisms of the Holy Spirit, the graces given for the upbuilding of the reign of God, groups without these characteristics will at best be well-meaning sects whose worlds begin and end with themselves.

CONSENSUS. If there has been a breakdown in anything since Vatican II, it has been a breakdown in consensus. Religious congregations have been sites of peaceful coexistence, of the cohabitation of opposites. One segment of the congregation has clung tenaciously to past philosophies of religious life and forms of ministry, kept the faith and drained the energy for new efforts and new thinking. Another segment of every congregation, the determined adventurers of the group, has moved to the margins of the congregation to preserve their own sense of purpose. Finally, an undigested middle attempts to negotiate between the two extremes, to mollify and to enable each, but this group never really faces the philosophical questions head-on. They simply go on going on, a number of good people doing a number of good things but without a common vision or a common commitment to do what is necessary in order to be for this age what the congregation was for another age now past. As a result, the congregation itself drifts and strains from issue to issue, from incident to incident, with no criteria and no character to cling to in difficult times.

Religious communities of the future, religious communities which manage to navigate the shoals of the present, will be communities that form—and reform—around a common vision and engage the support and gifts of every individual member to achieve it. Difficult times breed difficult topics. When congregations fail to come to grips with the implications of each situation for the integrity and purpose of the community, then the congregation itself becomes suspect. The central purpose of joining any group is to enable the individual to do with others what cannot possibly be done as well alone. The congregation without a consensus on its purpose and actions, therefore, is a congregation of little value to others and with no reason to exist for itself.

CORPORATE COMMITMENT. The great ministries of times past are long gone. The state provides a school system and the concept of universal health care is now the coin of the realm. The lay Catholic community is now prepared—thanks to over 150 years of commitment from congregations of sisters and brothers—both to support and to staff a network of Catholic schools, if the Catholic population still wants one. Hospitals are largely government-funded and government-regulated. Obviously the works of the ages before us are, for all practical purposes, accomplished. The question now is, what are the great works of the present to which religious congregations must attend and how can they do it with declining numbers?

The massive institutions and great concentration of resources that made Catholic health and education work so successful are now operating against the very perpetuation of the congregations which sacrificed to create them.

Empty buildings, large debts, taxes and staffing concerns all militate against the continuance of established ministries and impede the development of new ones as well. Congregations have neither the monies nor the facilities to embark on new institutional ventures. What is more, issues change at such a rate in this period of history that any convergence of personnel and physical resources must at least be undertaken judiciously. The fact is that what is begun today may be passé in less than a decade.

The concern is a real one: How can a congregation as congregation minister today in the shadow of yesterday's successes and tomorrow's needs?

It seems to me that congregations must begin to adapt regularly renewable corporate commitments: issues, ideas or concerns around which an order rallies its resources in conjunction with multiple others but out of the perspective of its charism and through the medium of each of its members' individual ministries rather than through exclusively owned or specific institutions. A Franciscan congregation, for instance, could set out to exert all of its corporate and individual efforts to highlight the needs and change conditions for the homeless poor, or the elderly poor, or the pre-school poor. A Dominican congregation could decide to bend its energies to teach about the conditions of women to all segments of society. A Benedictine community could devote itself to world peace by opposing nuclearization of the planet or the use of violence as an arm of U.S. foreign policy. A Mercy congregation could concentrate on achieving mercy for the hungry in this country whose allocation of food stamps has been reduced. Whatever the issue, if it is in accord with the original charism of the institute, it would draw from the same well that softened the ground of immigrant illiteracy and anti-Catholic sentiment in the century before us. Each member could contribute to the congregational commitment wherever they were and to such an extent that the congregation's concern would permeate every segment of society. Teachers would include materials on the subject in their classrooms. Chaplains would develop prayer services and homilies around the question. Pastoral administrators would engage their parishes in projects designed to understand and change the situation. The congregation itself would hold prayer-vigils on the subject and critique current legislation in their newsletters and tithe to support advocacy groups and sign petitions and hold public conferences.

The possibilities are, in fact, legion. And the effects are apparent. The charism of the congregation would shine once more, clearly, for all to see, at every level of society and in every corner of the local community.

Groups who hire a member of these congregations would know what charism was walking in the door. The poor would take hope. The rich would take notice. The congregation would take character again and brim with purpose and gospel meaning. What's more, the individual and the congregation would be in sync.

SOCIAL RELEVANCE. When there is a consensus to cling to and a corporate commitment to uphold, then the social value of a congregation is as clear to the world which it purports to serve as it is to its members. At the same time, the religious community of the future will have only one real concern: the plight of the poor and its dedication to be a voice on their behalf, not only to repair the wreckage left by the system but to change the system itself on their behalf.

The function of religious life is not to achieve endowed leisure. Religious congregations, monastic communities whose Benedictine spirituality requires special attention to "the poor and the pilgrim...[since] our very awe of the rich guarantees them special respect," as well as apostolic congregations founded to spread the Word of God, do not exist for their own sake. Each is to be a sign that the reign of God is possible, that the reign of God is near. To withdraw from the questions of the day in order to perpetuate ourselves is to deny the very ground of God out of which we grew.

When FORUS, the Nygren and Ukeritis study on the Future of Religious Orders,[1] reports that commitment to the poor is lacking in contemporary religious life and that anomie—a sense of purposelessness—characterizes our very existence, then the bell is tolling a sad, sad knell no matter how financially secure our congregations, no matter how comfortable and pious our lives.

SPIRITUAL ENERGY. Prayer is not work and work is not prayer. One may flow from the other but one cannot substitute for the other. It takes prayer to fuel what is apparently useless. It takes prayer to sustain what is difficult. It takes prayer to put on the mind of Christ when resistance wearies us and success seduces us into thinking that enough is enough.

At the heart of every religious congregation people must be able to find a spiritual center that speaks to laws above this law and keeps alive for people the mind of God. The social service and public advocacy that we take to the center of this culture is not meant to be a product, it is meant to be a witness to another vision of life. Congregations that have no demonstrable prayer life have no coherent spiritual vision to leave behind to those to whom life has given little when our projects do not succeed and the system does not change. Ronald Neibuhr wrote: "Nothing that is worth doing is achieved in our lifetime; therefore, we must be saved by hope. Nothing which is true or beautiful or good makes complete sense in any immediate context of history; therefore, we must be saved by faith. Nothing we do, however virtuous, can be accomplished alone; therefore, we must be saved by love." Faith, hope and love, not caution, pragmatism and gentility, must characterize the endeavors of contemporary religious life as much as they did the religious life of the past, or religious life will have no character at all.

It is a function of religious life to give a lived demonstration of union with

God, of seeing the world as God sees the world, of coming to growth, both through failure and through success. In the final analysis it may be the finest gift we have to give. But those who do not pray cannot teach it and without it the world is poor indeed. Without it, the poor will not be sustained and the rich will not be converted. Without it, we ourselves will be the weaker witnesses.

PROPHETIC ACTION. Religious congregations are not faced with a vocation crisis. Young people go on giving their lives to great human endeavors year after year after year. Religious life is faced with a crisis of significance and a crisis of spirituality.[2] Religious life is at the brink of renewal and faced with two choices: personal comfort or prophetic presence, individual commitments or charismatic congregations. Neither choice is an easy one but one does not preclude the other.

The problem for the future is no longer the structures of religious life. Structures have been bent to the breaking point. The problem for the future is the commitment of religious themselves.

If the basic commitment of individual religious and their congregations, after years of adaptation and adjustment and individual development, is to comfort, to security, to private spirituality alone, to the preservation of monastic museums or past apostolic institutions, then there is no reason for that kind of religious life to exist. But something else will surely rise up in their places because God never fails to "comfort the people," to send the prophet, to raise up a voice in the wilderness. What is yet to be certain is whether we will be the ones who decide to do it.

But one thing is sure: There is a great deal of life in this present death. More has happened in religious communities in the past twenty-five years, at least in U.S. religious life, than has happened since the early nineteenth century. Where old steps led nowhere, new steps have definitely been taken into soup kitchens and political advocacy work and women's shelters and poverty programs and peace work and new forms of education and countless other arenas where the need is great and the resources are sparse.

The only thing left to see is whether communities at large will continue to forge ahead courageously into a world on the edge of globalism, a church in the morass of sexism, a nation on the slippery slope of classism, or whether they will settle down into passivity, privatism and personal comfort, worn down by the struggles of the past twenty-five years, seduced by numbers, paralyzed by the evil of ageism and addicted to the warmth of the nest.

The question now is not whether we have a few prophetic people in every community trying to function under the dead weight of the past. The question now is whether we have prophetic communities who together are a sign of hope, where neither age nor numbers inhibit their call or suppress their voices, where quietism and despair do not blur the alternative models they must give, in every age, to a world at a loss for alternatives.

The question now is whether there is enough down-deep, bedrock, authentic gospel spirituality in us to go on past our personal prayers to the building up of the reign of God to which those prayers call us.

The church is waiting, the world is waiting, the young people of the world are waiting to see if there is such a thing as a religious life so immersed in the contemplative moment that it does significant things in significant ways at this significant moment in history.

They are all waiting, waiting to see whether this generation of religious has anything at all to bring to this age as they did to the questions of the past, to see whether this generation of religious is still really religious. If we will, surely religious congregations now have the opportunity to be more religious than ever before in our time.

The world, however, is waiting to see whether, prepared by twenty-five years of cosmetic change and adaptation, religious now have the commitment, the spirituality, the social vision and the prophetic presence to take religious life into the future.

Elton Trueblood wrote: "Faith is not belief without proof; faith is trust without reservation." It is time for religious to trust again that we are here now for more than preserving the past, for more than surrendering to old age and dying gracefully, for more than the gathering of retirement funds. We are here to move on with Abram, to begin again with Sarai, to spill the widow's oil. Indeed, the future that God has never abandoned is waiting with confidence and hope that the religious congregations who met the challenges of the past are up to the challenges of the present: theologically, psychologically and spiritually.

"If you carry your own lantern," the Hasidim teach, "you will endure the dark." It is time to see if the light of hope and courage, of commitment and risk still shines in religious life. If those lanterns are not dimmed we shall surely get where we are going.

Notes

1. David J. Nygren, C.M., and Miriam D. Ukeritis, C.S.J., "Future of Religious Orders in the United States," in *Origins*, CNS Documentary Service, Washington, D.C., September 24, 1992, pp. 257-72.

2. For a fuller development of this concept of significance and spirituality see "The Future of Religious Life," in Joan Chittister, O.S.B., *Women, Ministry and the Church* (Paulist Press: New York, 1983), pp. 27-35.

"A White Light Still and Moving": Religious Life at the Crossroads of the Future

Margaret Brennan, IHM

Quoting a passage from T.S. Eliot's *The Four Quarters,* "...a white light still and moving," Jean Shinoda Bolen, a noted Jungian analyst and author, reflects on the ancient archetype of the wise woman who is grounded in the midst of outer chaos, her character tempered by experience. She is elsewhere pictured as the goddess of the crossroads. Standing where several roads meet, she could see where others were coming from, and the choices that met them as they discerned directions in the journey ahead.[1] These images speak to me as significant symbols in our own continuing journey as women religious.

We do indeed stand at a crossroads in terms of our future as religious and the vision and hope we hold out for ourselves and for those whom we serve. In the last few years several very significant books examining the future of religious life have made their appearance.[2] Although each author focuses his or her reflection from a somewhat different perspective, they are alike in their acknowledgement of the positive transformation of the past, the continued need for change, the identity of sisters as church women.

Recently a young woman religious approached me with her own dilemmas in regard to these publications. While these authors spoke to her of her past and present experience, they failed to offer her a meaningful reflection on the future reality of religious life. Her hope, as I heard her, was to find their questions on religious life relating to the larger questions of a changing world view which will inevitably affect our life and understanding of both monastic and apostolic community. Some of these changes include the changing nature and context of religious experience; the power of the universe story as a primary source of revelation and an essential model of community; the manner in which feminist consciousness and spirituality can affect global liberative transformations.[3]

In this essay, while following the general theme of the Institute, I would like to make use of Jean Shinoda Bolen's imagery of the wise woman at the crossroads. In the contextualization of paradigm shifts, I will look back on the roads upon which we have traveled these last twenty-five years, reflect on the present challenges of the crossroads where we now stand, and, finally, scan the wider horizons of the future in terms of where we might go. This is not to suggest that I consider myself to *be* that wise woman but only that I am conscious that when women share their stories, hopes, and experiences they find a wisdom in new insights which are in turn translated into brave and bold decisions. I hope that my own "story" can offer something to that articulation.

As I attempt to express my own thoughts around these questions of past, present, and future, I recognize the contributions of the authors mentioned above as well as many others who have helped to shape the growing volume of reflection around and about the future. I am also conscious of other questions raised about the future in the light of paradigm shifts that point to a changing world view which is already upon us.

The framework for my own thinking has developed from my lived experience of religious life which falls into two almost equal periods of time and is now in the early years of a third. I spent the first twenty years of my religious life in what we would now call the pre-Vatican church. The second twenty years were lived in the tumultuous decades of renewal and aggiornamento following the council. The last half-decade or so I would describe as movement into an emerging post-modern world. Significant shifts marked the transitions from the first to the second and the second to the third periods, and there is no doubt that cultural shifts contextualized the change of consciousness I experienced. It is from these perspectives that I offer my own reflections.

THE JOURNEY FROM THE PAST

Our history as religious, as it has changed over the last twenty-five years, has been marked by two significant cultural shifts which have brought about an enormous change of consciousness. My own wide and deep exposure to the movement and momentum of those years, both nationally and internationally, *lead* to believe that the shifts I am about to describe *were* and *are* operative in the experience of women's congregations in general—especially in the western world.

The First Cultural Shift

The *first shift*, initiated by Vatican II, was the more dramatic of the two in that it brought changes of life and ministry that had not been questioned in any basic way for more than a hundred years.

After decades of declared discontinuity and mistrust, the church came to terms with the modern world. A paradigm shift of immense proportions has marked the church's thinking from Pius IX's anti-modernist policies of retrenchment and hostility to the whole tenor of the Vatican documents which enunciate again and again that the church is not inimical to modern culture but has something to offer to it as well as to receive from it.

It must be said, however, that new theological insights arising from both cultural and religious ferment in Europe were already making inroads in earlier decades that prepared the ground for Vatican II. Works of Henri de Lubac on the nature of the church and those of Yves Congar on an emerging theology of the laity stirred the fertile ground of our understanding and offered new and exciting challenges for what it meant to *be* church. In the United States, the liturgical movement, which originated among Benedictines in Europe, took on a new and exciting impetus with the work of Virgil Michael at St. John's Abbey in Collegeville, Minnesota. Before long the publication of *Orate Fratres*, later changed to *Worship*, became the liturgical "primer" for parishes as well as for religious congregations. Pius XII's encyclicals *Mediator Dei* and *Mystici Corporis* gave authoritative status to such movements and called us to new levels of our unity as the body of Christ and to the beginnings of active participation in the worship of the church rather than being passive observers. The encyclical letter *Divino Afflante Spiritu* opened the treasures of the scriptures to new methods of interpretation which in time would revolutionize our understanding of texts and our use of them in theological studies, in spirituality, and in ecumenical endeavors.

In the United States the 1950s were a time of growth and expansion for most religious congregations. The publication of Thomas Merton's *Seven Storey Mountain* opened up a new interest in the contemplative life and Trappist monasteries multiplied across the country. Houses of study called juniorates were built to accommodate the increased numbers of vocations in apostolic congregations and to better prepare young religious who in a very real way were looked upon—and were—the church's professionals. The Sister Formation Movement had already led many congregations in the teaching and healing apostolates to recognize the need for a more adequate formation and academic education of novices and junior professed. In colleges belonging to their own congregations, on secular campuses or at Catholic universities, young women religious pursued academic degrees that professionally prepared them to administer hospitals and work in educational institutions. The same attention was given to spiritual and human formation. In many cases, this movement led to conflict with the bishops as the years of preparation caused personnel shortages and brought in laity who began to work side by side with religious. Whereas previously the education of religious had been spread over seventeen or eighteen summers, religious were now fully prepared and equal to their lay colleagues as they began their apostolic life. A decade of such formation formed fertile minds and shaped the ability to make critical judgments. As a result, when Vatican II called the universal church to a revisioning of its nature and mission, the seed of renewal was able to fall on good ground in many communities of religious women in North America.[4]

Nevertheless, although some of these changes had already begun to alter our understanding of apostolic religious life, our way of being on the eve of the council remained a hierarchically structured, semi-monastic way of life. The 1917 Code of Canon Law had prescribed numerous regulations about religious governance, the profession and practice of the vows, the formation of novices, and the exercise of the apostolate. These were reflected in rules of life that governed every moment of the day. Elements of cloister and separation from the world curtailed contact with "seculars," which was limited to the hours dedicated to the apostolate and occasional visits from family. The works of religious were basically institutional and were carried out in most cases under the mandate of the local bishop. The apostolic impetus and charisms that had given birth to religious congregations were, as a result, often lost under prescriptions that hindered rather than enhanced the purposes for which they were founded.

In principle, the Vatican church encouraged and endorsed the changes that such an adaptation to modern culture would mean for religious life. But neither the church, nor we ourselves for that matter, knew what the consequences of such adaptation would entail. What the council meant for us in terms of dramatic shifts in both lifestyle and ministry is something that all of us know only too well.

An added factor in the turmoil of renewal was the realization that the cultural context into which we moved in the immediate post-Vatican years was one of struggle and turmoil. In the United States, the civil rights and peace movements of the 1960s taught us that justice was linked to systemic change. A consequence of this realization led many of us into ministries of advocacy for the poor, social work in government agencies, political lobbying for economic justice, and work with Christians and non-Christians alike for nuclear disarmament and the promotion of peace. This represented a move away from the more institutionalized ministries of education and health-care which were now shared and even taken over in some instances by the laity.

More importantly, contextualized by the growing momentum of the women's movement, we began to find our own voices as women—to name ourselves, and to state our own identity as we experienced it. This brought us into a painful conflict with the Vatican church, which failed for the most part to hear, understand or reverence our experience. The story of these struggles is told in the archives of most congregations as they record the difficulties encountered with seeking approval of new constitutions. More dramatic in the United States has been the tumultuous encounter of the Leadership Conference of Religious with the Vatican Congregation of Religious from the mid-1960s to the present day. The history of what Sisters Lora Ann Quinonez and Mary Daniel Turner call "the rightful coming to power of American Sisters" is insightfully chronicled in their recently published book, *The Transformation of American Catholic Sisters*. This struggle is about laying claim to rightful uses of power—the power from within which activates the inherent ability to become who we are meant to be.

Second Cultural Shift

Yet, even with all of these "sea changes," the *second cultural shift* which we are presently experiencing, while less dramatic, is, for me, far more radical in terms of the future of religious life. What is being called into question today is not the relevance of the church to modern world, but the very meaning of the modern world itself whose unbridled technology has led to the degradation of our environment, to newly articulated ideologies of militarism, institutionalized violence, superiority, and the will to dominate and control. Western civilization in particular is experiencing a fundamental shift in its view of the world.

In some ways, the shift has been very hard for a number of women religious to identify with. Many of us are still struggling to find our way in modern culture after such a long experience of separation from it. To be told now that we are on the threshold of another cultural evolution and world view, which in fact repudiates many of the values of modernity, is not only confusing but raises feelings of resistance and suspicion as well. Calls to fostering a more intentional community life, a more committed corporate apostolic witness and a lifestyle which reflects greater mutuality, interdependence and interrelationships, rather than seen as a critique of fragmentation and individualism, is viewed by some as a return to past models of conformity which we have so recently left.

THE PRESENT CHALLENGE

It appears to me that the present challenge we are experiencing is very much one of dealing with the tension and confusion that accompanies a shift in paradigms or world views.

As we enter the last decade of this century and move toward the third millennium, religious life, as indeed the whole of western civilization, finds itself at the crossroads of a newly emerging world view. One of the most influential voices in terms of the meaning of paradigm shifts and therefore correlatively of changing world views has been that of scientific historian Thomas Kuhn. Applying his thought from that of the world of science, we can sense that in times of transition such as our own, proponents of competing world views or paradigms see different realities even though they look from the same place in the same direction. When persons of opposing paradigms address each other, they often use the same language but they tend to speak *through* each other instead of *to* each other. Both groups may be looking at the world but they see things and realities in the world in different relationships, and some things they see differently. In Kuhn's thought, the transfer from one world view to another is a kind of conversion experience that cannot be forced. No one can be compelled to move into the circle, nor does one arrive there step by step. One of the most compelling arguments for promoting a paradigm shift is that the new paradigm claims to be able to solve the problems that led the old one into crisis. But even more compelling is to have faith that the new paradigm will be able to deal creatively with the many new problems that it will inevitably face.[5]

In the last few years manysocial analysts, historians, economists, theologians, artists and poets have been speaking and writing about an emerging post-modern global culture in an interfaith world. It is in great part a repudiation of the possessive individualism, fragmentation, and dehumanization that has characterized the overly optimistic predictions about the future that were promised by the modern world. Two world wars, the holocaust, and the possibility of nuclear annihilation and ecological devastation have severely undermined the uncritical conviction that human autonomy and reason would of themselves progressively lead us to greater freedom and justice. Our horizons have expanded and the landscape has shifted in ways that have shocked and surprised us.

For Vaclav Havel, former poet/playwright president of Czechoslovakia, the end of communism bears an important message to the human race. It has, in his opinion, brought about an end not only to the nineteenth and twentieth centuries but to the modern age as well. "One thing is certain," he wrote, "The Age of Modernity with its Eurocentrism is over. But what comes after Modernity? What should we call these times? How can we understand them? They are radically pluralistic—this perplexes, challenges, confronts us."[6]

For theologians such as David Tracy, knowing how to deal with radical pluralism authentically and responsibly will be the task of the future. In a very real way it has challenged and compelled us—and will continue to do so—to listen to the voices of the marginalized and those groups and persons oppressed by the agenda of modernity, and by our religious tradition as well which has not led and encouraged us to seek, to listen, to search for and to find the holy in other faith traditions while remaining committed to our own.[7]

This new challenge has come out of the political, the economic and, above all, the spiritual crisis of our times rather than from institutional religion. The spiritual crisis is not to be understood primarily in terms of prayer and contemplation as it is with questions of ultimate meaning and value. It is one that seeks to eradicate the subjugation of any race, class, religion or gender to any other and to create a social and spiritual vision marked by the quest for equality, mutuality and inclusiveness. Signs of this are present even though not immediately evident in the light of the Gulf War and its aftermath with newly created deiologies and declarations of western hegemony and superiority.

Feminism and Ecological Awareness

A growing ecological awareness developing from new scientific paradigms has raised our consciousness about the interconnectedness and interdependence of all reality which is seen as embedded in a cosmos that is ongoing and continually developing. The common bond of our interrelatedness within the cosmos suggests also that there are universal values on the cultural level as well. This realization can lead to the formation of new attitudes toward the world, the recognition of genuine pluralism, the ability to see things as they are in their individuality, the promotion of an atmosphere of solidarity, unity and diversity based on mutual respect and cooperation, rather than on control and competition. Here too the western dreams of domination, mastery, and control are again challenged and repudiated.

Creative and innovative thinkers point out that the political and economic structures of society should reflect this basic reality of interdependence which in reality grounds all our interaction. Already we are acknowledging the need for world agencies to solve global problems. Such action calls for a kind of world federation of nation states with a common world authority rather than allowing and leaning on the power and might of first world countries to control the agenda of the world.[8]

The growth of ecological awareness and consciousness in this fundamental sense has not only given birth—or perhaps rebirth—to a renewed religious awareness in general, but in particular has fostered a new kind of earth-spirituality and new context for experiencing the holy. Explorations on the frontiers of science and spirituality have been the subject of much fruitful reflection in recent years. Indeed, the religious implications of scientific theories can develop quite apart from the intention of the authors. The experience of physicist James Lovelock is a case in point. As originator of the *Gaia*

Hypothesis, named after the Greek earth goddess, Lovelock maintained that the planet is a living organism, alive, resilient, and capable of existence beyond our own misuse of her gifts and bounty. Indeed, our lives depend more on her than her life on ours. After publishing his first book entitled *Gaia: A New Look at Life on Earth*, Lovelock expressed shock and surprise that the majority of his readers interpreted his message within the framework of religious faith.[9]

I believe further that the fundamental commitment of *feminism* to the transformation of hierarchical and patriarchal societal structures, more than any other social movement for change, has within itself the potential for promoting such goals. More than seeking justice for women alone, feminism is about an egalitarianism that promotes mutual and equal relationships between all persons. Such equivalence and impartiality, hopefully, will be catalyst for opening new horizons and possibilities in the structures of our society and of our church.[10] While it is true that there is yet a great deal of healing and bridge-building that needs to be done among and within different groups of women, the basic challenge is to acknowledge and respect the diversities so as to move beyond such divisions to the question of promoting the survival and flourishing of life, a value to which all feminists are committed.

Religious Life at the Crossroads of a Newly Emerging World View

As religious life stands at the crossroads of a newly emerging world view, will we be reflective, still and contemplative enough to live in the "white light" that acknowledges the truth and reality of this shifting paradigm with its crisis and opportunity? Will we be able to loosen the structures of the existing frameworks out of which we live, work and move in ways that will permit the new paradigm to emerge?

As religious congregations, some hopeful and expanding signs of this shift are already operative among us even though the impact of their implications in terms of the future may escape us. Affirmations coming from chapters and assemblies reflect our own awareness of and commitment to movements and directions that point to cultural transformation, to greater awareness and understanding of feminism, fostering spiritualities that are prophetic, contemplative, holistic and mystical in the truest sense. Recommitments to work for justice are nuanced by a growing sense of the interdependence and unity of all creation as central to the emerging world view. We have also acknowledged our need to live out our constitutions and ministerial directions within expanding faith horizons that will include other world religions whose numbers have overshadowed our own Christian tradition.

Community documents which affirm such directions have given us an agenda of commitment to the hopeful and expanding signs of these times. However, community gatherings in which such hopes are forged can lose some of their focus and force as we return to our more or less separate ministry situations. Moreover, it is altogether likely that among our membership are those who, while endorsing ecological consciousness and responsibility, the pursuance of justice, and the rights of women, are still basically committed to a present world view. And so, lest we remain at the crossroads, we will need to be more intentional with regard to the brave and bold directions we have taken and of their consequences among ourselves. This is especially true because their hope also harbors a costly challenge as we try to live them out in our country, our church, and our own congregations.

For example, in our *nation* political and economic policies have not responded kindly to post-modern critiques of imperialism, militarism, ecological devastation and threats to its own power structures. The new world order described by President Bush does not reflect the interdependence and interrelatedness needed to bring an end to cruel and dangerous disparities in an unjust world and indeed within the United States as well. The Gulf War showed once more our penchant for using force as the way to resolve conflicts. What remains uppermost is the need to be the number one power structure of the world and to measure the extent to which our country will engage in environmental controls according to what degree it touches our own economy and employment possibilities.

The commitment to pursuing and promoting peace and justice that we have made as religious has often placed us in opposition to the policies of our country. As a result, we risk losing a place of privilege and former standing that we may have had as upholders of the status quo. More seriously, we may be looked upon as troublemakers or, worse, as disloyal dissidents.

More poignantly, the *Vatican church*, in spite of strong and compelling critiques of human rights violations and oppressive structures in world situations, has resisted critiquing itself on these very same points, leaving us with feelings of ambivalence, alienation, estrangement, and dislocation.

Recent statements/actions of Vatican control of CLAR (The Latin American Conference of Religious) and the Carmelite Order of nuns have caused further uneasiness. The concern generated in Rome over the United States bishops' pastoral on women offers another instance of the Vatican's difficulty in dealing positively with the theological implications of the women's movement. And most recently, the Vatican approval of a New Council for Women Religious, to take its place alongside of the Leadership Conference of Women Religious, has not only structured division among major superiors, but has opened the door to reviving of old wounds that religious congregations have struggled so hard to overcome during the past twenty-five years.

Within my own IHM Congregation, and I suspect in many other congregations as well, the many voices and faces of feminist theory among us have generated some fear and confusion, and the suspicion of the church as well.

The challenge of the Second Vatican Council, with its commitment to the poor, and its call to work for justice, was a clear and compelling gospel mandate for societal transformation which did not disturb the basic symbol system of the church. Initial resistance to change on the part of some of our membership could be countered and encouraged by appealing to the council and its documents. It was precisely in the name of the gospel and in its spirit that we were mandated in the *Pastoral Constitution on the Church in the Modern World* "to make our own the joys and the hopes, the griefs and anxieties of the human beings of this age, especially those who are poor or in any way afflicted."

What we did not foresee was that in pursuing the plight of women in the church and in society we would discover that the feminist movement within Christianity is *precisely about* such symbolic transformation. Our commitment to it as women religious in the Roman Catholic Church is not to overthrow our rich tradition but rather to overcome the dualisms that have taken root in its structures and its symbol system as well. For example, feminists in the church, and among ourselves, call for a revisioning of the church's theology, preaching, patterns of pastoral care and its liturgical and institutional life that will not only reflect women's experience, but will offer a corrective to all that continues to denigrate women and deny the exercise of their gifts.

As we engage in a more intentional study of the feminist perspective, to which many of us as women religious have committed ourselves, it will be important to remember, as we try to hear and to reverence the variety of experiences which inform our views, that what all feminists hold together in the search for a more just world is the desire to liberate all persons and systems from the will to control and to dominate others. This, of course, applies within our congregations as well as within societal and church issues with which we are engaged and to which we are committed.

FUTURE HORIZONS AND CHALLENGING QUESTIONS

The future challenges that we face as women religious are met in a world that is in a major transition. In such times when one world view is dying and another is struggling to come to birth there is some ambivalence and ambiguity about how to chart the future or whether it is even possible.

Much of the recent literature written about religious life reflects these concerns in one way or another. On the other hand, we still find questioning of whether or not such a paradigm shift is not rather a kind of capitulation to unreflected assumptions about a so-called post-modern world. I sense that most of our congregations and communities deal internally with these parameters on a number of issues.

The emerging signs of a changing world view and horizon are already becoming clear to us from the crossroads where we presently find ourselves. As we approach the next century we will have to face some very practical present realities as well as continue to be creative and daring dreamers in terms of a future that is full of hope and promise for the sustaining of a just and harmonious planet.

The immediate and challenging questions that face us regarding our diminishing numbers, rising median age, institutional decline and decreasing finances are serious concerns that cannot be dismissed. The way in which we interpret these realities is indicative, I believe, of how we view the shape of our future.

Some of us may see these diminishments as a result of having moved too uncritically in the adaptation of our lifestyle and ministries to modern culture. Having turned away from the essential elements of religious life, we no longer offer a counter-cultural witness that appeals and attracts the generous spirit of those who want to make a difference in our society. Our accommodation to the signs of the times may appear to have broadened and flattened our common sense of mission, coupled with an over-emphasis on personal growth and development. For these persons, a return to a lifestyle that stresses identification as religious with strong canonical bonds to the institutional church, simplicity of life in intentional communities and a general commitment to institutional ministries which offer a corporate witness would provide the image of religious life that continues the long tradition and rich contribution it has made to the church and to the world.

I believe also that there are and can be a number of variations of this model. Some, for example, would promote a more intentional connection with the church in terms of wearing religious habits, living in canonically erected religious houses where authority structures, although modified, remain hierarchically ordered. Other groups, while sharing the same general critique of over-adaptation to the status quo, would interpret church ministries as being less controlled by local bishops and pastors, promote life in small collegial communities among the poor whom they serve directly, and be strongly motivated by concerns of social justice.

On the other hand, there are numbers of women religious who, while not personally subscribing to such intentionality in community, feel nevertheless that their lives are committed to the poor and marginalized in other ways than direct contact. Such persons feel strong bonds with one another for the fostering and sustaining of their congregations though they may live in very diverse circumstances. Their commitment to the church is deep and real though often less visibly institutional—perhaps designedly so.

All the above described groups share a common concern for and about the future of their congregations, and all of them, I believe, sense that religious life will never regain the large numbers we experienced in the past. As a result, greater collaboration with laity and some forms of associate membership in which lay women and men can share in the congregations mission is fostered.

Without wishing to be judgmental in any way, and not without some temerity, it seems to me that this kind of reforming and refounding of religious life is still rooted within the context of present and past world views. This is not to deny its validity nor its viability for many years to come but simply to state a reality.

Earlier, when articulating some of the present challenges facing religious congregations today, I suggested that some of the hopeful signs of an emerging world view were already operative in the affirmations and directives arising out of assemblies and chapter gatherings of the late 1980s and early 1990s. My own question is to what degree the intentional pursuance of these movements can co-exist with religious life as we have known it. Might it not be possible that they will lead to the creation of essentially new forms? I would like to comment briefly on four such directions: new forms of membership, the changing locus of power, feminism, and spirituality.

The growth of *associate forms of membership* within the traditional frameworks of religious congregations, it seems to me, is more than simply a way to bolster our diminishing membership and to invite others in to share our charism and commitment. It is also, whether consciously articulated or not, a witness to the growing sense of inclusivity, of the interconnectedness and interdependence that parallels the scientific paradigm of the interrelationships which are at the heart of the cosmos and a growing sign of our times. Thoughts such as these were already operative among some congregational leaders as early as the late 1960s even though they were not articulated within paradigmatic cultural shifts.

In 1968 Felix Cardegna, who was then rector of Woodstock College, a Jesuit major seminary, addressed the Conference of Major Superiors of Men in Chicago. "I am personally convinced," he said, "that we are on the verge of the discovery of new forms of the religious life." The predictions that he prophetically described regarding a shift of emphasis in our understanding of the vows, the common life, forms of spirituality, shared decision-making, and diversification of apostolates appeared at the time to be shockingly radical. Few of us could relate to them, and yet most of these predictions have become an integral part of religious life today.

In 1989, about twenty years later, during a joint meeting of the Leadership Conference of Women and the Conference of Major Superiors of Men, the membership engaged in a process that envisioned ten transformative elements for religious life in the next twenty years which more expressly contextualized the changes foreseen by Cardegna but *now* within an understanding of a changing world view. Perhaps for many of us, these predictions will appear once more as shockingly radical and we will not be able to hear them. One of the transformative elements to be nourished for religious life in the future concerned the creation of broad-based, inclusive communities.

In 2010, religious communities will be characterized by inclusivity and intentionality. These communities may include persons of different ages, genders, cultures, races, and sexual orientation. They may include persons who are lay or cleric, married or single, as well as vowed and/or unvowed members. They will have a core group and persons with temporary and permanent commitments.

These communities will be ecumenical, possibly interfaith; faith-sharing will be constitutive of the quality of life in this context of expanded membership. Such inclusivity will necessitate a new understanding of membership and a language to accompany it.

Such broad inclusivity, and even much less radical forms of associate membership, is still a touchy and delicate issue in many congregations of women today. Fears of loss of identity and unwillingness to allow others, who are not vowed members, to share our way of life are still very much evident. As a result, reaching out to include others is often met with anxiety, apprehension, and sometimes hostility.

Further reflecting on a future world view where models of power will be more mutual and not only the prerogative of the most powerful and wealthy, the same joint conference committed itself to nourishing a change of the *locus of power.*

Religious in 2010 will have replaced models of domination and control with principles of mutuality drawn from feminist and ecological insights, so that collaborative modes of decision-making and power-sharing are normative. Priorities for service will be generated and shaped in the local arena, while impetus for such action will be influenced by global awareness.

Surely the implementation of such directives would truly be transformative elements in religious life, creating a new contour to its reality which would be more than adaptation and accommodation to changing times.

As the feminist movement continues to grow and develop, it will, as many have predicted, become one of the most powerful forces—if not the most powerful—for the building of global communities that will cross national, racial, and gender boundaries. Women have always been catalysts for moral change. The creation of a worldwide sisterhood that is committed to overcoming the obstacles and impasses that are within its circle as well as without, and to forging networks of compassion and solidarity, will be able to bring creative imagination to play in confronting the human problems of our planet. It will also offer us a challenge of major proportions.

Religious congregations of women have much to offer the feminist movement. Our centuries-long history and experience of life in community, struggles to be self-determining, and service to the fostering and sustaining of life can provide a rich source of encouragement and education to the nascent movements of communities of women. Will we be able to overcome some of our own fears and prejudices with regard to divergent positions and diversities of lifestyles so as to be open to listening, to loving, and to treating one another with justice?

Spirituality

The new scientific paradigms regarding the oneness of creation have opened up for us once again the richness of a *creation-centered spirituality*. I say "once again" because this tradition has had deep roots within our own Christian experience. For us as women, a more radical challenge has engendered and enabled a new articulation of our spiritual experience. As we have come to name our own likeness to the divine within our own embodiment, we have come to seek for and to discover the God/ess of compassion, nurturance, and fertility. Feminists within the Christian tradition have written powerfully and convincingly of the world as God's body. Such an understanding of God has led to rituals of worship which give time and space to bonding and creative movement that acknowledges the divine presence in the participants and in the world of nature. Moreover, it has led to a new awareness of thinking which includes an openness to God and to Jesus which includes an openness to truth, goodness, and beauty wherever they are found. This, in turn, opens the door to a greater respect for the spiritual traditions of native Americans, Africans, Asians and other tribal peoples whose worship of the Great Spirit is intimately connected with the living force in all things. It also provides a new space for dialogue where Hindus, Buddhists, Christians, Moslems and Jews can share insights toward acknowledging the same unifying force which roots us in a transcendent source of life and being.

Such movements of spirituality are very operative today in religious congregations of women, but again not always with ease and understanding. For some, practices such as these suggest a denigration of time-honored forms of prayer and worship and smack of neo-paganism. Again, time and education can do much to allay such fears.

CONCLUSION

It is my belief that our journey from the crossroads into the future is a call to leave a worldview and a way of religious life that have in reality come to an end. That means that we have to leave behind many of the images and memories we have lived by, many of which we have loved and valued. This is particularly true for religious of apostolic congregations whose very reason for being has been to serve needs that have not been met adequately, or at all, by either the church or society. The joint meeting of LCWR and CMSM spoke about the future as re-examining, reclaiming and setting free the charisms of their founders/foundresses. Perhaps such "setting free" will mean the loosening of current structures, spiritualities, and ways of life which never really fit. For example, might the kind of vows we take in the future reflect more the nature of our commitment to service? Will our own listening and learning from the poor and marginalized shape all aspects of our lives? Will racial and demographic changes, our interactions with persons of various cultures and races result in deeper inculturation, interdependence and openness to being evangelized by others? Can we engage in the challenge to be open to new forms of membership while we seek at the same time to retrieve the rich tradition of religious life even as we attempt to revision it?

Such a leaving behind may cause us grief, sadness, and even some depression. The call to go forward and to leave our sadness behind is in many ways to leave ourselves and to go empty, but expectant and open, into a future where the horizon is not clear. In the risk of this journey, we would do well to listen to the mystics who have told us and witnessed in their lives through many epochs of the church's life that it is only in time of endarkenment and emptiness that God can enlighten and fill us. In this way, we can be open to the new and free to play creatively with future forms of community life.

Evelyn Underhill, a great modern teacher of mysticism, has stated:

> To be a mystic is simply to participate here and now in real and eternal life, in the fullest, deepest sense which is possible to man. It is to share

as a free and conscious agent in the joyous travail of the universe, its mighty, onward sweep through pain and glory to its home in God.... The mystic act of union, that joyous loss of the transfigured self in God, which is the crown of man's conscious ascent towards the Absolute, is the contribution of the individual to this, the destiny of the Cosmos.[11]

The challenge of Underhill's description of the mystical life, while true in every period of history, seems particularly relevant today. To be a "free and conscious agent" in the joyous travail of the universe may indeed include the call to move away from structures and ways of life whose meaning may no longer reflect the "onward sweep" of the universe to its home in God. This is not to say that the gift of religious life no longer has place or meaning in an emerging post-modern world, but that its basic prophetic witness and contemplative attitude toward life will be marked by a commitment and intentionality that is reflective of newly articulated realities that challenge it anew.

The pursuit of God as experience in life and in the reality of history has been a struggle in the Christian church from its very beginnings. The prophetic words of Jesus uttered in complaint to the Pharisees who asked for a sign in testifying to the truth of his message are sounded anew in every age: "You know how to interpret the appearance of the sky, but you cannot interpret the signs of the times" (Mt 16:3). To be able to discern the word and action of God's Spirit in our own time requires that we be rooted in the best traditions of our past, but it also demands that our own lives be so in touch with God that we can trust the deepest desires of our own hearts in charting a future not yet clear to us. Here we would do well to ponder the words of Teresa of Avila, speaking of her own order's call to a continual renewal, in *Book of the Foundations:*

> Let it never be said of them, as it is said of some other Orders, that they do nothing but praise their beginnings. It is we who are the beginners now....

Finally, it is my hope that our commitment to and belief in each other can reflect the devotion of Ruth whose bondedness to Naomi led her to leave her own traditions and to go forward into a future that did not harbor signs of fruitfulness or fulfillment.

In the end, as we know, their journey is rewarded in ways far beyond their expectations. The great lesson of this book of the Hebrew scriptures, in the words of a woman biblical scholar, is that "brave and bold decisions of women embody and bring to pass the blessings of God."[12]

May we continue to walk in the company of such wise women...grounded in the midst of outer chaos...tempered by experience...trusting in the presence of God in the experience of our lives.

Notes

1. Jean Shinoda Bolen, M.D., *Goddesses in Everywoman* (San Francisco: Harper and Row, 1984), pp. 112-13.

2. Cf. for example: Gerald A. Arbuckle, *Out of Chaos: Refounding Religious Congregations* (New York: Paulist Press, 1988); Barbara Fiand, *Living the Vision: Religious Vows in an Age of Change* (New York: Crossroad, 1990); Mary Jo Leddy, *Reweaving Religious Life: Beyond the Liberal Model* (Mystic: Twenty-Third Publications, 1991); Diarmuid O'Murchu, *Religious Life: A Prophetic Vision, Hope and Promise for Tomorrow* (Notre Dame: Ave Maria Press, 1991); Lora Ann Quinonez and Mary Daniel Turner, *The Transformation of American Catholic Sisters* (Philadelphia: Temple University Press, 1992); Patricia Wittberg, *Creating a Future for Religious Life: A Sociological Perspective* (New York, Paulist Press, 1991).

3. Hopefully these thoughts of Heather MacKinnon will appear shortly in her own article.

4. For a further elaboration on the effects of Vatican Council II's Decree on Religious Life, see my article entitled "Commentary on the Decree on the Appropriate Renewal of Religious Life," in *The Church Renewed: The Documents of Vatican II Reconsidered,* ed. George P. Schner, S.J. (Maryland: University Press of America, 1986), pp. 63-73.

5. Thomas Kuhn, *The Structure of Scientific Revolutions* (Chicago: The University of Chicago Press, 1970), pp. 144-59.

6. Interview in *New York Times,* February 1992.

7. Cf. Werner G. Jeanrond and Jennifer L. Rike, *Radical Pluralism and Truth* (New York: Crossroad, 1991), pp. ix-xxiv.

8. See Fritjof Capra and David Steindl-Rast, *Belonging to the Universe* (San Francisco: Harper, 1991), pp. 199-203.

9. See my article "...It's Like Looking at God," *The Way* (October 1992).

10. For an analysis of what a feminist-revised Catholic social theory might look like, see Maria Riley's *Transforming Feminism,* pp. 76ff.

11. Evelyn Underhill, *Mysticism: A Study in the Nature of Man's Spiritual Consciousness* (New York: Dutton, 1961), p. 534.

12. Phyllis Trible, *God and the Rhetoric of Sexuality* (Philadelphia: Fortress Press, 1978).

The Present Moment: Creative Death[1]

Austin Smith, CP

My birth is a subject of historical debate. When was I born? Some see my conception outside or beyond the very religious tradition, I mean the Christian, to which I belong. I mean my religious tradition is rooted in Jesus, the Jew, so my tradition is historically much older than Christianity itself. There was a religious community, at the time of Jesus, living in the desert at the northwestern end of the Dead Sea. Some would say, though I feel a little tenuously, that was where I was born. I really don't want to get into this debate. I only mention it to make clear to you how old I am. Many claim I was actually born in the very first, frightened and insecure, community of Christians. As far as my own identity is concerned, I feel that claim to be a little arrogant. But there's an element of truth in the claim. Sharing goods together, prayer, love, hospitality—I can see the point. But I have to say I feel a little uneasy with the idea. That was my Christian birth. My religious life birth is simply an expression, though an important one, of that earlier birth. It is with my religious life birth I am concerned and, of course, its consequences.

WHERE I WAS BORN

One thing is certain I was born in the east. That is the origin of my family, brothers and sisters, the east. Deserts and small towns, indeed hamlets, villages, even caves. The family has little to boast about in environmental terms. The family sprang up quite spontaneously, though not without deliberate choice. It is difficult to pinpoint our beginnings.

We may seem to have done quite well in later centuries. In fact, we've done very well. Pulled ourselves up by our spiritual bootstraps, as they say. Though there are some now, and even quite a few in the early days of the family, who felt we had pulled ourselves down. The problem is you've got to keep up to things. But it's a dangerous game. Mind you, we have never

109

been short of the few here and there, in the eyes of some, party spoilers, drinking far too heavily and deeply the neat and pure spirit of the gospel. They ruin every comfortable stop-over. You get them everywhere. Anyway, we've had them and, to be honest, we have them. The rest of us may sink into self-pity reflecting on the rough ride they have given and are giving us. But I can tell you it's not nearly as rough as the one they get. Ask Francis of Assisi, one of my distant brothers. But I must get back to my birth, and, perhaps more importantly, the circumstances of my birth. What I say on this matter may well be open to dispute. Still, what's not open to dispute?

THE PROGRESS OF MY FAMILY

As I was saying, the family has really done well. We're all over the world. We own a vast amount of property and large tracts of land. We have schools for the poor and schools for the rich; we have hospitals for the poor and hospitals for the rich. Many members, a vast number in fact, became priests, bishops, and even popes. There have been a lot of family arguments about this latter fact. But, then, every family has its arguments. Mind you, some arguments are more serious, even more crucial, than others. Anyway, thousands have taken care of local Christian communities. We are in universities as professors and lecturers and, having educated the poor children in the back streets, taking them literally off the streets, we built teacher training colleges to take them further educationally. Some members of the family have a longer organized set-up than others. Many live completely removed from the day-to-day world, committing themselves wholly to prayer. It has even been suggested that we are responsible for the movement of social welfare and, at the far end of the spectrum, guardianship and creators of art and scholarship. Certainly the family can boast some of the most dedicated historical figures in the care of the sick and the powerless; the family has also fostered some of the most brilliant minds in history. And, yes, some have been shot to death in the light of the moon because of their awkwardness with the state, their conviction of the truth of Jesus and their defense of the vulnerable. As the familiar hymn says, we've known "dungeon, fire and sword." Oh, by the way, I should tell you that members of the family carried the teaching of Jesus all over the world. I can speak for Europe only, but you'll find their tombs all over the continent. I could go on and on. The stories, the anecdotes, the journeys and the achievements are innumerable. And, needless to say, so are the tragedies. After all I'm talking about, at least, one thousand seven hundred years of life. That's how old I am. My birthday was way back. And it was, as I have remarked, in the east.

A RADICAL BEGINNING

When the church settled down, having been accepted by the state, there were some people not altogether too happy with this turn of events. They were just that little bit afraid of getting into the respectability game. I mean, they saw the church making the state respectable and the state making the church respectable. This took place formally in the early years of the fourth century. It came about not only by a formal acceptance, but was signaled by what had been a permanent threat to the church—martyrdom. But with this acceptance martyrdom had come to an end. Martyrdom was a symbol. You may worry about this. After all, there's nothing intrinsically good in being burned to death. I think, however, there's much more to it. Martyrdom can arrive in your life with a certain subtlety. The poor of this world, for example, are hardly ever invited onto the cocktail circuit. And you know yourself, if you start talking too much on the same circuit about racism or poverty or marginalization, indeed even if you so speak in the local church, the invitations dry up. I think it was this social, not to say political, respectability which worried them. Martyrdom has a lot to do with exclusion, and at its most extreme you simply vanish at the cockcrow in a South African or South American dawn. That's an extreme example. But any exclusion socially, politically, even theologically, is martyrdom.

THE PROBLEM OF POWER AND LOVE

With this fear of respectability went an unease with power expressed in political collusion or power expressed in riches. They wanted power defined in the light of the gospel. And on top of this they saw no radical obedience to authority worth its name outside the Jesus of the little ones or the servant of all or the model of the first being last. Virginity and celibacy were also at the heart of their anxiety. It was reaching for a transcendent love. It may not be a very good way of describing the issues of virginity and celibacy. But I would prefer to leave it there, though I must take up, however briefly, and indeed superficially, this question. Virginity has a long history. Indeed, it goes back beyond the life of the Christian church itself, never mind my own particular family in the church. As far as the church is concerned, "(s)ome commentators have concluded that the original inspiration for the ideal arose from a Greco-Roman culture whose licentiousness may have provoked a cult of virginity as an antidote."[2] There are serious and compelling reasons for such an opinion. I do not wish to simply reduce an ideal, inspired by a deep union with God, to political or cultural causes. At the same time, the latter cannot be excluded. Ancient history, including early church history, suffers the gender oppression. That is to say, most records are written by men. When one ancient witness could actually say, "The creator had purposely made one half of the whole race imperfect, and, as it were mutilated," referring to women, I can't ignore the social influences at work in the expression of virginity. Or, to put this another way, I can understand the virginity issue, preached by Paul the apostle, being grasped by women in terms of liberation. It has been wisely remarked, "There were other, more social factors. Thus celibacy was particularly important for women as it made them equal participants, with men, in a common search for perfection. It also created a space for other than that allotted to wife, mother or courtesan."[3] Needless to say, I am far from ignoring the deeper theological issues in celibacy and virginity. But I believe the social and, for that matter, the theological unrest in terms of the women in the contemporary church should highlight this area of reflection. Woman exploding from the domination of man, like all historical movements, psychologically at least, has a longer history than the past hundred years. I'll come back to this in terms of my family, but leave it there for the moment.

EXTREMES AND PROTESTS

There is surely hardly any need for me to record for you, or remind you, the family has produced innumerable extremists, eccentrics, and even out and out dangerous individuals. But every worthwhile and creative idea will always give birth to extremes and eccentricity. Some of the family started living on the top of pillars! But you must remember they felt themselves face to face with, recalling a recent example of protest, a cultural and spiritual Greenham Common. Some things you just can't let go. No matter how mad you may seem to the rest of the world, protest is the only choice. Times were critical. It was an era when the spiritual state of things could be considered a major crisis. As I have remarked more than once, there are all kinds of opinions about this. Still distinguished members of the family and, for that matter, of the church and secular society have seen it this way. It has been well said:

> It was not by chance that...the retreat to the desert spread so suddenly just as the State made its peace with the Church. There is certainly a very close connection between these two contemporaneous historical facts. When a world in which Christians as such were separated and proscribed was succeeded by a world in which they came to be in honour, but a world whose spirit had hardly changed for all that, the best Christians, by instinct, would freely choose the state of proscription no longer imposed on them by circumstances. In a world which no longer

treated them as enemies, they would feel obliged to live as enemies of the world: they sensed too well that, without this, they would soon become slaves.... The reaction was so natural that it seems more and more to have been spontaneously the same in more than one place at the same time..... Antiquity, having been born in Egypt, was diffused everywhere from there.[4]

GEOGRAPHICAL POSSESSION

Everywhere is not an exaggeration. It is starkly true. Through France it made its first journey, and even, from Egypt itself, some say, a distinctive journey to Ireland was launched. It is hard to believe that by the year 1534 in England alone, there were between eleven and twelve thousand members in the family with nearly nine hundred homes. I do not want to get into technical argument about the difference between monks and clerks or nuns and sisters. I call them all members of the religious life or, simply, religious. When just on fifty years ago, I joined the family in a little church in a Cotswold village, one winter's evening, in the presence of my father and mother, I was spiritually nearly eighteen hundred years old. So I see myself born in Egypt, at least this is how I see it now, in circumstances of creative tension with the powers of this world and, more specifically, belonging loyally to a church perceived drifting into social and political respectability.

So the journey of the family has been a long one. The fact that the family has been around a long time, by the way, says nothing more than that it has been around a long time. Longevity in itself proves nothing except longevity. I say this because I would want to make it clear there is no reason for the family to go on existing. But it would be a tragedy were it to die out. Peter Brown in his wonderful life of St. Augustine who, by the way, was a very distinguished member of the family, speaking of Augustine's world, Roman North Africa, which had virtually come to the end of its days, offers the sober reflection, "Yet, as so often happens, this world on the edge of dissolution had settled down to believe that it would last forever." I really hope the family is not on the edge of dissolution, but I do worry about our tendency to settle down believing we can last forever. I so quote with purpose.

REMEMBERING ROOTS

I believe the family, as a whole, and all the varying rich movements, organizations and expressions of the family, needs to remember those early stark, even frightening, tensions between church and state, respectability and acceptance, the power of the gospel and the power of the political, economic, social and cultural power pyramids of the times, and, with due loyalty and commitment, the tensions between the family and the church, seeing them not simply as history but, rather perhaps, a pointer into our own task and times—the dying decade of the twentieth century. The tensions, creative tensions, of early days are acutely with us today.

In a word, I believe it is a task of religious life, not alone but with others, to be a source of creative tension. It is important that the religious life is not seduced by its own institutionalization. Anything as enormous as the religious life must submit to institutionalization. It is accountable to the world and the church. But it must always be alive with its own distinctive historical consciousness and the consciousness which is awakened by the demands of the voice of God in the world of its times. This sounds so very simple and straightforward. It's not, I assure you.

I have given you the impression, late twentieth century religious, that I am the result of some kind of easy linear, event after event, century after century, year after year, religious man. Forget that, I am not. What happened in the eastern desert was in the nature of a spiritual explosion. The spiritual explosion was not the facing of a problem; it was rather amassive and troublesome asking of a question. What's Christian woman and man about? I am trying to say, the monasteries didn't come after the desert, the wandering friars after the monasteries, the teaching religious orders and the preaching religious orders after the friars, the nursing and welfare and educationally committed orders after the preachers and the teachers, Mother Teresa in the Bombay slums after Charles deFoucauld in the North African desert, right down to our retreat houses and inner city commitments of today. In a word, it was not some kind of inevitable and pre-ordained progress, the subject of ecclesiastical institutionalization. Theologies and spiritualities of it may make it appear this way. I've done this myself in the past.

INSTITUTIONS

It was rather a question, institutionalized and codified in all kinds of ways to be sure, and maybe overly so, carried on the waves of history. Incarnated in living, contemplative, active, enthusiastic, riotous men and women. And weaknesses? Too many to spell out, believe me. Compromise with ourselves and compromise with the institutions of this world, all too often because of our institutionalized position, caring more for self-preservation, like all institutions, and running from risk. In a word, the very fact that *we are essentially a ministering question* allowing too often, perhaps, our very questioning nature to slip, too easily, into pragmatic comfort. And, I must add, being too ready to accommodate the institutional church when the time has come for challenge. Accountable we must always be but accountability never excludes questions, even arguments. The hope is they are embraced in a creative and sincere conversation.

A COMMON CHRISTIAN VOCATION

What is powerlessness, what is love, what is subjection to the vision of Jesus? That radically was the question, I believe, asked in an eastern desert, when Christian women and men feared, as we say nowadays, doubtful and even dangerous inculturation. Sometimes, I feel, our very institutional success has been our death warrant.

Rightly, you ask me, "Is not that question for the whole of Christian life, for every single Christian?" Actually powerlessness, love and subjection to the vision of Jesus is the Christian life. There are ways without number to respond to and live out this life. Religious life, as I have indicated it, is one of those ways. But it takes to itself, a task taken up, in my opinion, in its very beginnings and repeated by thousands of women and men down the years, to keep alive the question along with all members of the family, but even deeper to make sure the question is interpreted in the light of historical demands. It is, therefore, called into a constant flow of becoming within the tensions of history. It is to be more concerned with the mutability both of itself, church and world face to face with history, and must be careful of the seductive attractions of immutability. Mutability is not synonymous with imperfection. It is about growth, about development, about liberation and, above all, about creativity. This is not a question of change for change's sake, to quote that rather tired axiom, which all too often is a sign of escape or trumpet sound for retreat. To put this another way, and more theologically, recalling the words of John XXIII, it is responding to "the signs of the times." This, too, has become a tired phrase but only because it is always hedged in with a timidity mistakenly called caution or prudence. The very act of servanthood to which we are called requires religious to be alert interpreters of the signs. Religious life betrays that task if it fails to live the question up to the very point of tension.

STRESSING THE PAST

You may feel, and I sympathize with your feeling, I have given too much attention to history; I mean in terms of times past. You may also feel I am being somewhat gimmicky. I refer to all this business about being over a thousand years old. It is a bit gimmicky, but there are explanations for this.

I honestly do not believe that you can talk about anything, I mean "serious" anything, outside of an historical perspective. I am over a thousand years old. I carry the burden, not to mention the enrichment, of over a thousand years. Just as the black kids on Granby Street carry the imprisoning confinements of the slave ships sailing down the Mersey River to "catch niggers," not my words, the words of the captains who guided the ships beyond the bar. I can't gaze at a River Mersey sunset or dawn, and I gazed at a dawn with these thoughts in mind only the other day as I read the gospel passion of Jesus, without a consciousness of those ships. To be honest I have done this a few times in recent years. Meditating upon the loneliness of Jesus has never been more powerful, more disturbing, than in that dawn silence on the banks of the River Mersey. I've watched the ships breaking anchor and setting sail for the west coast of Africa. I became a white watcher of the passion. I have seen blood and water gush from black flesh. Then someone knocked the bench, as they did in a monastery, to say time up on meditation. Time for breakfast. I drove past a black man waiting for the bus and thought, "Well you're not waiting to embark on the slaveship—or are you?" It's doubtful because a distinguished black man today has told me about white men ruffling his hair in a local factory. His hair was so different from theirs. Then there was fun in the factory canteen as he, a lone black man, nudged along the line with his tray. Such was the story he told me.

DRAWING UPON HISTORICAL STRENGTH

What is the source of his strength? To be sure, the personality developed by himself, family and the solidarity of friendship. But it has also come from the reflection upon a past. It emerges indirectly from a history of thousands, indeed millions of black people who have set their faces against middle passage, of the slave trade. He is as old as, even older than, John Newton, captain of the Liverpool ship, Duke of Argyle, brought into St. John's Harbor, Antigua, in the Caribbean on July 3, 1751. It took him forty-two days to make the middle passage from Sierra Leone to the Caribbean, May 23 to July 3, having left Liverpool the previous summer. The log of the middle passage reads, "Thursday 23rd May...Buryed a man slave (No. 34)...Wednesday 29th May...Buryed a boy slave (No. 86) of a flu...Wednesday 12th June... Buryed a man slave (No. 84) of a flu, which he had been struggling with near 7 weeks...Thursday 13th June...This morning buryed a woman slave (No. 47). Know not what to say she died of for she has not been properly alive since she first came on board."[5] Yes, our Liverpool black friend is as old as the ten million Africans transported across the Atlantic in the space of two and a half centuries, 1600 to the 1840s. Their suffering and oppression are his. And their richness, their culture, their strength and their power are his. I mention this latter point of strength, for as black history is reclaimed, we are not reclaiming weakness and inferiority, we are reclaiming the dynamic of strength and calling in the debts of history in the struggle for equality. It is one, though very distinct, with all the powerless of this world—the movement toward authentic liberation.

INTERPRETING

It is with deliberation I draw upon your history, for I believe racism and marginalization, on every level, is the major demand upon the members of my own family today. But, needless to say, returning to my theme, I reflect in my way on history. You will have heard the trite statement about history repeating itself. It doesn't. It is rather a fact that ideas and questions in the very heart of humanity never die. They come back again and again in new contexts—just as the ideas, even very new and insighted ones, the questions new and very demanding, of our own times will not die. They return, and will continue to return, in different ways and in different contexts. The crucial issue is, however, that we cannot live, even survive, by simply repeating the ideas of the past. They must be interpreted in the present, renewed in the present, and, perhaps, ignored in the present, left in an historical silence.

This issue of interpreting the past in the light of our own times is a critical one. In all exercises of interpretation there is what I wish to call a moment of "creative death." I speak not of the death of questions or ideas. I speak rather about that necessary, perhaps painful, moment of allowing to die something, which may indeed, though falsely, seem to offer security, perhaps a hope, in a contemporary hour of discomfort arising from the need for new decisions. There is always a failure point in all examples, but I'll risk offering you one.

You, with so many of our mutual friends, have in the past struggled, and continue to struggle today, against all forms of racism. We have seen this as our call to counter powerlessness. We have shared also our struggles too, face to face with the oppression of the woman and the poor in our own area. One night, let's imagine, you talk to your mother about this. "Well," she says, busy with tea, "your dad and myself knew it. But we stayed together and our love of each other brought us through it. Never forget that!" You treasure this statement. You admire the statement. You even envy it. You know it is a portent of graveside tears one day. Deep down, however, in your heart and experience, you know it's just not enough. It still carries meaning for a new day. There is a creative power in the words and the meaning the words signify. Still, it's not enough. There is a sense in which the statement must die. There is about it a creative dying. "Oh, Mum, that's a load of nonsense," you would never dream of saying. "Mum, it's different and it's because of you and dad we're into what we are," you are more likely to say. You are grateful for your inheritance. But you cannot repeat her prescription in the illness of your own times. Respectfulness and reverence bring about a creative death, the memory will always remain, but there is a new time.

REPEATING AND EXTENDING

I worry about this in my religious life institutions, which analogously I have called my family. We too often, I feel, sometimes with profound honesty and fear, and, it has to be said, often enough out of stubbornness and sheer pigheadedness, run from creative death. And this can happen when we get into the language game. We change the language but fail to change the game. It is what I call the dangerous philosophy of repetitionism. The world's new agenda does not lead to a new creativity in the family because we have failed to accept, in our contemporary interpretation, the fact of creative death. I stress here I am not abandoning reverence, respect and gratitude for the past. Indeed, there is a power in the past which must continue to flow into the present. But the flow into the present demands that element of creative death. I speak of this in terms of my own religious life family. Actually it exists, and in a corruptive manner, through so many of our institutions. On a very deep spiritual level, I believe we fail to let loose the creativity of God's unfolding in us. Sometimes, perhaps unconsciously, this can lead not so much to the death of God, but to the manipulation of God. And there's a further danger in this.

We have lived and worked together in this area for a number of years. There were times, indeed there are times, when we have been able to create something very distinctive in our struggle with powerlessness. I feel, sometimes, when new demands emerge we extend what we've got, when we should be allowing the new that is emerging to redefine us. This tendency, and excuse the language (I did warn you about this when I began attempting to answer your questions, Who am I? and What am I?), is a logical consequence to the philosophy of repetitionism; it is the philosophy of extensionism. To put this concretely within your own context, the liberation of the black in society will mean a new definition of the so-called liberated white, as the liberation of the woman in society demands a new definition of the so-called liberated man. This is a crucial question, I must add, for my own family and even for the church to which it is accountable. In a word, you don't face new days and new demands by simply extending what you have already. It is time for a retreat to face the theme of creative and reverential redefinition.

In all this I feel we are not facing something unique. If you institutionalize anything of importance, and institutionalize you must to pass on vital and charismatic moments of history, there will come historical moments when the self-preservation of the institution subordinates, even silences, the articulated voices of new days. It is not inevitable, however, as long as honest reflection is married to committed discernment. Using your history, I have tried to stress my history. Without such historical understanding I cannot understand my present, still less creatively develop themes for a future.

TENSION AGAIN

Few of us, I know this is my own tendency, seek tension for its own sake. At the same time, tension is too often perceived as, by nature, destructive. Tension is, however, or at least can be, inspiringly creative. Creativity is developed when there is conversation. And conversation is, in personal terms, the way by which I find my way, pick my way around, the mind and life of another. It is not proving points, it is not about winning, it is not about convincing, it is about a gentle exchange of a group of people, an exchange of failures, hopes and, if in these days one dare use the word, vision. For this reason conversation is both the cause and the effect of *amicitia*, friendship, the love of another for the good of the other. I don't simply like your company, I do not feel you are simply useful to me; to use the distinctions of an ancient Greek philosopher, we rather seek the good of each other and, therefore, the good of the world in which we live.

BELONGINGNESS

When, therefore, you ask me who and what I am, my answer is about you as much as about me. It's a common search. So my distinct family cannot go on only existing and acting for you, but, much more radically, we must seriously exist and act with you. This has very profound consequences. Our conversations, based upon the friendship I've described, may lead to a total reflection upon a new belongingness for you in or with the family. The family will need to seriously discuss and understand its separateness. In many of our homes, we used to have a door over which was inscribed the word Enclosure. In many of them those days are gone. They are open homes and, like all families, maintaining certain distinctive family areas. But the family of the future may have to rethink the very meaning of belonging to the family. Remember the word family is used throughout what I have written to you in a very analogous way.

VOWING TO GOD

I mention this point for a very special reason. I have already mentioned to you the distinct areas of poverty, chastity and obedience, though very briefly and indirectly. As present in the family they have distinct, even legal, meaning. I don't want to go into the accepted or historical meaning of these terms. And, I must add, by not going into them here I am not denying the distinctive meaning. When I reflect, however, upon those terms in my own times, sometimes during my riverside meditation, I find them such powerful concepts in very distinctive ways. They become for me not only aspects of life which I must honor, but must be signs of the wonder of the human story and the earth story as told by God, the creative author.

ALIENATION AND BELONGING

There seems to me to be a terrible cultural alienation in my own times. Powerlessness has been taken for granted, the sexual oppression of millions is part of my hearing and so many are excluded from the control over their own destiny by self-created, and sometimes community created, political, economic, social and cultural elites. This alienation, like all alienation, results in the vandalizing of human and earth dignity. In a word, though realized and total, community may not always remain an aspiration, humanity living in a blend of a "now" and a "not yet"; the experience of communion must not be some vague dream dismissed by the pragmatists as some kind of idealism. Those who stand for the vision of the kingdom of Jesus and those who are part of the institutional church will need to face up to the crisis of God's creation. This means more than highlighting sin and sinner; it means more than marking out what it sees as obvious immorality. It means accepting what I believe was at the birth of my family, a tension with the respectable manipulators of God's creation, on all levels, some of us sitting in church benches on the sabbath. If you ask me, then, to say in one word (you always put it that way and I ignore you shamelessly) what I believe should be the guiding word for my family, at this point of its rethink, my answer is POWERLESSNESS. So simple? Not complicated enough? Well, those questions bring me to a final reflection.

EXISTING WITH THE SIMPLE AND THE COMPLEX

"There are far too many politicized people on earth today for any nation readily to accept the finality of America's historical mission to lead the world."[6] I wish to use this statement analogously; I use it for the sake of my own response to your questions.

Just on fifty-two years ago I entered what was called a junior seminary. I had decided I wanted to join a branch of the family. It was called "The Passionists." I still belong to it. I was very young; I think too young. It was the pattern, indeed the road, to becoming a member of the order and a priest in those days. The reason, indeed the origin, for this step I have already explained to you. But there is a "Who," namely me, surrendering to a "What," namely a branch of the family and the priesthood. I was at a point socially and politically. I was a mere fourteen years out of the womb of my mother. I had so early in life become a part of this ancient movement, the religious life. I was on my way to a different and new birth.

Only a few years after this event, I was taking vows of poverty, chastity and obedience. And only nine years after that moment, the year 1954, I was ordained a Catholic priest. A line had been drawn under my "Who" by a "What." The "Who" is obvious, the "What" is the religious order and the priesthood. I had become a member of an ancient historical family. It was being part of a movement subjected to vast institutionalization and structural-ization. Theological, spiritual and, I believe, cultural interpretations took over my life. I surrendered to them, accepted them willingly. In this hour of my life I have no regrets. Yet in a very few years relatively, the "Who" was wondering about and asking questions of the "What." There was simply no denial, certainly no betrayal, in such questions. I was simply, in the name of my own faith, reason and commitment, asking questions. Where did the questions come from? A broader understanding of religious life, priesthood and the historical world in which I was unfolding and evolving. The respons-es of the "What" were too predictable and, I must say, too ahistorical.

This was not a question of unbelief struggling with belief. It was rather belief struggling with another belief which seemed insensitive to the cultural and political energies of history. I believe now my vocation to the life of the family and the priesthood within the family and the church had been too his-torically transcendent. This is not to deny certain radical and fundamental realities. But it is to say that even radical and fundamental realities must be subjected to the creative, and God-given, unfolding of history.

A tree at dawn is not the same tree at eventide. The tree remains, but the light changes. I see it differently at dawn from the way I see it at eventide. I must not dismiss the factor of the light as something quite irrelevant. For I see the light, as well as the tree. They are both real, the light and the tree. In a word, like human beings becoming politicized in our times and, consequently, finding themselves unable to accept undisputed and unquestioned one political force, so in all vocations the institutions to which we belong will be disputed and questioned. This does not necessarily take place out of some inner personal dissatisfaction. It rather comes from the inevitable dialogue, indeed dialectic, between the human being and the movements of history through which and in which an institution, to which I have willingly chosen to belong, makes its journey. In this analogy, the tree is the institution, the light is history. But the light is not an accidental element.

In parentheses I must make an important point. I make it briefly because I will say more about it later. The "What," the family to which I belong, has, as a family, submitted itself to very profound moments of reflection and self-critique. I played a part in such events nearly thirty years ago. I can't help wondering, however, if we begin our reflections and self-critique without a sufficient openness to the word of God within the flow of history. Religious life is a dynamic historical force in our western world. I believe we have, largely through a submission to certain monastic influences, given way to over-organization. The tendency of a too tight exercise in organization, in its turn, resists the power of historical forces—and too often, in doing so, silences important voices within its own family membership. This is not to be dealt with by simply saying one must accept pluralism. It is much deeper than that in our own times. It is rather to ask the question. In our own times is what we call pluralism the very nature of the family, the institution, itself? I know this is a major question in the whole understanding of authority in our times; it must be faced at all levels. We live in a world, which after too many totalitarian experiences, struggles for pluralistic creativity.

This statement is not without relevance. I often feel the dreams of socialism are not totally out of touch with the dreams of my family. The word "communism" weeps, I feel, for rehabilitation. While, especially from the 1960s, a whole world was into the "community thing," one could hardly go to a meeting without hearing the word. Christians were running away from the term "communism." Why? It had taken to itself its own unique historical and political meaning. Community had been executed on the block of ideological interpretation. What we all perceived was not community; we saw the horror of totalitarianism. I believe Sheldrake has expressed this with a distinct sharpness. "The original fluidity was lost as the personal and autonomous was subordinated to the common life." Indeed, if I may adopt a concept from recent Soviet history, a more generous understanding of community gave way to "collectivization." In a philosophy, not to mention a theology, of collectivization, the human imagination, so often the receptacle of God's dialogue with history, slips out of human and divine sight.

All this I say to you for a very simple, though very complex, reason.

When you asked me "Who am I?" and "What am I" you placed a very difficult question. Yet at the same time, probably all unknowingly, the distinction between the "Who" and the "What" is crucial. To be sure, in the day to day existential and active conduct of life they are fused. But, I repeat, the distinction is crucial, and not for purely personal reasons. It is much more than that. Loyalty and commitment, for example, are wonderful, not to say necessary virtues in life. But in that to which any person is loyal and committed, be it another person, systems of ideas or institution, the person must be permitted her or his own process of discernment. Disharmonies in interpretation must be given the conversational time and space to be worked out. If we do not do this, all too often in life, we blame the singer and not the shared song.

If here in the inner city, and this was the case, you and many other friends introduced me to the marginalization of powerlessness and the horror of racism, then the "Who" I am approaches the "What" to which I belong and am committed a different person, a changed person. I have been brought into your suffering and the suffering of others and such suffering has become mine. This is not an accidental or superficial aspect of my life journey. Far from it! It goes very deep into something I have already shared with you and explained in my own terms. It goes deep into my spirituality and theology.

In the "What" to which I belong, I have, throughout my whole adult life, been asked to see and, indeed, understand the world in the light or, if you will, the loving darkness of the suffering of Jesus. I have been encouraged to purgate myself from my own self-seeking and to seek union through Jesus with God in the suffering of this world. I feel, no more than that, for too many years the journey has lacked a perception of suffering in real lives. Above all things I have not really understood the living tension between the gospel of Jesus and the actual social, political, economic and cultural models of power within the world through which I pass and in which I am called to minister. So I come not only to a point of self-reflection and critique, but this changed "Who" I am leads me to see the "What" to which I belong and offer total commitment in a new way. This is not to say there is no longer any ministry to the powerful and those who suffer no marginalization. But it is to say I can only minister, in such a milieu, through the lives of the powerless and the marginalized. This is not a personal opinion or interpretation. It is the essence of the mystery, the life and the vision of Jesus. It is the fundamental tension taken up in the eastern desert well over a thousand years ago. Facing up to this is the grounds for the freedom of the daughters and sons of God. It is, indeed, the noble and authentic liberation of all.

Our lives together, the struggle we have experienced, calling to mind that 1981 summer of riots and the tension between police and community, force us to accept a life caught within the simple and the complex. We can see even now some glaring simple facts, but are we ready to accept the facts also of complexity. It is a distinction, the simple and the complex, at the very roots of all human life. What I have said to you already (I have yet to discuss my priesthood) is faced with life and action caught between simplicity and complexity? A modern example of this may help. I remember a discussion, with someone of some influence, about the Gulf War. He was an American. How come, I asked him, we can dispatch from the United States 650,000 troops across 6,000 miles with all the supplies and back-up involved into the midst of the desert, yet we seem unable to feed the hungry, the starving and the exposed in our streets? He told me I was being very simple; it is a very complex question. I assured him I understood the complexity, but there's no harm in raising the simple question.

You know, I have really begun to understand the vision of Jesus, the relationship between the "Who" I am and the "What" of the religious life, indeed the relationship between church and world, in these terms. Here's a story from the recorded vision of Jesus. He and his friends came to a town one day, "and when he was in the house he asked them, 'What were you arguing about on the road?' They said nothing because they had been arguing which of them was the greatest. So he sat down, called the twelve to him and said, 'If anyone wants to be the first, he must make himself last and servant of all.' He then took a little child, set him in front of them, put his arms around him, and said to them, 'Anyone who welcomes one of these little children in my name welcomes me; and anyone who welcomes me welcomes not me but the one who sent me'" (Lk 9:46-48). This has been a recurring theme. Whenever I read it my imagination runs riot. I can hear someone, perhaps getting the meal ready, whispering to someone else, "It can't be as simple as that." At that point I hear the urgent and demanding Jesus, and though we get the impression he spent life dawdling down country lanes, he was urgent and demanding, suddenly shouting across the room, "Of course, it's not as simple as that. I've been fighting the colonial and religious establishments about Caesar's taxes; I came drinking and eating and they said I was a glutton, yet when my cousin fasted they said he was possessed by Satan. I've had to defend a prostitute at an upper-class dinner; the mob wanted to make me a king and I ran for it; Herod's crowd have struck up an alliance with the temple lot to get me. Don't talk to me about my vision not being as simple as what I have just said. Don't insult me by saying I don't know the complexity. Of course I do. I live with it, pick my way around it every day. At the same time, it is as simple as I say."

Wild imagining? Up to a point, yes. But we are faced with the simplicity and complexity of the paradox day in and day out. How can people starve in a food-stuffed supermarket world and how can we construct every kind of border control imaginable in a world geographically peppered with travel agencies? Millions planning their holidays and millions looking for some escape to food and peace. I believe, accepting the paradox, searching for informed simplicity, the task of the religious life is to drag the world fearlessly, even to the point of looking foolish, to the fact of simplicity. It is for the religious life to accept the fact that this Jesus called out to friends "Follow me" and never once really spelled out the destination. He couldn't because the destination was in the midst of the marginalized, the stigmatized and the powerless. And who, in the name of God, wants that kind of destination? It's simple and it's complex. The danger is we get lost in the elaborate theories of the complexity. This is always a danger. We are all, I certainly am, too often mugged by it, at every dimension of life. My family has suffered from it.

I have attempted in the answer to suggest that the origin of my family was rooted in a warning precisely about this. It is rooted in a warning about the flight from simplicity. We came to birth in the midst of a tension between the power of the vision of Jesus and the power of political, economic, social and cultural elitism. The identification of the powerless, solidarity with the powerless and articulation of the corruption of elitism were not perceived as a specialized work to be done; it was rather a life and action at the very heart of all life and work in the family.

My own family, a few years ago, decided to redefine the very core of its reason for existence, with this in view. The family was called to see the crucified of this world in the crucified one. This is a summons into the heart of the tension of so long ago. It is a creative tension. But in a world in which we are now talking about "the underclass" with such ease, it is a reclaiming of our roots—and not the roots only of my own branch of the family, but of the whole family. Jesus once spoke about the poor being always with us. My only interpretation of that is the powerful will always be looked after. The family must be about the powerless. We must see this, I believe, not with that cynicism which too often afflicts us as so-called experienced people (it is impossible to hold a real conversation with a cynic), but with the open and believing eyes of children. Of course, there will be complexity in such discernment. One can only be truly upheld, sustained and inspired by the simple.

Remember the words I quoted at the very beginning of my response?

It is sometimes said, either irritably or with satisfaction, that philosophy makes no progress. It is certainly true, and I think this is an abiding and not regrettable characteristic, to keep trying to return to the beginning, a thing which is not at all easy to do. There is a two-way movement in philosophy, a movement towards the building of elaborate theories, and a move back again towards the consideration of simple and obvious facts.[7]

Notes

1. It is important for me to stress that this reflection is part of a much longer reflection. The reflection as a whole is a response to some local friends in the inner city who asked me one night, "Who are you and what are you?" This context must be taken into consideration by the reader.

2. Philip Sheldrake, S.J., *Spirituality & History* (SPCK, 1991), p. 108.

3. Ibid.

4. Louis Bouyer, *A History of Christian Spirituality* (B & O, 1983 reprint), Vol. 1, pp. 305-06.

5. James Walvin, *Black Ivory* (Harper Collins, 1992), pp. 39-40.

6. Edward Said, *Culture & Imperialism* (Chatto & Windus, 1993), p. 348.

7. Iris Murdoch, *Sovereignty of God* (Ark Paperbacks, 1983), p. 1.

Meeting the Challenges of the New Century: Through the Eye of the Needle

Marie Augusta Neal, SND de N

During the past thirty years, religious institutes of apostolic women have been absorbed in reshaping their constitutions the better to fit their ministries among the people into the realization of the new direction the Catholic church's mission has taken since the early 1960s. It was then that Pope John XXIII called for the opening of the Second Vatican Council to bring the Church to a new awareness of what it is expected to do in a coming new world of interdependent peer groups.

There is a transition in process in religious life today but, though many are aware of that fact, some are still puzzled about what is actually going on and why. I will venture a thesis. A social class system, based on race and ethnicity, long in place and reinforced by religion, ceased being functional in the early 1960s. This happened because of emerging realities, the first one global. Third world countries began to throw off colonialism with a measure of awareness of their human rights. The second one was a simultaneous ending and flowering of two parallel events in the United States: 1. the end of a century-long struggle of European immigrants striving to succeed in the United States, with some members of all ethnic groups making it in the system; 2. the beginning of our seeing descendants of the freed slaves of the nineteenth century conducting a responsible civil rights movement as competitors of equal status demanding their place in the emerging world community of peer groups.

A pragmatic manifestation of the change as a global reality was the discovery by Brazilian peasants, using Paulo Freire's method of literacy learning, conscientization, that they could learn to read and write in time spans from six weeks to six months, despite centuries of illiteracy. Further they found that such learning happened when the words they read were the ones they used in planning action toward the elimination of the oppression which they experienced in working the land they were prevented from owning when defined as serfs and enslaved in ignorance (Freire, 1970). This phenomenon suggests the need to understand as teachers how education involves both a freeing and an indoctrinating function.

The philosophical manifestation of the end of this classism was the declaration of human rights by the United Nations in 1948 and the subsequent efforts to turn that declaration into law by the working out of the covenants that later became *The International Bill of Human Rights.*[1] These tenets affirm everyone's right to freedom and resources for life as equal human beings, sharing the same nature and hence the same rights and responsibilities and needing the same education together to teach and to learn from each other.

There was an emerging recognition by organizations of men and women that there are no lesser human beings. This made the possession of enormous wealth and power by some, while others have none or not enough to live with dignity, a problem for the church embedded in the system that embodied sinful social structures. The Catholic Church as well as churches of other denominations called for change. For us Catholics the call came from Pope John XXIII in *Pacem in Terris.* The church had already passed judgment on the unjust treatment of industrial workers and affirmed their right to organize in order to have the power to demand a just family wage, thus giving the labor movement a needed boost.[2] So now it was time to take a second step by responding to the just demands of the oppressed in the world community as they awakened to the possibility of achieving their human rights (Neal, 1987).

Just thirty years ago Pope John XXIII promulgated *Pacem in Terris,* his contribution to the twentieth century's advancement in the developing awareness of human rights. In order to examine the current reality from which we can reflect on the future of religious life of women in the United States, it is useful to quote the following passage from *Pacem in Terris:*

39. Our age has three distinctive characteristics.

40. First of all, we note that the working classes have gradually gained ground in economic and public affairs. They began by claiming their rights in the socio-economic sphere. They extended their action then to claims on the political level. And, finally, they applied themselves to the acquisition of the benefits of a more refined culture. Today, therefore, workers all over the world bluntly refuse ever to be treated as if they were irrational objects without freedom, to be used at the arbitrary disposition of others. They insist that they be regarded as men with a share in every sector of human society: in the socio-economic sphere and in public life and in the fields of learning and culture.

41. Secondly, it is obvious to everyone that women are now taking a part in public life. This is happening more rapidly perhaps in nations with a Christian tradition, and more slowly, but broadly, among peoples who have inherited other traditions or cultures. Since women are becoming ever more conscious of their human dignity, they will not tolerate being treated as inanimate objects or mere instruments, but claim, both in domestic and in public life, the rights and duties that befit a human person.

42. Finally, the modern world, as compared with the recent past, has taken on an entirely new appearance in the field of social and political life. For since all peoples have either achieved, or are on the way to achieving, independence, there will soon no longer exist a world divided into peoples who rule others and peoples who are subject to others.

43. Men all over the world have today—or will soon have—the rank of citizens in independent nations. No one wants to feel subject to political power located outside his own country or ethnic group. Thus, in our day, in very many human beings the inferiority complex which endured for hundreds and thousands of years is disappearing, while in others there is an attenuation and gradual fading of the corresponding superiority complex which had its roots in socio-economic privileges, sex or political standing.

44. On the contrary, the conviction that all men are equal by reason of their natural dignity has been generally accepted. Hence, racial discrimination can in no way be justified, at least doctrinally or in theory. And this is of fundamental importance and significance for the formation of human society according to those principles which we have outlined above. For, if a man becomes conscious of his rights, he must become equally aware of his duties. Thus, he who possesses certain rights has likewise the duty to claim those rights as marks of this dignity, while all others have the obligation to acknowledge those rights and respect them.

45. When the relations of human society are expressed in terms of rights and duties, men become conscious of spiritual values and understand the meaning and significance of truth, justice, charity and freedom. They become deeply aware that they belong to this world of values. Moreover, when moved by such concerns, they are brought to a better knowledge of the true God, who is personal and transcendent. Thus they make the ties that bind them to God the solid foundation of

their lives, both of that life which they live interiorly in the depths of their own souls and of that in which they are united to other men in society (John XXIII, 1963).

It was Pope John's recognition of the radically new world order that would come after the United Nations recognition of human rights that resulted in the calling of the Vatican Council to update the church with the intent of eliminating those customs and rules that violated these principles. It was in the updating that the new understanding of the mission of the church was articulated, i.e. "a special option for the poor." This constituted the focus from which the renewal would spring. The church would take its stand with the aware poor nations instead of with an enlightened elite.[3]

This option was adopted by apostolic institutes,[4] especially those of the women, and incorporated into their statements of mission in their revised constitutions. A decade of intense review of life in mission was initiated. Some, however, remained unaware of the depth of this analysis, misinterpreted the intent and moved to the periphery of their groups, or dropped out. Others could not accept the new direction of mission. In their view, the church's being a part of their exclusive ethnic enclave was a good. Since the class bias in their experience was not a conscious choice, it was not examined critically or even raised to awareness. In short, congregations differed radically in their mode of response and interpretation of evidence.[5]

The mission of the apostolic institutes has always been that of implementing the mission of the church. One of the functions of apostolic institutes, as prophetic bodies, is to bring the institutional church to new levels of awareness when it becomes embedded in the status quo and forgetful of its biblical roots in love of neighbor and in being neighbor to those in need. In fact apostolic institutes came into existence to perform a prophetic role. This happened when, in an earlier era, Catholic enclaves held on to the feudal model of serf/landlord long after the industrial revolution was operating by rewarding personal initiative and democracy in its economic and political model for initial development of industrialization. In the process the new industrial workers, having lost their traditional rural roots, were being treated in the new urban centers as a commodity in market exchange. They suffered hunger, homelessness and illness. Alone and distanced from their rural family ties, they sought help in their new environment. In response to this new need some cloistered religious congregations, despite papal skepticism, left the security of the enclosed contemplative life of withdrawal from the world, and, keeping the vows of poverty, chastity and obedience, modified cloister so that they could go out into the street to serve their neighbors' needs. They invented a lifestyle that enabled women and men to provide the health care, education and social services necessary for human development of ex-serfs migrating to industrial centers. The women suffered the indignity of being labeled "not real nuns" for modifying some of the restrictions of cloister that seriously limited their contact with the world outside the convent. These restrictions remained because of the control by men who were over-protective of women whom they perceived as vulnerable. Despite this limitation, however, a semi-contemplative way of life flourished in the nineteenth century, providing European immigrants in America communities of support and spiritual life, and colonial countries in Latin America and Africa their introduction to Christianity. Asia too was evangelized (Neal, 1990).

This way of life for women religious in the United States peaked in 1966, one year after the promulgation of the Second Vatican Council's *Decree on the Renewal of Religious Life* (Flannery, 611-79). Religious congregations had begun to recognize the beginning of a new era of justice education and action. Thus, this council document mandated a pervasive review of all aspects of life in religious communities, to eliminate naivetés which were preventing the effective fulfillment of the new direction mission was taking. This mission, to participate with the laity in the transformation of the world according to principles of justice and peace, was itself being redirected to assist the dispossessed in effectively claiming their rights as human beings. It is best expressed in these words of the Synod assembled to implement the call to action mandate of *Octogesima Adveniens* in 1971:

Action in behalf of justice and participation in the transformation of the world fully appear to us as a constitutive dimension of the preaching of the gospel, or in other words, of the church's mission for the redemption of the human race and its liberation from every oppressive situation (Synod, p. 4).

This time the official church's vision of what needed to be done preceded any significant action toward reform on the part of the apostolic institutes. The media in film and drama portrayed caricatures of the other-worldly sister trying to play a responsible role in this world before the institutes formally initiated action to change naive customs. The urgency of the action needed to implement the new mission was the motivation for expediting change. An obedience was called for and the sisters responded with determined speed. They acted according to the mind of the church as expressed in the *Decree of the Renewal of Religious Life*. The language of the decree mandating "an up-to-date renewal" was clear:

The manner of life, of prayer and of work should be in harmony with the present day psychological and physical condition of the members.

The mode of government of the institutes should also be examined according to the same criteria. For this reason constitutions, directories and books of customs, of prayers, of ceremonies, and such like, should be properly revised, obsolete prescriptions being suppressed, and should be brought into line with conciliar documents (Flannery, p. 613).

Both of these questions came from section three of the *Decree on Renewal of Religious Life*. This kind of detail characterizes the entire document. It makes it clear that the realization of the mission of the church is the agenda for apostolic institutes (section 6), that it is the function of general chapters to establish the norms for the appropriate renewal and to legislate for it (section 4) and to provide for suitable experimentation (section 4). It instructs superiors to consult with their members and provide a means for implementing decisions made (section 4). It reasons that, since the church accepted their profession of vows, religious are to be dedicated to the service of the church (section 5); that apostolic and charitable activity is of the very nature of religious life; that the entire religious life of the members should be imbued with an apostolic spirit and their apostolic activity with a religious spirit (section 8); that each institute should adjust its observances and customs to its particular apostolate (section 8) (Flannery, pp. 611-16).

All these details were attended to by most of the institutes of women religious with a commendable alacrity, though not without some serious criticisms, even conflict and some indiscretion. The most positive dimension of the thirty years since the renewal began is the direct link of religious congregations of women with the church's emphasis on action for social justice as "a constitutive dimension of the preaching of the gospel" (Synod, p. 4).[6]

Today the link of the renewal of religious life with the social justice agenda of the church is an accepted fact (Walsh and Davies, 1984). During the period of renewal, however, even some church administrators feared that the justice agenda was dangerously socialist and hence too this-worldly oriented to be part of the constitutions of religious institutes. In fact, the church's formal espousing of its own social teachings as "a constitutive dimension of the preaching of the gospel" has been defined as "our best kept secret" (Schultheis). It was only with the preparation for the hundredth anniversary of *Rerum Novarum* in 1991 that many church personnel realized that the concern for the rights of workers in the late nineteenth century had extended to those of all poor peoples of the world by 1961 (cf. *Mater et Magistra*) and that seeking to eliminate sinful social structures of power and wealth had been a function of evangelization by 1971.[7] It is to the credit of the sisters in many different institutes that their chapter deliberations during the 1970s incorporated the social justice agenda as the goal of their ministry. It is in terms of this criterion that we will examine the present situation in apostolic institutes of women and speculate on their future.

What I plan to do is to reflect briefly on three national surveys of sisters completed in the past two years: *A Report on the National Profile of the Third Sisters' Survey*, which I published in 1991, the LCWR report by Anne Munley entitled *Threads for the Loom*, 1992, and David Nygren and Miriam Ukaritis, *The Future of Religious Orders in the United States.*[8] I will examine the conclusions of the three surveys in the light of what they say about mission and ministry.

The Sisters' Survey of 1967 was specifically designed to incorporate the combined mandate of *Pacem in Terris* promulgated in 1963 and the *Decree on the Renewal of Religious Life*, promulgated in October of 1965.[9] It was a population survey sent to all members of the institutes in the Conference of Major Superiors of Women Religious (now the LCWR). The number of returned surveys was 139,691 (Neal, 1971). The same groups were randomly sampled again in 1989 with a 74% return. There are 147 items that are repeats, so comparisons can be made.

In summary the sisters are 90% aware that the option for the poor is central to church mission and 72% want their institutes to be involved in doing it. Two-thirds of them think that critical social analysis is a skill needed for participating effectively in this mission. They expect to be getting more training in it but only about 44% are eager to do the actual work related to the elimination of the causes of poverty, whether it be working with the poor to help them to reach out to take what is rightfully theirs or working with the non-poor to help them to release their grasp on what the poor need in order to survive. In fact, in 1989, 77% of those sampled were not working with the poor and 63% did not think the work they were doing was related in any way either to the alleviation of the results of poverty or to the elimination of its causes. Despite this contradiction, 87% believe they personally were called to religious life and 76% think their congregation has a distinct spirit that distinguishes it from all others. This spirit they associate with the doing of the mission of the church. Although 78% believe God speaks to us today through the voices of the poor, as they organize themselves to claim their rights as human beings, when asked where they would turn, if they had a choice to hear God's voice, 50% chose "my own inner spirit" out of eight options, including: "my religious superior," "my bishop," "my community gathered to deliberate a question," "the cries of the dispossessed," or "the organized poor." Only 1% chose the organized poor while 30% chose their community. I think the juxtaposition of these two items gets to the heart of the questions about the future of religious life. How will the transforming work get done and who will be here to do it? Before discussing this, however, we need to look at the conclusions from the LCWR/Munley and the

Nygren/Ukaritis studies to see what advances have been made in the under-standing of why apostolic institutes exist and what their future is.

The LCWR survey gathered its information from the current administra-tors of the apostolic institutes which constitute their membership. This pro-vided contact with about 90% of the institutes in the country.[10] The LCWR study was undertaken to determine what ministries, given current needs, would be increasing and which declining in the next five years. The current reality is described as a "time of diminishment and down-sizing" (Munley, p. 197). The findings indicate that there is a national trend away from tradition-al works associated with sponsoring and administering schools, hospitals and social service centers toward choice of work in ministries that serve vulnera-ble poor people. It shows that institutional ownership of places to do a min-istry is declining, as is diocesan sponsorship; that employment is becoming job oriented, matching the individual sister's skills with the job description. It concludes from the data that, though the intention is to choose ministries compatible with the "institute's mission and charism" and emphasizing "ser-vice with the poor and marginated and efforts for systemic change," the real-ity is that "maximizing the abilities of the individual is the determining factor in job choice" (Munley, p. 192). Looking to the future, 74% of this popula-tion of administrators anticipate that multiculturalism will be a factor to reck-on with. This finding suggests that there is an awareness that ethnic homo-geneity of the membership of women's institutes is not a positive element for realizing the mission of the church nor for the recruitment of new members. This seems inevitable in a country characterized both by mixed inner-city neighborhoods struggling with little success to become communities of peers, and by homogeneous rural towns filled with fears of the spread of inner-city violence.

The trends, ably described in the LCWR research, indicate that an era of secure staffing of what were, not so long ago, stable ministries has ended and that already in place is a desire to serve with the most vulnerable segments of society. But huge problems loom. Without buildings one can use and without diocesan sponsorship, how can innovation proceed?[11] Secondly, how will the willing workers learn the skills they need in new ministries? These realities are related to the current state of the church as regards personnel and finance: to the decline in vocations to priesthood and religious life and diminished financial support on the part of the laity. Also, probably another factor is that of ideological differences about the kind of church we want to be.

The LCWR study concludes that, given the actual trends in ministry choices and distribution today, institutes need leaders who can convert ideol-ogy into action. This is necessary now because actually only 8% of jobs cho-sen currently were selected because they provide service to the poor. Pragmatic factors dominated choices in many instances. But, although the evidence demonstrates this expediency in making choices, it equally shows a clear commitment on the part of the LCWR, the Leadership Conference of Women Religious, whose members are all leaders of apostolic institutes, to take seriously the option for the poor. The "how to do it" is for them a question.

The study done by Miriam Ukaritis and David Nygren entitled *The Future of Religious Orders in the United States* examined the life in numerous religious institutes of both women and men through survey, interview, psychological tests and seminars. From these data they concluded that major changes must occur in most religious institutes if they are to remain a vital force in the church (Nygren, Ukaritis, p. 42). The findings are rich in insight and comprehensive in report. I will focus on just a few that are related to the mission of these institutes.

Their study claims that basic to the ongoing mission of religious communities are "fidelity to the founder's charism" and "responsiveness to critical and unmet human needs" (Nygren, Ukaritis, p. 42). They also note that, if the theology of religious life is right in claiming that the preferential option for the poor is "normative for religious life" and "constitutive of the religious vocation," then their finding that "a significant number of religious feel no personal commitment to this espoused value" (p. 45) is a serious problem. Secondly, they recommend that "resolving the discrepancy between espoused and operative values will reduce the dissonance between the cultural value of individualism and the religious value of vocation," which, they claim, is currently one of the eight struggles needing to be worked through if an apostolic institute is to reach its desired future.

The third and last conclusion I will select out of this study is discussed as the sixth of their critical factors interacting toward achieving or preventing the emergence of a desired future: racism and multiculturalism (Nygren, Ukaritis, p. 48). In reference to these factors, they note that religious institutes of women are 96% white. (The Sisters' Survey yields the same finding.) They see this very high percentage of white membership as a "cultural isolationism" that harbors unconscious racism, making it difficult for minorities to join an established community. Here then is the place to focus the question of recruitment, since it is essential to the doing of any ministry in the long run. The global migration of peoples has already begun. The mandate to respond where need is manifest suggests that the institute responding should witness to the values it is committed to as an institute. Those congregations whose membership is multi-ethnic have something to teach us.

When *Pacem in Terris* noted in 1963 that "racial discrimination can in no way be justified at least doctrinally or in theory," we can see now that that rider—"at least doctrinally or in theory"—was not a detraction from the power of the statement but an indication of the grounding for all choice of ministry and action. Relationships in multi-ethnic communities could attract from all races those young people who want to work for social justice and peace. So 96% whiteness of the membership does not speak to the multi-ethnic community from which new members will now be drawn. Unless our basic doctrine and theory is a belief in one human community of peers, potential members from other than white origin will sense exclusiveness and pass by. How to do multi-ethnic living in community is the problem this era is challenged to resolve. We must be what we aim to serve. There is no witness to the mission of the church in communities that do not attract members from other ethnic groups living in their midst. Some kinds of multi-ethnic community building must be developed because we are no longer living in a stable, compartmentalized and homogeneous world society. The South African doctrine of apartheid generated an ethnically unjust system that, in theory and sometimes in fact, the world community rejected. These oppressed peoples themselves prove by their response that they were not lesser ineffective beings. It took thirty years from the initial effective protest but today a multi-ethnic constitution is slowly being negotiated.[12]

In the light of this, if we reread the prophetic words of Pope John XXIII quoted at the beginning of this chapter we will understand better the main reason why the mandate to renewal was given to religious institutes living the vowed life. Up to that time many men and women dedicated in poverty, chastity and obedience to the biblical invitation to divest themselves of riches, and to respond to human need, clung to the western culture traditions they found familiar. They were willing to help the stranger adjust to the situation as those of the dominant group defined it. But they resisted a redefinition when those whom our way of life excluded from community organized with sufficient power to demand a fair share in the world's resources. This was so, even though the same doctrine that defined our rights to own or to control defined the rights of others to demand a share, for, in the words of Pope John XXIII:

> those who possess certain rights have likewise the duty to claim those rights as marks of their dignity, while all others have the obligation to acknowledge those rights and respect them (John XXIII, 1963, section 44).

An emerging global society, with media bringing instant communication and translation to every part of the world, calls for an apostolic style that is inclusive. We need both to learn and to teach. So much of what we do not know and are unaware that we do not know rules our behavior that older styles of community life, worship and ministry need revisioning. In order to develop a spirituality for such a reality, multi-ethnic communities are essential. Total commitment of some is called for, lest in the struggle to find a common life, we lose sight of God already obscured for some by the language of patriarchy. But this is another story.

The findings of these three studies reflect a range of beliefs about the relationship of God to social action and to societal transformation which vary from remote transcendence to even intrusive immanence. Ideas about God and the ways in which God acts in society are a major determinant of what efforts sisters will make to contribute to "establishing true peace and justice in this world" currently defined as "serving the pastoral work of the church."[13] This relationship between ideas about God and openness to efforts to transform sinful social structures is the major finding of the Sisters' Survey of 1967, 1980, and 1989.[14] It is related to the question of who will do the work and with what insights.

Certainly this new orientation to social justice addressing the gap between the rich and the poor calls to the apostolic institutes for partnership in the struggle of the poor reaching out to take what is rightfully theirs and the rich learning to let go what the poor need to survive (Neal, 1987).

What action is needed challenges our whole life commitment. It is best expressed by the camel and the eye of the needle. Jesus looked after the rich young man who had turned sadly away after Jesus answered his query about how to gain eternal life by saying: "You lack one thing. Go, sell what you have and give to the poor and you will have treasure in heaven, and come follow me." Remember, the man turned away "because he had so much wealth." Jesus did not call him back or modify his position by saying that he meant spiritual poverty not material poverty. No, he looked after him and said: "How hard it will be for those who have riches to enter the kingdom of God, harder than for a camel to go through the eye of a needle" (Mk 10:17-25). That is mighty hard. It calls for real choices. We can no longer sit on the fence and just watch. As Pope Paul VI challenges us in *Octogesima Adveniens* in 1971:

> Let each one examine herself, to see what she has done up to now and what she ought to do. It is not enough to recall principles, state intentions, point to crying injustices and utter prophetic denunciations; these words will lack real weight unless they are accompanied for each individual by a livelier awareness of personal responsibility and by effective action. It is too easy to throw back on others responsibility for injustice, if at the same time one does not realize how each one shares in it personally and how personal conversion is needed first (Paul VI, *Octogesima Adveniens*, section 48).

The call to divest of wealth and to give it to the poor is addressed to all the followers of Jesus. So also is this call of Pope Paul's to action to transform unjust structures. The uniqueness for vowed religious women is that we were specifically addressed in the *Decree on the Renewal of Religious Life* to carry out the mission of the church. During the period of renewal the mandate for action became more and more explicit as the social justice agenda (Paul VI, *Apostolic Exhortation on Religious Life*, 1971, section 17). It reached its clearest expression in 1988 with the publication of *Sollicitudo Rei Socialis* in which structures of both capitalism and communism are condemned because they generate a wide gap between the rich and the poor, where a few have wealth and power and the many have nothing. We now know through the media where in our society these inequalities exist. It follows then that fulfilling the mission of apostolic institutes in the church today to offer needed human services with a priority for the poor, whether it be through education, community organizing or providing for health or other services, should embody this directive: intentional action to work toward the elimination of societal injustices and toward our becoming a human community of peers sharing the resources of the world based on human need primarily. This is the challenge to religious in apostolic institutes. It calls for actions specific to the urgent problems of our times.

Human need and racism cannot be effectively responded to by sisters acting alone. The groundwork is set in the formation programs rooted in congregations' new mission statements. The formation can be developed from the social teachings of the church in its hundred year development.[15] The division of labor comes through individual institutes' charisms, the election of excellent leaders, and commitment of the members to the making of good decisions about effective action. Prayer and liturgy as well as life in community sustain the will and enthusiasm through difficult times, and God's steadfast love is the enduring support as well as the very reason for there being the vowed life. The institute that can meet this challenge has a future worth striving for.

Notes

1. This document combines two covenants: "The Covenant on Civil and Political Rights" and "The Covenant on Economic, Social and Cultural Rights" (United Nations, p. 2). Both of these covenants became a part of international law for the countries accepting them in 1976. The United States accepted the first one only in September of 1992. It does not as yet accept the second one which "recognizes everyone's right to work, to fair wages, to social security, to adequate standards of living and freedom from hunger, and to health and education. It also undertakes to ensure the right of everyone to form and join trade unions," calling these goals but not rights. This position of the U.S. is recorded in a 1988 State Department document entitled "U.S. Human Rights Policy: An Overview" by Paula Dobriansky, Current Policy, Department of State, No. 1091, 1988.

2. This happened in 1891 when Pope Leo XIII promulgated his now famous encyclical on labor relations, *Rerum Novarum,* which ushered in the hundred years of Catholic social teaching celebrated in 1991 in the encyclical *Centesimus Annus.*

3. There is a striking development in the hundred years of formal Catholic social teaching from the focus on just wages for workers in 1891, to doing social analysis from the perspective of the poor in 1971, to defining as "sinful structures" elements of both capitalism and communism by 1991. See especially John XXIII's *Mater et Magistra,* and Paul VI's *Populorum Progressio,* and John Paul's *Sollicitudo Rei Sociales.* This thesis is derived from the study of over two hundred chapter reports and constitutions. See Neal, 1990, Chapter 3.

4. I am using the phrase "apostolic institutes" and "religious congregations" interchangeably to refer to groups of vowed women or men in the active life in the church.

5. These observations are derived from analyses of items in the Sisters' Survey of 1980 which sampled twenty-eight congregations selected on the basis of their scores on a measure of belief in the 1967 Survey.

6. Section 48 of Pope Paul VI's apostolic letter commemorating the eightieth anniversary of *Rerum Novarum* is an eloquent call to action to get to work transforming unjust social structures. It is addressed to the laity, but in another document published the same year, sisters are urged to participate. See section 17 of *Evangelica Testificatio.*

7. See *Justice in the World,* p. 4.

8. *A Report on the National Profile of the Third Sisters' Survey* is currently available only in xerox form. It can be ordered from Sisters' Survey, c/o Neal, Sociology Department, Emmanuel College, Boston, MA 02115.

The LCWR study is completed: Ann Munley, IHM, *Threads for the Loom,* LCWR Planning and Ministry Studies, Leadership Conference of Women Religious, Silver Spring, MD, 1992.

Only an executive summary of the FORUS is currently available: David Nygren and Miriam Ukaritis, *The Future of Religious Orders in the United States: Transformation and Commitment,* Praeger, 1993.

9. The Sisters' Survey of 1967 was sponsored by the Leadership Conference of Women Religious. It was followed up in 1980 and 1989. I designed all three studies and did the analyses.

10. Some of the missing 10% are congregations whose administrators have chosen to join an alternate leadership ground now called the Council of Major Superiors of Women Religious.

11. Most religious congregations have only fragile connections with buildings in which to initiate new works. Without diocesan support for experimentation in new methods a work begun can die.

12. The complexity of the South African struggle and the length of time it has continued demonstrate how much unlearning must be done and how hard it is when one is in the midst of the struggle to continue to believe in the goal of equality. Yet, it is that commitment that constitutes ministry.

13. These two descriptions are from the "Lineamenta" for the Synod, 1994, entitled: "Consecrated Life in the Church and the World," published in *Origins,* Vol. 22,

No. 26, December 10, 1992, p. 441. It refers to brothers, not sisters but why is not clear.

14. The "Sisters' Survey" of 1967 included a scale measuring beliefs about God and God's relationship with human society. The orientation of church to the world found in *Sollicitudo Rei Socialos* has a similar definition of the situation. See Neal, 1971. Items 1–28 in the Third Sisters' Survey are all taken from *Sollicitudo Rei Socialis*. See Appendix 1, pp. 1-5, Neal, 1993.

15. One of the best sources through which to see this development of mission in the encyclicals on the social teachings of the church is Donal Dorr's *Option for the Poor: A Hundred Years of Vatican Social Teaching,* 1983. See also Adriance, Aristide, Avila, Cardenal, Cleary, Cone, Cussianovich, Ferree, Freire, Gutierrez, Hanks, Holland, John XXIII, Medellín Documents, Nessan, O'Brien and Shannon, Sobrino, Steidl-Meier.

References

Adriance, Madeleine Cousineau, *Option for the Poor: Brazilian Catholicism in Transition.* New York: Sheed and Ward, 1986.

Aristide, Jean-Bertrand, *In the Parish of the Poor: Writings from Haiti.* Maryknoll: Orbis, 1990.

Avila, Charles. *Ownership.* Maryknoll: Orbis, 1983.

Cardinal, Ernesto, *The Gospel of Solentiname.* Maryknoll: Orbis, 1976. The story of one village and one priest, 1985.

Cleary, Edward L., ed., *Born of the Poor.* Notre Dame: Notre Dame University Press, 1990.

Cone, James H., *God of the Oppressed.* New York: Seabury Press, 1975.

Cussianovich, Alejandro, S.D.B., *Religious Life and the Poor: Liberation Theology Perspectives.* Maryknoll: Orbis, 1979.

Dorr, Donal, *Option for the Poor: A Hundred Years of Vatican Social Teaching.* Maryknoll: Orbis, 1983.

——, *Spirituality and Justice.* Maryknoll: Orbis, 1984.

—— *The Social Justice Agenda: Justice, Ecology, Power and the Church.* Maryknoll: Orbis, 1991.

Ferree, William, *The Act of Social Justice.* Dayton: Marianist Publications, 1951.

Flannery, Austin, ed., *Vatican Council II: The Conciliar and Post-Conciliar Documents.* Northport: Costello Publishing Co., 1975.

Freire, Paulo, *Pedagogy of the Oppressed.* New York: Herder and Herder, 1970.

——, *The Politics of Education: Culture, Power and Liberation.* Massachusetts: Bergin and Garvey, 1985.

Gutierrez, Gustavo M., *A Theology of Liberation.* Maryknoll: Orbis, 1971.

——, *The Power of the Poor in History.* Maryknoll: Orbis, 1983.

Hanks, Thomas D., *God So Loved the Third World.* Maryknoll: Orbis, 1983.

Holland, Joe and Peter Henriot, S.J., *Social Analysis: Linking Faith and Justice.* Maryknoll: Orbis, rev. ed., 1983.

John XXIII, *Mater et Magistra (Christianity and Social Progress).* New York: America Press, 1961.

——, *Pacem in Terris.* Boston: St. Paul Editions, 1963.

John Paul II, *Laborem Exercens (On Human Work).* Boston: St. Paul Editions, 1981.

——, *Sollicitudo Rei Socialis (On Social Concern).* Boston: St. Paul Editions, 1987.

——, *Centesimus Annus (On the Hundredth Anniversary of Rerum Novarum.* Boston: St. Paul Editions, 1991

Leo XIII, *The Condition of Labor (Rerum Novarum,* 1891). Washington, D.C.: National Catholic Welfare Conference, 1942.

Lernoux, Penny, *Cry of the People.* New York: Simon and Schuster, 1980.

Medellin Documents. *The Church in the Present Day Transformation of Latin America in the Light of the Council.* Official English Edition. Washington, D.C.: United States Catholic Conference, and Bogota, Columbia: Latin American Episcopal Council, 1970.

Munley, Anne, *Threads from the Loom.* Leadership Conference of Women Religious. Silver Spring, 1992.

Neal, Marie Augusta, Part I, "The Relation Between Religious Belief and Structural Change in Religious Orders. Developing an Effective Measuring Instrument." *Review of Religious Research,* Vol XII, No. 1, Fall 1970, pp. 2-16; Part II, "The Relation Between Religious Belief and Structural Change in Religious Orders: Some Evidence." *Review of Religious Research,* Vol XII, No. 3, Spring 1971, pp. 154-64.

——, *The Just Demands of the Poor.* New York: Paulist Press, 1987. (Out of print—available only at Emmanuel College Bookstore, 400 The Fenway, Boston, MA. 02115).

——, *From Nuns to Sisters.* Mystic: Twenty-Third Publications, 1990.

——, *A Report on the National Profile of the Third Sisters' Survey,* through Sisters' Survey, c/o Marie Augusta Neal, Emmanuel College, 400 The Fenway, Boston, MA 02115.

——, "American Catholic Sisters," in *Abraham's Daughters*, edited by Catherine Wessinger. University of South Carolina Press, in press.

Nessan, Craig L., *Orthopraxis or Heresy: The North American Theological Response to Latin American Liberation Theology.* Atlanta: Scholars Press, 1989.

Nygren, David and Miriam Ukaritis, "The Religious Life Futures Project:

Executive Summary," in *Review for Religious,* January-February 1993, pp. 42-50.

O'Brien, David J. and Thomas A. Shannon, eds., *Catholic Social Thought: The Documentary Heritage.* Maryknoll: Orbis, 1992.

Paul VI, *Pastoral Constitution on the Church in the Modern World,* Boston: St. Paul Editions, 1965.

——, *A Call to Action (Octogesima Adveniens),* Apostolic Letter on the Eightieth Anniversary of *Rerum Novarum.* Washington, D.C.: United States Catholic Conference, 1971.

——, *Apostolic Exhortation on Religious Life.* Official Vatican Translation of *Evangelica Testificatio.* Boston: Daughters of St. Paul, 1971.

——, *The Development of Peoples (Populorum Progressio).* Boston: St. Paul Editions, 1967.

Pius XI, *On Reconstructing the Social Order (Quadragesimo Anno).* Washington, D.C.: National Catholic Welfare Conference, 1931.

Schultheis, Michael J., Edward P. De Berri, Peter J. Henriot, *Our Best Kept Secret: The Rich Heritage of Catholic Social Teachings.* Washington, D.C.: Center of Concern, 1987.

Sobrino, Jon, *The True Church and the Poor.* Maryknoll: Orbis, 1984.

South African Christians, "Kairos: The Moment of Truth" (a theological reflection against apartheid issued on September 25, 1985), in *Connections,* October 1986.

Steidl-Meier, S.J., *Social Justice Ministry: Foundations and Concerns.* New York: Le Jacq Inc., 1984.

Synod of Bishops, *Synodal Document on Justice in the World,* Second General Assembly of Synod of Bishops, Rome, November 30, 1971. Boston: St. Paul Editions, 1971.

Tamez, Elsa, *The Bible of the Oppressed.* Maryknoll: Orbis, 1982.

United Nations, *The International Bill of Human Rights.* New York: United Nations, 1978.

United States Catholic Conference, "Brothers and Sisters to Us," *Origins,* Nov. 29, 1979, Vol. 9, No. 24 (on racism).

Vatican II, *Decree on Renewal of Religious Life.* Boston: Daughters of St. Paul, 1965.

Walsh, Michael and Brian Davies, eds., *Proclaiming Justice and Peace: Documents from John XXIII– John Paul II.* Mystic: Twenty-third Publications, 1984.

World Resource Institute, *World Resources 1992* (an assessment of the resource base that supports the global economy). New York: Basic Books, 1992.

Religious Life:
The Continuing Journey—Vision and Hope

John Manuel Lozano, CMF

The Present Moment

Religious life has been evolving since the early times of the church, taking on different forms and directions. Its history has been characterized by a constant development, with high points and low points, periods of transformation and times of marvelous expansion.

The Crisis

Many Christians are asking: Where is religious life today? In crisis, many would answer. And who could deny it? The symptoms of a crisis are all there. But two things need to be said about this situation of crisis. In the first place, religious life has gone through several periods of crisis in the past and has come out of them transformed and strengthened. In the second place, a crisis is not a purely negative phenomenon. An individual's life is periodically subject to critical stages of transformation from infancy to childhood, adolescence and successive steps in adulthood. Stagnation would mean death for living organisms. Institutions, too, pass through critical periods. The Catholic Church has known many.

Generally speaking, religious life enters into a stage of change whenever the church itself is in crisis, and both the church and religious orders enter into a period of transformation and adjustment whenever the human world (civil society) of which they are a part is undergoing a deep change of its own.

The Facts

Today, religious life offers many surprises and not a few challenges. We intend to examine the most significant facts that are shaping this kind of

Christian existence at present. When differences appear in several continents, we will first describe those facts that are most visible in North America (the United States and Canada) and then go on to underscore converging or diverging phenomena in other parts of the church.

Religious life today seems to be characterized by the following traits: (1) a radical change in the attitude of religious toward the world and the church; (2) this new attitude is leading them toward a new, collective form of ministry; (3) their spirituality is passing through a period of deep renewal; (4) the poor have become a point of reference for their spirituality, ministry and lifestyle; (5) there is a certain evolution in their ministerial activities; (6) this is accompanied by a new understanding and experience of community life; (7) finally, one must mention the present scarcity of candidates for religious orders.

A Challenging Presence. Perhaps the most important fact is the new attitude that religious have been taking toward the "world," in other words, toward civil society. The old notion of "separation from the world" has given way—especially, though not exclusively, among apostolic orders—to one of being a "challenging presence in the world."

The history of religious life is somewhat amazing in this respect. Did it not begin with a flight from the city and its problems to the desert? Yes—and it has spent centuries trying to return to the city. Periodically, religious would re-enter the city through the wrong gate of economic power and political influence (eleventh century monasticism, for example), and then try to escape again (Carthusians, Fonte Avellana, Camaldoli).

When the religious life has occasionally tried to move away from the city, it has always had to confront the "world." Religious are now more aware of a trait that is essential to their profession: from the time of the desert solitaries on, every form of religious life has been a response to a need of the church and of the "world." But this awareness is not something new. After surfacing timidly among some of the canons regular and growing bolder in the mendicant orders, it was deeply felt by the early Franciscans, the first Jesuits and the Daughters of Charity, among others. Recall the passage from the Legend of the Three Companions, where Lady Poverty asks the Franciscans where their monastery is. The friars answer by pointing to the four points of the compass: "This [the whole world] is our monastery."[1] It is in the world and in the eyes of the world that we must be faithful to the gospel. Francis of Assisi, Ignatius and Louise de Marillac brought a sense of solidarity to the relationship of religious with civil society, a sense that is equally visible in the many foundresses and founders who came after them. They all viewed it as a needy, suffering world. Francis "reinvented" poverty as sharing the condition of the outcast. Ignatius wanted to "help souls." For Louise de Marillac, the "world" was not the splendor of Versailles, where Richelieu's purple mingled with the pastel silks of duchesses. The "world" to which her religious commitment brought her was the place where God's children were suffering. This is the world that religious are discovering again.

In our own time, the case of Thomas Merton is paradigmatic. Having abandoned the "world" where sin and futility predominated, he was led by the Spirit back to the world, first by making him experience the people in a square in Louisville as God's beloved children and then by pushing him to confront social injustice from his hermitage. Mary Luke Tobin has stated it once for all: "For me renewal has opened the doors of the world. In this sense the world is people—a broader cut of people, a whole suffering world."[2] Who would dare to blame her?

Prophetical Stance. This new attitude has led religious orders to take a stance in facing problems affecting civil society and the church. A prophetic sensitivity has been gradually spreading among them. Statements on social justice, on political and economic oppression, on discrimination, on the status of women in the church and in society have been appearing in texts emanating from general and provincial chapters all over the world. Statements have been accompanied by actions, especially in Latin America, the United States, the Philippines and South Africa. In the Philippines, sisters played a decisive leadership role in the people's revolution that overthrew the Marcos regime.

A Renewed Spirituality. The new relationship with the world created by God but wounded by sin has also had an impact on the level of spirituality. The present spirituality of religious takes up those values of creation that religious do not renounce by their vows. There is a growing personalism among religious and more attention is being given to personal journeys and needs. This obviously creates new tensions with communal demands and expectations. Although in varying degrees in various cultures, there is an increasing appreciation for the total human being (body / soul / spirit, the dimension of Genesis, the gift / gifts of the Spirit, spiritual / psychological health, inwardness / relatedness...). A sense of personal dignity and freedom is being incorporated into the theology and practice of obedience. Religious are taking a more positive look even at those human values they renounce in their profession: married life, for example.

From the "side chapels" in which religious orders used to sit (each with their own advocacies, devotions and privileges), they have moved out into the "main aisle" of the church. There is a strong ecclesial orientation in their spirituality and a sense of communion with the rest of God's people. Of course, religious have been affected by the energies unleashed by Vatican II: biblical and liturgical movements, Christ-centered spirituality.

In North America we must add another trait: the rediscovery of contemplative life and an emphasis on the contemplative dimension of religious life.

It all began in the 1950s, with an increase of vocations to contemplative orders. Houses of prayer were opened. Directed retreats became extremely popular among religious. Some members of apostolic communities have become hermits, while still remaining members of their congregations. This is a part of the search for the Spirit (prayer groups, the charismatic movement) that is observable in America. Miriam Theresa Demjanovich, a Sister of Charity of Convent Station, New Jersey, and, later, Thomas Merton, have been prophets and forerunners among us of this search for the Spirit. But, at least among sisters, it seems also to reflect a reaction against the intensely active life that they were obliged to live in the past.

The Poor. Another significant fact is the presence of the poor in the reflections and decisions of today's religious, as a preferential object of their love, as a central focus of their ministries and as a criterion whereby to judge the authenticity of their life. Vatican II opened the way, but the most decisive event was the fact that Paul VI, in his *Evangelica Testificatio*, began his presentation on religious poverty with the "cry of the poor."[3] Then came the Puebla documents and the influence of Latin American theologians and confessors. A certain Hellenistic, even abstract, understanding of poverty as a means to individual perfection was left behind, as evangelical poverty returned to its gospel roots. Interpreted as kenosis and solidarity, it became once more a descent into the hell of human suffering.

Ministries. In the ministerial field, sisters and brothers in North America are fairly teeming with creativity. They have undertaken a number of personal ministries that priests had been carrying out during the last centuries: spiritual direction, retreats, teaching in seminaries and universities. Moreover, they have launched out on other contemporary kinds of ministries as social workers, therapists and counselors. Religious sisters, brothers and priests are now engaged in new forms of services to alcoholics, drug addicts, abused children, in houses of affirmation, in peace and justice teams, providing spiritual leadership and support to gays and lesbians. Sisters work with battered women. Older sisters are often in charge of home visits to the sick and the elderly.

Western Europe and some Latin American countries are also moving in this direction, although at a slower pace. In these countries, sisters and brothers usually work within their own institutions (schools, hospitals), but some sisters have gone outside them to minister in certain sensitive areas, such as assistance to prostitutes and drug addicts. While spiritual direction is still largely reserved to priests, a certain number of men and women religious are involved in the fields of psychotherapy and counseling.

Local Communities. While men religious are by and large (except in mission territories) attached to older forms of local community with a few living in the same house, women religious in North America have created a more flexible kind of community life. They have done this in order to broaden the strongly disciplined kind of communal living to which they were restricted in the past, but also in many cases to adjust to the works available to them. On the other continents sisters have largely kept to traditional forms of communal living.

Nearly everywhere, the more or less ritualized and structured form of community existing until Vatican II has disappeared and community now tends to focus on its essential core: interpersonal relationships of support, mutual evangelization and collaboration.

Everywhere, too, but in different degrees depending on the cultural context, community government is based on a sense of communion and co-responsibility, and is exercised in dialogue.

Vocations. Finally, we have to face up to a phenomenon that is viewed as negative by many, but not so much so by others: the lack of vocations to religious orders. In the United States, men's orders are now suffering from the same shortage that women's communities have been experiencing since the early 1970s. As a consequence, more and more scholasticates have been closed of late and their students have been sent to common theological schools. It is significant, however, that while more men's orders have joined various theological unions, the total number of scholastics has remained about the same or has decreased. In western Europe, both and women religious complain of a similar scarcity of candidates.

The situation is quite different in Africa, southern India, the Philippines and eastern Europe, where vocations are still abundant, and in some Latin American countries where the number of candidates is *beginning* to expand again. Anyone from the northern hemisphere who visits these countries seems to be reliving part of his or her own past: most candidates come from working class and often large families. In all of these countries, entering a novitiate still means taking a step up on the social ladder, and the habit is a badge of distinction. In most of these areas, religious orders provide a level of education that would have been beyond the reach of most candidates, had they not entered a novitiate.

How We Came To Be Where We Are

Large historical phenomena are always the products of many intertwined causes. As we said before, religious life has never ceased moving with civil society and with the church. The present situation is the result of a long development and the effect of many causes.

Our Roots

First of all, we must remember that most of the present religious congregations have their remote origins in the sixteenth century movement that created the modern apostolic orders. Most of them were originally founded in order to carry out a series of services for which there was a widely felt need, but which civil society did not provide: education, the care of the sick and the elderly, orphanages. It was a decisive step in the evolution of religious life. Then as now, this kind of Christian existence flowed from a commitment to offer a service to humankind and to the church.

What Ignatius Loyola and later Vincent de Paul and Louise de Marillac actually did—and what Francis de Sales tried to do, but was prevented from doing, first by the archbishop of Lyon and finally by Rome—was a decisive step. Already in the twelfth and thirteenth centuries, some orders had been founded for ministries: Trinitarians, Dominicans, Mercedarians. What distinguished apostolic institutes from the sixteenth century on was the fact that ministry became their typical form of serving God, and therefore their concrete way of life evolved around it. By this very fact, religious life drew closer to civil society, to the infamous "world."

Initially, the first generation of apostolic religious were, as a general rule, even closer to civil society. But in the second or third generation a phenomenon of involution usually appeared, in which attention to strengthening internal structures predominated, and older and more prestigious forms of theology and spirituality tended to take the place of the original apostolic inspiration. Sisters, brothers and priests continued to work very hard, but their work often appeared to be in tension with the generic religious structures and spirituality that they had borrowed from older forms of religious life: they tended to look more and more like nuns and friars. Whereas the first generation, under the leadership of the founder or foundress, had tended to look outward and toward the future, the second and third generations tended to look inward and toward the past. Most of our renewal efforts have consisted of reaching back to our original freshness, beyond the pale of these later, added accretions.

Our Immediate Past

Historians of the religious life often seem to be unaware of the deep impact that the French revolution and its aftermath had on European institutes, both by simply attacking them ideologically and by actually suppressing them. Many things happened in reaction to it.

After the revolution, many apostolic congregations were founded all over

Europe. Thousands of women and men committed themselves with untiring generosity to a broad spectrum of ministries: parish missions and retreats, education, care of the sick, the elderly and orphans, rehabilitating prostitutes, foreign missions.

But when they committed themselves to the service of the needy, these men and women entered a theological ambience where the idea of self-sacrifice was central. Wasn't this so for the French school, especially for Condren? Jansenism exhorted religious to annihilate themselves before the awesome holiness and sovereignty of God. Next, in response to the enlightenment's hostility toward religious who, in its view, had abdicated their freedom, the romantic apologists (Chateaubriand, in particular) insisted that this was precisely the source of their grandeur: religious were the Christian heroes of the day, offering themselves as a holocaust and orienting their life toward the moment of their death. All this had a strong influence on the ideological milieu of religious: in opposition to the ideals of a growing secular humanism, austerity and mortification and self-denial were now viewed as the leading forces of an authentic religious life.

The church, reacting to the many attacks inflicted on it, drew up its bridges and put on a fortress mentality. There was a divorce between the gospel and human values. The world became the enemy of the church. We need only recall a pronouncement of the Syllabus of Errors: "Let whoever states that the church must accommodate to the modern world be anathema." The term "freedom," used by the revolutionists against the *ancien régime*, of which the church was an important part, became extremely suspect in European Christianity until recently. More than a few of the church's faithful children were ostracized on this score.

In reaction to modern individualism, which had been exalted by the enlightenment and the French revolution, a strongly disciplined form of community developed throughout the nineteenth century, and silent obedience was valued as the highest form of sacrifice.

Thus it was that the numerous religious of that time entered the world of human suffering, while at the same time they made a point of abandoning the world in spirit and in mindset. They left it by the habits they wore, by the overly strict interpretation of enclosure they observed and by their opposition to the world through sacrifice and obedience. Religious garb initially arose as a sign of commitment to poverty (the Benedictine Rule, the Franciscans). Many nuns and later sisters had adopted the garb of plain and decent women. In the nineteenth century we can see the culmination of a process whereby a habit had to be different from any other form of attire in order to express difference and separation from secular Christians.

The structure and manner of wearing a habit were also connected with the well-known enmity against the body, an attitude that had ancient roots (the desert solitaries) but was reinforced by Jansenism, a movement which, even though it had been condemned, had a strong influence on religious communities, an influence that was later compounded by various forms of Puritanism.

The American Experience

Haven't we been talking too much about the European situation? No, especially if we recall how many communities were transplanted from Europe to the States in the course of the nineteenth century or were founded here by European-born Catholics. Yet the history of American religious life has become more and more different and distinctive as a result of several converging movements,

The Hispanic and French parts of the country had religious from the first times in which the Spaniards and the French occupied them: Franciscans, Jesuits, Ursulines. In the English colonies there were also a few religious, mostly Jesuits (John Carroll, for example), until their order was suppressed by Clement XIV in 1773. Then, soon after independence had been won, the first cloister was established in Maryland, a foundation of Discalced Carmelite Nuns, followed by another of the Visitation in Georgetown. But around that time the first American communities of women were established: the Sisters of Charity of Mother Seton in Emmitsburg, Maryland, the Sisters of Loretto at the Foot of the Cross, the Sisters of Charity of Nazareth—both in Kentucky—and the Sisters of Charity of Our Lady of Mercy in Cincinnati.

The Sulpicians arrived in Baltimore on July 10, 1791. The Augustinians, Dominicans and Vincentians soon followed. The Jesuits were reinstated. The Religious of the Sacred Heart and the Sisters of St. Joseph of Carondelet came to Saint Louis and the Sisters of Providence to Terre Haute, Indiana. Finally, during the period when the church had become mostly a church of immigrants, numerous orders and congregations crossed the Atlantic, most of them at the invitation of their co-nationals in the States, others escaping from persecution. Due in large part to the distance from and lack of communication with their old world counterparts, many groups became autonomous communities or congregations, or even gave birth to several institutes (e.g. the Sisters of St. Joseph of Carondelet).

A process of inculturation took place. Initially, American Catholics were very much aware of the differences that distinguished them from the various shades of European Catholicism. This was part of their cultural environment. Independence produced in the former British subjects a strong tendency to differentiate themselves from the "old world." John Quincy Adams, then secretary of state, admonished a German baron that immigrants "must cast off the European skin, never to resume it." Bishop Carroll wrote that the idea of affiliating Mother Seton's Institute with the French *Filles de la charité* failed due to the different characters of both nations.[4] Differences became attenuated in the church of the immigrants, but tensions arose between American candidates and their European-born superiors. Rutland (Isaac Hecker's superior), Bishop Dubourg and Mother Theodore Guerin all looked with suspicion on certain traits of the American character: the American cult of freedom versus European discipline (as they put it), American equality versus the European sense of hierarchy.[5] There was more to it than that. Some American-born religious figures, like Hecker, and later on some European-born churchmen, like Bishop John Ireland, came to dislike the foreign aspect that the church was taking on in this country.[6] On the other side of the Atlantic some differences in emphasis were perceived, and the spiritual atmosphere described by Hecker gave rise over there to the imagined specter of "Americanism."

A common historical experience began to shape the life and mindset of American religious. While men religious remained very similar to their European counterparts (most of them belonged to international institutes), women religious began to appear with characteristics all their own. Unlike their European counterparts who owned the schools they taught in, most of the American sisters began to work in schools that belonged to a diocese. They appeared as groups of hard-working women whose life was divided between the convent, ruled by the superior, and the parish school, where the pastor had the last word. In the eyes of the immigrants, most of whom were unable to speak English, sisters embodied the church's motherhood, and both they and the pastor were a bond with the culture they had left behind. Like their European sisters, they lived and worked strictly within the framework of their communities. But their lifestyle appeared, in our opinion, to be marked by three distinctive features: strict discipline, hard work and, for those who were teachers, full economic dependence on the school system (the parish).

Deep Changes

This world was bound to disappear, and it did. The socio-cultural environment that had shaped the lifestyle and mindset of American religious began to break into pieces. A process of differentiation from the European experience began to appear in spirituality. This process set in rather early, since even during the nineteenth century a number of European superiors had problems with American candidates. But the differences have become much more visible in recent times. To the extent that religious in the United States became really American, their spirituality began to be influenced by the national character and thus to manifest some features typical of the American approach to spirituality.

Elsewhere, we have described what we consider to be its main features: (1) an image of God as generous giver (as opposed to the "God under whom we stand" of the Puritans—which still crops up from time to time in many public attitudes) and a grateful response to the gifts of God; (2) a surpassing of traditional dualisms (nature/grace, spirit/body, inwardness/action) and a tendency toward synthesis; (3) personalism, respect for freedom, a strong sense of basic equality; (4) a pronounced love of nature and a sense of communion with it (both very visible in Mother Seton, Isaac Hecker and Thomas Merton); (5) a strong apostolic orientation (John Carroll, John Ireland), recently balanced by a sensitivity toward the "contemplative" dimension of any form of Christian existence (more books on prayer and spiritual direction are published in the United States than in the rest of the church); (6) a particular attention to experience and therefore to the action of the Spirit in individuals; (7) a growing sensitivity in favor of social justice and against any form of discrimination; (8) finally, a greater openness to other believers and other Christians.[7]

While this transformation of spirituality was taking shape, the church itself was changing. The immigrants' church became the American Catholic Church and joined other denominations in the mainstream of American society. Many Catholics began to ascend the social ladder and moved to the suburbs, leaving their old inner-city churches and schools to the new immigrants or to non-Catholic minorities. To have their children educated in Catholic institutions was no longer a high priority for many American Catholics.

Equally important or even more important than all of this was the fact that sisters began taking the church's invitation to pursue higher education quite seriously, with the result that not only were new forms of ministry available to them, but sisters themselves became a different kind of persons. The movement toward women's affirmation and emancipation affected convents and placed serious demands on the church. New women and new men were being born, with a different sensibility and a different mindset.

MOTIVES FOR CONCERN

A Shrinking Membership

There are moments in every religious community when serious concerns begin to surface.

The first of these, which appears at every meeting, is the awareness that the community is aging. One needs only open her or his eyes at any assembly, chapter or celebration to see the passage from gray to white hair, the appearance of walking sticks, etc. At times the sight of it all can be a little depressing.

Sometimes religious feel forced to ask themselves: Is there any real future fur us?

Economic Problems

Because of shrinking recruitment, leaders of women's communities have to spend a good deal of time trying to broaden the economic basis to ensure a simple, decent life for their retired sisters. And leaders of men's communities are worrying, too.

In quite a few communities, retired religious will soon form the largest segment of the population. This is a general trend in civil society, in the northern hemisphere, due to the prolongation of human life and the widespread practice of birth control. In the religious communities of the north (of both Europe and America) aging has become a more aggravated phenomenon, due to decreasing recruitment.

An aging membership tends to cause more or less serious problems in the area of economy. Traditionally, ever since the times of Pachomius and Mary (fourth century Egypt), religious orders were very successful enterprises from an economic standpoint, and this for two reasons. First, because their members formed a very broad-based pyramid: a much larger segment of active workers supported a small passive population. Second, because, given their austerity, they "produced" (to use an economic term) much more than they consumed.

At present, this pyramid is reversed in a certain number of communities, and for all communities religious education and health care are much more costly than in former centuries.

Economic difficulties would seem to have some impact on pastoral activities. In a meeting of the Conference of Bishops and Religious Superiors of the Northwest (NABRS) held in Seattle a few years ago, a leader of a women's community publicly stated that because of economic problems, a number of sisters are no longer free to choose their ministries according to pastoral criteria. Indeed, some communities feel pressed to choose the work that is best remunerated.

However, we should not generalize: not only are there hundreds of sisters all over North America working with the poor and the destitute, but there are many of them who share with them their poverty and the risks inherent in living in violent neighborhoods. In order to illustrate a larger trend, let us cite but one instance of the larger tendency in an American community. The Missionary Servants of the Most Blessed Trinity have decided to remain faithful to their mission of evangelizing the poor, leaving to God's providence the task of supporting them through fund-raising.

Economic problems also have consequences for community life. On the one hand, work placement determines the place of residence, which is not infrequently at a distance from other members of the community. In some cases, sisters of different congregations live together. On the other hand, we hear that there is a trend for some congregations to live together in order to reduce expenses.

ATTITUDES AND FEELINGS

Some of the attitudes we have just described do not seem apt to uplift spirits! One would imagine, then, that the common mood among religious is one of preoccupation and, in some cases, of depression.

It is not. We cannot, of course, make absolute statements in this matter. First, we must distinguish between larger international orders and smaller communities, both national and international. The decrease of membership in the international groups is proportionally less visible. Worldwide, the membership of some communities (the Claretians, for example) has remained approximately the same as it was twenty years ago: the decrease in North American candidates has been compensated by an increase in Indian, Filipino, Polish and African candidates and by a recent surge in Latino vocations. The Franciscans seem to be growing particularly in eastern Europe and Africa. The School Sisters of Saint Francis are receiving many candidates from India and Central America. Among the School Sisters of Notre Dame there is what one of them calls "a shift in life." While they are experiencing a reduction in older provinces (such as Germany and the United States), they are growing in Africa, Asia and Central America. The Franciscan Missionary Sisters of the Immaculate Conception, an international institute founded by British Sister Elizabeth Ignatius Hayes, are receiving most of their candidates from Papua New Guinea and South America. We should, however, notice that the Sulpicians are doing better in the States than in Europe, and that some North American provinces of the Order of Preachers are also doing well.

The state of spirits differs from one religious to another. There are those who are nostalgic for the large novitiates and crowded ordinations of yesteryear. There are also those who resisted recent changes or were unhappy with them and still claim that the negative aspects of the crisis only prove that they have been right all along. But the general trend among religious is one of feeling alive and full of hope.

Instead of embarking on the long and arduous task of compiling statistics and interpreting them, we have preferred to question some representatives, who are appreciated in and beyond their own communities, whom we know to be bearers of a personal spirituality and to be clearly aware of the values proper of religious life.

Sister Miriam Ross, SSND, a well-known spiritual director and member of the next general chapter of her congregation in Rome, recently told the author of this article: "Our aging and shrinking as a community is freeing us from many burdens and moving us to cross new frontiers. There is an upbeat spirit among our sisters. I have never experienced so much love for one another and so much creativity in ministry. In ministry we are trying to do the most with the least amount of people. We ask ourselves how we can take risks for justice in worldwide structures; how we can vitalize existing world structures for transformation. Our present creativity depends on two things: first, we are reaping the fruits of many sisters' being faithful to their own journey and therefore assuming their own power; second, there is a transformation in leadership as well. Leaders, too, are being faithful to their own journey. Therefore they are an empowered, rather than dictatorial, leadership. The result is mutual leadership. We have empowered grassroots and leadership. In dialogue, everyone is taking up leadership and contributing to the vision—to what the vision is and how it is to be carried out. Dialogue is essential."

Sister Catherine Dooley, a Dominican of Sinsinawa, Wisconsin, and professor at the Catholic University of America, stated just a few days ago: "Every time we come together, we seem to become more convinced about the importance of our life and ministry in spite of decreasing numbers, aging and financial insecurity. Our energy comes from deep faith, solid tradition and a strong sense of community bonding. Our ministries keep us committed to the future." Another Sinsinawa Dominican, Sister Marie Anna Stelmach, a member of an interfaith group working in the Hawaiian leprosarium on Molokai, looks back on the past of her Order and to the present in a written statement: "I have great hope in our Dominican Order, because of our faithfulness to our charism—truth. Our leadership throughout the centuries has creatively responded to God's invitation to keep alive *the Word* through the ministry of preaching. The members of my Sinsinawa Dominican Congregation are good listeners—to one another, to the persons among whom we minister, to the world, to God. I personally feel that this collaborative encouragement, support, and ministry with enthusiasm, nurtures our continued hope in a religious life rooted in prayer and community life."

Sister Judy Cole, a Sister of Saint Joseph of Cleveland, spiritual advisor and lecturer, answers: "We are at the opposite pole from pessimism. I feel a strong energy flowing from within each sister of my community that is mobilizing and freeing all of us. There is a great acceptance of each sister for what they are and for the unique journey each has had. Before, we were locked in goose-step together; now, we are really celebrating the uniqueness of each other and it is so liberating for sisters to go and do what they are gifted to do and being blessed by the community. As a result, the community is reaching more people. There is much mutual support. Of course, there is still struggle, for example in the fact that we now have to go out and do things, while before things were placed in our laps."

"There is hope for religious communities if we remain faithful to our uniqueness, to our own charism," say three Missionary Servants of the Blessed Trinity, Sister Sara Butler, professor at Mundelein Seminary, Chicago, Sister Helen Gaffney, member of the general government, and Sister Theresa Bretthauer, formation director. "For us it means evangelizing the poor, promoting lay Christians' awareness of their vocation. Our community was forbidden by its founder to own institutions. We proclaim the gospel in contact with people and concentrate on helping them to become more aware of God's presence and action in their lives, and of their missionary call."

"We are hopeful, very hopeful and alive," answer two Missionary Franciscan Sisters of the Immaculate Conception, Sister Rose Bill, a pastoral minister in Syracuse, N.Y. and Sister Lorraine Chipman, a teacher in a Haitian school in Boston. "We see a future in which we will continue to serve God in the church. We may undergo some changes, but God will still continue to work in us and through us."

The impression of the writer is that, whatever the feelings of other religious might be, those religious who have adjusted to the changes are happy with the kind of ministry they are active in, are members of a community where spiritual ideals and values are strong and where leadership meets with broad approval, are optimistic about the future, even in the face of dwindling membership.

THE FUTURE

Can we imagine some of the traits of the future that lies ahead for the religious life?

Since it would be rather presumptuous of us to lay claim to the charism of prophecy, we will try to find an answer to this question in the lessons of the past and in an analysis of current trends.

In the World Church

Karl Rahner seems to have received a prophet's enlightenment when, in a short essay, he distinguished three stages in the history of the church: the very short Jewish period, the European church made possible by Paul's opening up of the faith to the Gentiles, and the world church that is being born in our days. The shortening of distances, the speed of communications, the phenomenon of migration, the transformation of planet earth into a global village (where everybody seems to know everybody) are putting strong pressure on the church and pushing it to lose its Euro-centered mindset. Everywhere we hear the same complaint: to the extent that the church is still so European in mentality, it is not yet fully Catholic. A new synthesis has to be forged between communion and the plurality of theological horizons, between spirituality and life experiences.

In the foreseeable future, the world church will be predominantly a southern hemisphere church. It is there that the Catholic population is growing considerably, and that vocations to the priesthood and to the religious life are numerous. A growing number of international orders and congregations are receiving their novices from the so-called "third world" countries. The influence of these new arrivals is beginning to be felt. This would seem to call for a greater flexibility and pluralism within the same charism, and a situation where general chapters reaffirm the common call, while provincial chapters deal with the problems of inculturation.

Some international institutes are now working hard at strengthening cross-cultural contacts between their members. Missionary congregations of men (the Comboni, the SVDs, the Scalabrinians) will of course continue their work of blending students from many countries in their scholasticates. It is interesting to note that Vietnamese, Filipino, Italian, Mexican, Ethiopian, Spanish, Ugandan and Kenyan students now form a good portion of seminarians attending the Catholic Theological Union of Chicago.

A Prophetic Minority

Will the decrease in the number of candidates in the northern hemisphere come to a halt and initiate a reverse trend? In the past there have been several periods of retrenchment followed by periods of expansion. But we doubt that vocations in these regions will again be as numerous as they were half a century ago. The sociological conditions that underlie the present reduction seem to be of a lasting character. We even suspect that these same cultural conditions will begin gradually to invade the third world and bring the present expansion to a standstill.

If we look back in history, we can clearly see that every time a new form of public commitment to the service of God has appeared in the church, the older forms of commitment have tended to shrink. Cenobitic monasticism took the place of solitary life. When the mendicant orders appeared and rapidly came to occupy the whole of Europe from Poland to Ireland and

Portugal, the number of monasteries began to decrease. Apostolic congregations had the same effect as the mendicant orders, and when sisters appeared,
the number of cloistered nuns began to dwindle. Today there is a new form
of commitment to public service in the church: that of the laity. Lay
Christians are taking many places formerly held by religious.

In the past, whenever a woman felt called to ministry, it was automatically interpreted as a call to the religious life. Men had two options: priesthood
and brotherhood. This is no longer so. One can have a personal call to ministry without feeling called to ordination or to profession. Many of those who
in the past would have become religious are now giving their life to God in
the church as lay ministers. Religious men seem destined to be what they
were in their earliest days: a prophetic minority.

Ministry Versus Services

From the sixteenth to the nineteenth centuries, society lamented the preva-
lence of some serious deficiencies that governments seemed unable to
resolve, such as lack of education among the great majority of the population
and lack of even basic health care for the poor. Numerous religious congregations were founded to provide these services, but since these services had to
be supplied by civil society itself, religious institutes therefore played a sup-
plementary role in them. The gospel works of mercy and education in
Christian faith came to be embodied in humanitarian services and institutions.

It would be utterly unjust to deny the work that large institutions (hospitals
and schools) are still accomplishing. Many religious feel that through them
they are serving God in God's children. But it is obvious that the Spirit has
been moving many religious and secular Christians alike to work outside of
large institutions in homes for battered women, abused children, centers for
the treatment of drug addicts and for assistance to both women and men who
have been engaged in prostitution. Other religious are committed to visiting
the sick, the elderly and the poor in their own homes. These are new ways of
promoting education in Christian faith and carrying out the works of mercy.

In the immediate future, religious congregations will probably keep moving from places where society is already active, and move in to the margins of
society, where God's children are suffering and are not being attended to.

Religious and Secular Christians

The growing presence of lay Christians who are active in the church has
been accompanied by a trend toward communion and cooperation between

members of religious institutes and secular Christians. In the past, there was a trend toward separation. At best, secular Christians were supposed to belong to a religious family, in a clear situation of dependence, as members of a "third order" or of an association orbiting around a male order. They clearly constituted a sphere of influence of religious in the church and therefore, whatever the original idea may have been, a demonstration of the power of the order.

The present tendency places religious and secular Christians together, in a cooperative and communional model. There are no longer "third orders": secular Franciscans and Dominicans share in the legacy of Francis and Dominic, together with Franciscan and Dominican religious. Discalced Carmelites pursue their experience of God (their contemplative call) together with groups of lay people. Congregations founded for evangelization are remembering that they were founded to proclaim the gospel. Proclamation was the pivot around which everything revolved in them. There lies the very core of their charism and the main task that they must fulfill. Now, they are beginning to conclude, their task implies promoting the apostolic call of the laity and facilitating their work. Here we can see one of the features that will characterize the apostolic religious life in the near future: communion and cooperation with the laity. New forums are being created in order to institutionalize this dialogue and cooperation, such as the presence of lay members of the family in chapters and assemblies with active participation in matters that are not purely internal to the community, and participation in mixed committees and commissions. Some secular Christians are living in community with religious, sharing in their life and spirituality.

Struggling To Survive

In conversations about the current situation, some religious as well as secular Christians are pronouncing a dire prognosis on what they consider to be the terminal state of some institutes: some (many?) communities are going to die out. The fear of death falls mostly on smaller communities that have not been receiving any candidates, or very few, for a number of years.

History may support these fears. At every turning point in the church, whenever religious life has entered into a crisis of transformation, some communities have died. They did so in patristic times (the Pachomian Congregation), in the middle ages (mostly autonomous monasteries or abbeys), in the reformation period, and in the aftermath of the French revolution.

Religious orders tend to flourish and expand during those periods in which they seem to respond well to the needs of the church and to the common sensitivity: cenobitic monasticism dominated all Europe until the twelfth century, and it was marvelously adjusted to the political and economic system of the early middle ages. Mendicant orders (especially the Franciscan family) spread like wildfire as soon as they were established in the thirteenth and fourteenth centuries. They expressed the values that the church needed most at that time and they were better adapted to new social conditions (better communications, the rise of the middle class, etc.).

Large religious orders tend to remain alive, even when their time of splendor is past, but they tend to shrink and enter a period of hibernation until the church's spirituality again becomes more consonant with their spirit. Since the thirteenth century and even more so after the sixteenth, Benedictine monasteries were not what they used to be in earlier times. They experienced a resurgence in the second half of the nineteenth century (Solesmes, Beuron, etc.) and they are very active centers of irradiation in our time, with our emphasis on communion, liturgical prayer, etc. Trappist monasteries were rather isolated and went largely unnoticed in America until the recent rediscovery of the contemplative dimension of Christian life.

Survival is a matter of internal spirit and external adjustment. The many communities established in the nineteenth century to provide certain services will have a hard time unless they learn to reinterpret their ministry. But having said all this, we must emphasize the fact that religious have the duty to fight for the survival of their communities. They owe it to the Spirit who gave them life. While we are alive, we must struggle to defend our life. The God of Jesus is a living God: "Our God is not a God of the dead, but of the living," as Jesus himself said (Mk 12:27). But some would object: What if God wants us to die? I would be a little wary of blaming God for a death that is clearly the consequence of natural causes. Of course, even if we do everything we can, yet disappear, then we will simply recede peacefully into the past.

The Blending of Communities

Finally, we cannot avoid mentioning a trend that has grown stronger and stronger in the last few years. Groups of communities deriving from the same foundress or founder have united to form one community (the Sisters of Mercy). Others are now involved in a federation, whether institutionalized (the Sisters of Saint Joseph) or not (the Sisters of the Incarnate Word and Sisters of the Blessed Sacrament). There is a tendency to reflect on their common charism and vision, and to pool their formation resources.

This is quite understandable, since these institutes lay claim to the same spiritual heritage. Their fragmentation during the nineteenth century was largely due to external causes: the long distance from the center, difficulties in communicating, and pressures by various local bishops who wanted to have "their own" sisters. All this is over and gone now. The problem comes from differences of mentality arising from their different particular histories.

Reuniting—for those who came from the same foundress or founder—and blending—for those who belong to the same large family (Dominican, Franciscan, Carmelite, Passionist) or have a similar mission—will open up, for some communities, the way to survival.

Notes

1. *Sacrum Commercium*, c. 6 in *Omnibus of Sources* (Chicago: Franciscan Herald Press, 1972), p. 1593. Cf. J. de Vitry, *Historia Orientalis*, c. 32: The Friars Minor live "in the vastness of an open cloister."

2. In Ann P. Ware, ed., *Midwives of the Future: American Sisters Tell Their Story* (Kansas City: Leaven Press, 1953), p. 197.

3. *Evangelical Witness*, n. 18.

4. Quoted by Annabelle M. Melville, *John Carroll of Baltimore* (New York: Scribner, 1955), p. 162.

5. Cf. John M. Lozano, *Grace and Brokenness in God's Country. An Exploration of American Catholic Spirituality* (New York: Paulist, 1991), pp. 65, 71-73.

6. John Ireland, *The Church and Modern Society* (Chicago-New York: D.H. McBride, 1896), p. 73.

7. *Grace and Brokenness in God's Country. An Exploration of American Catholic Spirituality* (New York: Paulist, 1991).

Religious Life:
The Challenge of the Ecozoic Era

Thomas Berry, CP

It is indeed a high honor to be with you today and to discuss with you the significance of these terminal decades of the century—which are also the terminal decades of the millennium. Far beyond any of these in its significance, we are presently in the terminal phase of the Cenozoic period of earth history. In these fateful years we are terminating sixty-five million years in the biological history of the planet. It is most important that we appreciate this order of magnitude of what is happening in our times.

We have mentioned Lewis Mumford in commemoration of his career as our foremost historian of cultures in this century. He extended the horizons of our vision to include a vast range of human cultural development. In doing this he was extremely sensitive to the rootedness of human affairs in the geological and biological systems of the planet. This perception we need to extend now beyond anything that he could envisage in his times.

The changes presently taking place in human and earthly affairs are beyond any parallel with historical change or cultural modification as these have occurred in the past. This is not like the transition from the classical period to the medieval period or from the medieval to the modern period. This change reaches far beyond the civilizational process itself, beyond even the human process into the biosystems and even the geological structures of the earth itself.

There are only two other moments in the history of this planet that offer us some sense of what is happening. These two moments are the end of the Paleozoic era, two hundred and twenty million years ago, when some 90% of all species living at that time were extinguished or sixty-five million years ago at the terminal phase of the Mesozoic era when there was also a very extensive extinction.

Then in the emerging Cenozoic period, the story of life on this planet flowed over into what could be called the lyric period of earth history. The trees had come before this, the mammals existed already in a rudimentary form, the flowers had appeared perhaps thirty million years earlier. But in the

Cenozoic period there was wave upon wave of life development, with the flowers and the birds and the trees and the mammalian species particularly, all leading to that luxuriant display of life upon earth such as we have known it.

In more recent times, during the past million years, this region of New England went through its different phases of glaciation, also its various phases of life development. In its trees especially it developed a unique grandeur. Possibly no other place on earth has such color in its fall foliage as this region. It was all worked out during these past sixty-five million years. The songbirds that we hear, they too came about in this long period.

Then we, the human inhabitants of the earth, came into this region with all the ambivalences that we bring with us. Not only here but throughout the planet we have become a profoundly disturbing presence. In this region and to the north of here in southern Quebec the native maple trees are dying out in great numbers due to pollutants in the atmosphere and in the soil and in the waters of the region.

This is largely due to the carbon compounds that we have loosed into the atmosphere through our use of fossil fuels, especially of petroleum, for fuel and energy. Carbon as you know is the magical element. The whole life structure of the planet is based upon the element of carbon. So long as the life process is guided by its natural patterns the integral functioning of the earth takes place. The wonderful variety expressed in marine life and land life, the splendor of the flowers and the birds and animals, all these could expand in their gorgeous coloration, in their fantastic forms, in their dancing movements and in their songs and calls that echo over the world.

To accomplish all this, however, nature must find a way of storing immense quantities of carbon in the petroleum and the coal deposits, also in the great forests. This was worked out over some hundreds of millions of years. A balance was achieved and the life systems of the planet were secure in the interaction of the air and the water and the soil with the inflowing energy from the sun.

But then we discovered that petroleum could produce such wonderful effects. It can be made into fertilizer to nourish crops, it can be spun into fabrics, it can fuel our internal combustion engines for transportation over the vast highway system that we have built, it can produce an unlimited variety of plastic implements, it can run gigantic generators and produce power for lighting and heating of our buildings.

It was all so simple. We had no awareness of the deadly consequences that would result from the residue that would be consequent on our use of petroleum for all these purposes. Nor did we know how profoundly we would affect the organisms in the soil with our insistence that the patterns of plant growth be governed by artificial human demands achieved by petroleum based fertilizers rather than by the spontaneous rhythms within the living world, nor did we understand that biological systems are not that adaptable to the mechanistic processes we imposed upon them.

I do not wish to dwell on the devastation we have brought upon the earth but only to make sure that we understand the nature and the order of magnitude of what is happening. While we seem to be achieving magnificent things at the microphase level of our functioning, we are devastating the entire range of living beings at the macrophase level. The natural world is more sensitive than we have realized. While we have thought to be of enormous benefit for the human process, we now find that by disturbing the biosystems of the planet at the most basic level of their functioning we have endangered all that makes the planet earth a suitable place for the integral development of human life itself.

Unaware of what we have done or its order of magnitude, we seek to remedy the situation by altering our ways of acting on some minor scale, by recycling, by diminishing our use of energy, by limiting our use of automobiles, by fewer development projects. The difficulty is that we do these things, not primarily to cease our plundering of the earth in its basic resources, but to make possible a continuation of our plundering industrial life patterns by mitigating the consequences. We mistake the order of magnitude of what we are dealing with.

Our problems are primarily problems of macrophase biology. Macrophase biology, the integral functioning of the entire complex of biosystems of the planet, is something that biologists have given almost no attention to. Only with James Lovelock and some of our more recent scientists have we even begun to think about this larger scale of life functioning. This is not surprising since we are caught in the microphase dimensions of every phase of our human endeavor. This is true in law and medicine and in the other professions as well as in biology.

Macrophase biology is concerned with the five basic spheres: the land sphere, the water sphere, the air sphere, the life sphere and how these interact with each other to enable the planet earth to be what it is. Then we have a very powerful sphere—the mind sphere, the human mind sphere. Consciousness is certainly not limited to humans. Every living being has its own mode of consciousness. We must be aware, however, that consciousness is an analogous concept. It is qualitatively different in its various modes of expression. Consciousness can be considered as the capacity for intimate presence of things to each other through knowledge and sensitive identity. But obviously the consciousness of a plant and the consciousness of an animal are qualitatively different. So too the consciousness of fish and the consciousness of birds or insects are all qualitatively different. So too with the human. For the purposes of the fish human modes of consciousness would be more a defect than an advantage, so with the differences of consciousness between the bird and the tiger.

It is clear also that the human mode of consciousness is capable of unique intrusion into the larger functioning of the planetary life systems. So powerful is this intrusion that the human has established an additional sphere that might be referred to as a technosphere, a way of controlling the functioning of the planet for the benefit of the human at the expense of the other modes of being. We might even consider that the technosphere in its subservience to industrial-commercial uses has become incompatible with the other spheres that constitute the basic functional context of the planet.

The biggest single question before us at present is the extent to which this technological-industrial-commercial context of human functioning can be made compatible with the integral functioning of the other life systems of the planet. We are reluctant to think of our activities being inherently incompatible with the integral functioning of the various components of the planetary systems. It is not simply a matter of modifying our energy use with such things as recycling, since this already supposes a cycling that is devastating in its original form.

Nor can we resolve the situation simply by mitigating the pollution so that the system itself can continue in its same basic form as at present. The system in its present plundering phase is certainly over with. It cannot continue. The industrial world on a global scale, as it functions presently, can be considered to be definitively bankrupt.

There is no way out of the present recession within the context of our existing commercial-industrial processes. This recession is not simply a financial recession or a human recession even. It is a recession of the planet itself. The earth cannot sustain such an industrial system or its devastating technologies. In the future the industrial system will have its moments of apparent recovery but these will be minor and momentary. The larger movement is toward dissolution. The impact of our present technologies is beyond what the earth can endure.

We can differentiate between an acceptable technology and an unacceptable technology quite simply: an acceptable technology is a technology that is compatible with the technologies of the natural world. An unacceptable technology is one that is incompatible with the integral functioning of the technologies that govern the functioning of the natural systems. Nature has its own technologies. The entire hydrological cycle can even be considered as a vast engineering project although it is an engineering project vastly greater than anything humans could devise with such beneficent consequences throughout the life systems of the planet.

The error has been to think that we could distort the natural processes for some immediate human benefit without incurring some immense penalty, a penalty that might eventually bring the well-being of the human as well as the well-being of most other life forms into danger. This is what has happened in this twentieth century petroleum economy that we have developed.

The petroleum base of our present industrial establishment might at its present rate of use last another fifty years; probably less, possibly more. But a severe depletion will occur within the lifetime of young people presently living. The major part of the petroleum will be gone. Our youngest children could see the end of it. They will likely see also the tragic climax of the population expansion. With the number of automobiles on the planet estimated at 600 million in the year 2000, we will be approaching another saturation level in the technological intrusion into the planetary process.

It is awesome to consider how quickly events of such catastrophic proportions are happening. When I was born in 1914 there were only one and a half billion people in the world. Children of the present will likely see ten billion. The petrochemical age had hardly begun in my early decades. Now the planet is saturated with the residue from spent oil products. There were less than a million automobiles in the world when I was born. In my childhood the tropical rainforests were substantially intact. Now they are devastated on an immense scale. The biological diversity of the life forms was not yet threatened on an extensive scale. The ozone layer was still intact.

In evaluating our present situation my proposal is that we have already terminated the Cenozoic period of the geo-biological systems of the planet. Sixty-five million years of life development are terminated. Extinction is taking place throughout the life systems on a scale unequaled since the terminal phase of the Mesozoic.

A renewal of life in some creative context requires that a new biological period come into being, a period when humans would dwell upon the earth in a mutually enhancing manner. This new mode of being of the planet I describe as the Ecozoic era, the fourth in the succession of life periods thus far identified as the Paleozoic, the Mesozoic, and the Cenozoic. But even when we propose an emerging Ecozoic era to succeed the Cenozoic era, we must indicate the unique character of this emergent period.

The Ecozoic era can only be brought into being by the integral life community itself. If other periods have been designated by such names as the Reptilian or Mammalian periods, this Ecozoic period must be identified as era of the integral life community. For this to emerge there are special conditions on the part of the human, for although this period cannot be an anthropocentric life period, it can come into being only under certain conditions that dominantly concern human understanding, choice and action. Here we might enumerate some of the particular conditions to be fulfilled on the part of the human if the Ecozoic era is to come about.

First as regards the name, Ecozoic. I propose Ecozoic as a better designation than Ecological. Eco-logos refers to an *understanding* of the interaction of things. Eco-zoic, a newly selected term, is a more biological term that can be used to indicate the integral *functioning* of life systems in their mutually enhancing relations.

When we consider the conditions required of humans for the emergence of such an Ecozoic era in earth history we might list these as follows:

The first condition is to understand that the universe is a communion of subjects, not a collection of objects. Every being has its own inner form, its own spontaneity, its own voice, its ability to declare itself, to be present to other components of the universe in a subject-to-subject relationship. While this is true of every being in the universe it is especially true of each component member of the earth community. Each component of the earth is integral with every other component of the earth. This is especially true of the living beings of the earth in their relations with each other.

The termination of the Cenozoic period of earth history has been brought about by the incapacity of humans in the industrial cultures to be present to the earth and its various modes of being in some intimate fashion. Ever since the time of Descartes in the early sixteenth century western humans, in their dominant life attitudes, have been autistic in relation to the non-human components of the planet. Whatever the abuse of the natural world by humans prior to this time, the living world was recognized until then in its proper biological functioning as having an "anima," a soul. Every living being was by definition an ensouled being with a voice that spoke to the depths of the human of wondrous and divine mysteries, a voice that was heard quite clearly by the poets and musicians and scientists and philosophers and mystics of the world, a voice heard also with special sensitivity by the children.

Descartes, we might say, killed the earth and all its living beings. For him the natural world was mechanism. There was no possibility of entering into a communion relationship. Western humans became autistic in relation to the surrounding world. There could be no communion with the birds or animals or plants since these were all mechanical contrivances. The real value of things was reduced to their economic value. A destructive anthropocentrism came into being.

This situation can be remedied only by a new mode of mutual presence between the human and the natural world, with the plants and the animals of both the sea and the land. If we do not get that straight then we cannot expect any significant remedy for the present distress experienced throughout the earth. This capacity for intimate rapport needs to be extended into the atmospheric phenomena and the geological structures and their functioning.

Because of this autism my generation never heard the voices of that vast multitude of inhabitants of the planet. They had no communion with the non-human world. They would go to the seashore or to the mountains for some recreation, a moment of aesthetic joy. But this was too superficial to estab-lish any true reverence or intimate rapport. No sensitivity was shown to the powers inherent in the various phenomena of the natural world, no depth of awe that would have restrained their assault on the natural world to extract from it some human advantage—even if this meant tearing to pieces the entire fabric of the planet.

The second condition for entering into the Ecozoic age is a realization that the earth exists and can survive only in its integral functioning. It cannot sur-vive in fragments any more than any organism can survive in fragments. Yet the earth is not a global sameness. It is differentiated unity and must be sus-tained in the integrity and inter-relations of its many bioregional contexts. This requires an immediacy of any human settlement with the life dynamics of the region. Within this region the human rights to habitat must respect the rights to habitat in the region possessed by the other members of the life community. Only the full complex of life expression can sustain the vigor of any bioregion.

A third condition for entering the Ecozoic era is recognition that the earth is a one-time endowment. We do not know the quantum of energy contained in the earth, its possibilities or its limitations. We must reasonably suppose that the earth is subject to irreversible damage in the major patterns of its functioning and even to distortions in its possibilities of development. Although there was survival and further development after the great extinc-tions at the end of the Paleozoic and the Mesozoic, life was not so highly developed as it is now. Nor were the very conditions of life negated by such changes as we have wrought through our disturbance of the chemical balance of the planet.

Life upon earth will surely survive the present decline of the Cenozoic but we do not know at what level of its development. The single-cell life forms found throughout the planet, the insects, the rodents, the plants, and a host of other forms of life, these will surely survive. But the severity of devastation as regards the extinction of rainforests, the fertility of the soils, species diver-sity, survival of the more developed animals, the consequences throughout the animal world of the diminishment of the ozone shield, the extension of deserts, pollution of the great freshwater lakes, the chemical balance of the atmosphere, these are all subject to disturbance that might not ever be restored to their present grandeur, certainly not within any timescale that is available to human modes of thinking or planning. Almost certainly we have witnessed in these past centuries a grand climax in the florescence of the earth.

A fourth condition for entering the Ecozoic age is a realization that the earth is primary and that humans are derivative. The present distortion is that humans are primary and the earth and its integral functioning can only be a secondary consideration. Thus the pathology manifest in our various human institutions, professions, programs and activities. The only acceptable way for humans to function effectively is by giving first consideration to the earth community and then dealing with humans as integral members of that community. In economics the first consideration cannot be the human economy, since the human economy does not even exist prior to the earth economy. Only if the earth economy is functioning in some integral manner can the human economy be in any manner effective. The earth economy can survive the loss of its human component but there is no way for the human economy to survive or prosper apart from the earth economy.

The absurdity has been to seek a rising gross human economy while diminishing the gross earth economy. This primacy of the earth community applies also to medicine and law and all the other activities of humans. It should be especially clear in medicine that we cannot have well humans on a sick planet. So in jurisprudence to poise the entire administration of justice on the rights of humans and their limitless freedoms to exploit the natural world is to open the natural world to the worst predatory instincts of humans. Medicine must first turn its attention to protecting the health and well-being of the earth before there can be any effective human health. So in law the prior rights of the entire earth community need to be assured first; then the rights and freedoms of humans can have their field of expression.

A fifth condition for the rise of the Ecozoic age is to realize that there is a single earth community. There is no such thing as a human community in any manner separate from the earth community. The human community and the natural world will go into the future as a single integral community or we will both experience disaster on the way. However differentiated in its modes of expression, there is only one earth community, one economic order, one health system, one moral order, one world of the sacred.

As I present this outline of an emerging Ecozoic period I am quite aware that such a conception of the future, when humans would be present to the earth in a mutually enhancing manner, is mythic in its form just as such conceptions as the Paleozoic, Mesozoic, and Cenozoic are mythic modes of understanding a continuing process, even though this continuing process is marked by an indefinite number of discontinuities amid the continuity of the process itself.

The effort here is to articulate the outlines of a new mythic form that would evoke a creative entrancement to succeed the destructive entrancement that has taken possession of the western soul in recent centuries. We can only counter one entrancement with another, a counter-entrancement. Only thus can we evoke the vision as well as the psychic energies needed to enable the earth community to enter successfully onto its next great creative phase. The grandeur of the possibilities ahead of us must in some manner be experienced in anticipation, otherwise we will not have the psychic energy to endure the pains of the required transformation.

Once we are sufficiently clear as to where we are headed, once we experience its urgency and the adventure of what we are about, we can get on with our historic task, we can accept and even ignore the difficulties to be resolved and the pains to be endured because we are involved in a great work. In creating such a great work the incidentals fall away. We can accept the pathos of our times, the sorrow that we will necessarily go through. Hopefully we will be able to guide and inspire the next generation as it takes up this creative effort. Otherwise they will simply survive with all their resentments amid the ruined infrastructures of the industrial world and amid the ruins of the natural world itself. The challenge itself is already predetermined. There is no way for the new generation to escape this confrontation. The task to which they are called, the destiny that is before them, is, however, not left simply to themselves. The human is supported by the entire universe, by every earthly being. The entire planet is involved. The successful emergency of the Ecozoic age can be considered presently as the great creative task of the universe itself.

This destiny can be understood, however, only in the context of the great story of the universe. All peoples derive their understanding of themselves by their account of how the universe came into being in the beginning, how it came to be as it is, and the role of the human in the story. We in our Euro-American traditions have in recent centuries through our observational studies created a new story of the universe. The difficulty is that this story was discovered in the context of a mechanistic way of thinking about the world and so has been devoid of meaning. Supposedly everything has happened in a random meaningless process.

It is little wonder then that we have lost our great story. Our earlier Genesis story has long ago lost its power over our historical cultural development. Our new scientific story has never carried any depth of meaning. We have lost our reverence for the universe and the entire range of natural phenomena.

The difficulty is that our scientific story of the universe has no continuity with the natural world as we experience this in the wind and the rain and the clouds, the birds, the animals, and the insects that we observe. For the first time in all of human history, the sun and moon and stars, the fields and the mountains and streams and woodlands fail to evoke a sense of reverence before the deep mystery of things. These wondrous components of the natural world are somehow not seen with any depth of appreciation. Perhaps that is why our presence had become so deadly.

But now all this is suddenly altered. Shocked by the devastation we have caused we are awakening to the wonder of a universe never before seen in quite the same manner. No one ever before could tell in such lyric language the story of the primordial flaring forth of the universe at the beginning, the shaping of the immense number of stars gathered into galaxies, the collapse of the first generation of stars to create the ninety-some elements, the gravitational gathering of scattered stardust into our solar system with its nine planets, the formation of the earth with its seas and atmosphere and the continents crashing and rifting as they move over the asthenosphere, the awakening of life.

Such a marvel this fifteen billion year process, such infinite numbers of stars in the heavens and living beings on earth, such limitless variety of flowering species, and all forms of animal life, such tropical luxuriance, such natural scenery in the mountains, such springtime wonders as occur each year.

What is needed now is that we be able to tell this story, meditate on this story, listen to this story as it is told by every breeze that blows, by every cloud in the sky, by every mountain and river and woodland, by the song of every cricket.

The role of elders at the present time is to assist the next generation in fulfilling their role in this transformation moment. We can, I think, assist them mainly by indicating just where they can receive their instructions. Here I would like to speak of an incident on Cape Croker along Georgian Bay in northwest Ontario. Some years ago I was invited to participate at a meeting there of the indigenous Indian peoples, mostly Ojibwa, Cree and Six Nations, concerning their future and what direction their lives should take.

When I spoke with them I mentioned that the night previously I was watching the moon flickering on the waters of the bay and I asked the moon, "What should I say?" and the moon answered "Tell them the story." I asked the wind "What should I say?" and the wind said, "Tell them the story." Then before I came into the big tent I asked the clover in the meadow, "What should I say?" and the clover said, "Tell them the story, my story, the mountain story, the river story, the bird story, your story, their story, the great story."

Then I remarked, "What I say here is not important. But what the mountains and the rivers say is important. What the birds and the animals and the creatures in the sea say, what the flowers and the trees say and the sands of the shore, what the wind and the sun and the moon and the stars say; all this is important." Of course the indigenous peoples all knew this. I was in a manner speaking to myself and to the society whence I come.

I mentioned then that my generation had been autistic in relation to the entire range of natural phenomena. Since we could not enter into evocatory relations with these surrounding powers we found it necessary to plunder these sources in order to survive, but the more we plundered the less fertility was found in the soils and the less abundant the natural resources, the less available water suited for drinking or air for breathing. Because we could not listen we could not learn.

We have lost contact with our story, with the great story, and that is why the instructions being given to me by the moon and the wind and the clover were to tell the story to remind us all what is happening and where we must look for guidance. For we can come together, all the peoples of earth and all the various members of the great earth community, only in the great story, the story of the universe.

For there is no community without a community story, no earth community without the earth story, and no universe community without the universe story. These three constitute the great story. Without this story the various forces of the planet become mutually destructive rather than mutually coherent.

We need to listen to each other's way of telling the great story. But first we in the west, with our newly developed capacity to listen to the universe through our vast telescopes and to hear the sounds of the universe as these come to us from the beginning of time and over some billions of years, we need really to listen to this story as our own special way of understanding and participating in the great story.

Whenever we forget our story we become confused. But the winds and the rivers and the mountains, they never become confused. We must go to them constantly to be reminded of the great story, for every being in the universe is what it is only through its participation in the story. We are resensitized whenever we listen to what they are telling us. Long ago they told us that we must be guided by a reverence and a restraint in our relations with the larger community of life, that we must respect the powers of the surrounding universe, that only through a sensitive insertion of ourselves into the great celebration of the earth community can we expect the support of the earth community. If we violate the integrity of this community we will die.

The natural world is vast and its lessons fearsome. One of the most severe expressions of the natural world has to do with nuclear energy. When we go deep into the natural world and penetrate into the inner structure of the atom and in a sense violate that deepest mystery for trivial or destructive purposes, we may get power, but nature throws at us its most deadly consequences. We are still helpless with regard to what to do once we have broken into the mysterious recesses of nuclear power. Forces have been let loose far beyond anything we can manage.

Earlier in this paper I mentioned five conditions for the integral emergence of the Ecozoic era. Here I would continue with a sixth condition—that we understand fully and respond effectively to our own human role in this new era. For while the Cenozoic era unfolded in its full splendor entirely apart from any role fulfilled by the human, almost nothing of major significance is likely to happen in the Ecozoic era that humans will not be involved in. The entire pattern of earth functioning is altered in this transition from the Cenozoic to the Ecozoic. We did not even exist until the major developments of the Cenozoic were complete. In the Ecozoic, however, the human will have a pervasive influence on almost everything that happens. We are crossing over a critical threshold in the entire modality of earth functioning. While we cannot make a blade of grass there is liable not to be a blade of grass unless it is accepted, protected and fostered by the human—protected mainly from ourselves, so that the earth can function from within its own dynamism.

There is finally the question of language. A new language, an Ecozoic language, is needed. Our late Cenozoic language is radically inadequate. The human mode of being is captured and destroyed by our present univalent, scientific, literal, unimaginative language. We need a multivalent language, a language much richer in the symbolic meanings which language carried in its earlier forms when the human lived deeply within the world of natural forms and the entire range of earth phenomena. As we recover this early experience in the emerging Ecozoic era, all the archetypes of the collective unconscious attain a new validity, also new patterns of functioning, especially in our understanding of the symbols of the heroic journey, the death-rebirth symbol, the great mother, the tree of life.

Every reality in the natural world is multivalent. Nothing is univalent. Everything has a multitude of aspects and meanings, as sunlight carries within itself warmth and light and energy. Sunlight awakens the multitude of living forms in the springtime. Sunlight is not a single thing. It awakens poetry in the soul, it evokes a sense of the divine. It is mercy and healing, affliction and death. Sunlight is irreducible to any scientific equation or any literal description.

But all these meanings are based on the physical experience of sunlight. If we were deprived of sunlight the entire visible world would be lost to us and eventually all life and immense realms of consciousness. We would be retarded in our inner development in proportion to our deprivation of the experience of natural phenomena, of mountains and rivers and forests and seacoasts and all their living inhabitants. The natural world itself is our primary language as it is our primary scripture, our primary awakening to the mysteries of existence. We might well put all our written scriptures on the shelf for twenty years until we learn what we are being told by unmediated experience of the world about us.

So too we might put Webster on the shelf until we revise the language of all our professions, especially such professions as law and medicine and education. In ethics we need new words such as biocide and geocide, words that have not yet been adopted into the language. In law we need to define society in terms that include the larger community of living beings of the bioregion, of the earth and even of the universe. Certainly human society separated from such contexts is an abstraction. Life, liberty, habitat and the pursuit of happiness are rights that should be granted to every living creature, each in accord with its own mode of being.

I might conclude with a reference to the exodus symbol which has exercised such great power over our western civilization. Many peoples came to this country believing they were leaving a land of oppression and going to a land of liberation. We have always had a sense of transition. Progress supposedly is taking us from an undesirable situation to a kind of beatitude. So we might think of the transition from the terminal Cenozoic to the emerging Ecozoic as a kind of exodus out of a period when humans were devastating the planet to a period when humans began to live upon the earth in a mutually enhancing manner.

There is a vast difference, however, in this present transition. This transition is not simply of the human but of the entire planet, its land, its air, its waters, its biosystems, its human communities. This exodus is a journey of the earth entire. Hopefully we will make the transition successfully. Whatever the future holds for us, however, it will be shared experience between humans and every other earthly being. There is one community, one destiny.

Religious Life:
A Prophetic, Dynamic Movement

Cassian J. Yuhaus, CP, HED

RENEWAL REPERCUSSION

One of the more fascinating aspects of religious life in our day is the repercussion that the response to the mandate for renewal has had and is having on the entire church. Pope, bishops, priests, laity: all are perplexed and disturbed. The perplexity and disturbance pre-date the council; they were in evidence at the first world congress on the then declared "states of perfection" convened by Pius XII in 1949 and became full-blown in the heart of the council itself when the tiny document *Perfectae Caritatis* was beaten to a near pulp, to one-sixth of its original size because little agreement could be reached on its declarations and proposals about what came to be known as *Institutes of Apostolic Life*. It is no wonder the decree on religious, *Perfectae Caritatis*, remains one of the three weakest documents of the council, a compromise, and in the view of some scholars scarcely worthy of a conciliar document.

To this debate we must add the even more serious concern of religious themselves at the council. The most important document of the council, the key to all others, was in its fourth draft and still did not carry a single word of reference to religious. We are speaking about nothing less than the Dogmatic Constitution on the Church, *Lumen Gentium*. Fortunately, and we must regard the ensuing debate as a singular manifestation of the presence of the Holy Spirit, the dissatisfaction resulted in the finest, clearest and most profound declaration on the religious life in five hundred years! Chapter VI of *Lumen Gentium* on the life of religious in the life of the church contains more theological renewal of the religious life than the entire decree *Perfectae Caritatis*.

I have often remarked how unfortunate it has been for the church in the United States that the small, aggressive and protesting group of religious known as the Consortium, after years and years of insistence, public and private, finally succeeded in wresting a charter-of-a-kind from the Holy See.

How unfortunate, I say, that they did not base their efforts on Chapter VI of *Lumen Gentium* rather than the decree from which they have assumed their name, *Perfectae Caritatis*. Had they done so with clarity of intention and an openness to its full implications, I doubt we would be experiencing the present dissension and harmful divisiveness.

I say all this because, at root, the renewal of religious life is doctrinal! Nothing less. It is not a question of externals of structures or customs or the habit. It is not a question of vows, their number and their precise canonical requirements. It is not a question of the great work that religious have done or may not be doing. It is not a question of "who's in charge," a question of authority and its correlate obedience. It is not a question of community and the famed "regular observance" (which, in reality, meant silent conformity more than prayer). Above all it is not a question of the habit, as divisive and disturbing as that false issue has been.

It is none of these. Or, rather, it is all of these wrapped up into one issue: the theology of religious life, that is, the nature, the meaning, the purpose and the functioning of religious life not just in the church, particularly not the institutional church, but in the church as it pertains to kingdom and in the world as it groans for the reign of God.

The key to every single problem that has vexed congregation after congregation, often wounding and dividing communities—witness the hot issue of dress among women religious—is doctrinal: What is religious life? The council could hardly have been aware of the Pandora's box it was opening when it called upon religious around the world to initiate, with the collaboration and participation of all the members of the community, a participative program for total renewal. And herein we discover the key to successful renewal. The extent, depth and sincerity of the collaboration and participation of *all* the members, not the chosen few, is the determining factor.

Taking the council seriously, religious embarked on the rocky road, picking and pecking their way through thicket and thorn, seeking to learn what the journey was all about and where it was leading. Many were the obstacles and surprises, not the least of which were the hierarchy and ordained clergy themselves, both as obstacles to genuine renewal and surprise over the direction renewal began to take.

NOT BY HIERARCHICAL FIAT

With this we arrive immediately at one of the most important understandings of a renewed theology of religious life, albeit one of the most vexing and difficult to handle—even though the church has the witness of the centuries on its side. The fact, doctrinal and historical, is that religious life does not exist by hierarchical fiat. The church did *not* create religious life. No pope however great and holy—and there were many of that caliber—ever claimed to be the originator of religious life. No council, ecumenical or regional, no synod, no conference, accredits itself with the distinction. The truth at once awesome and compelling, complex and sophisticated, is simple in its enunciation: religious life is a gift of the Lord to his church and his world. Now what do you do about that! Popes and cardinals and bishops and priests may inveigh against religious, but the life endures. The church can suppress and has suppressed this or that religious community, but the life endures. Efforts may be made to prevent young men and women from "burying" themselves within cloistered walls. Bishops may dissuade young men from entering the novitiate, but the life endures. Kings and emperors, prime ministers and lords may deceive and entice religious away from enclosure but the life endures. Tyrants and dictators, bigots and reformers may burn convents, destroy monasteries, incarcerate religious, torture and maim them, obliterate them in gas chambers and tombs, but the life goes on.

The truth is: when we touch religious life, we are touching one of the greatest mysteries of the church, a profound mystery of God. When we touch religious life we are touching one of the most fascinating phenomena of human history. The life goes on.

GOSPEL: NORM AND JUDGMENT

The origin of Christian religious life is the gospel life and teaching of Jesus. That is why the Second Vatican Council so wisely declared that the first principle for the renewal of religious life in our day is fidelity to the gospel. Here is the message of meaning and the test of fidelity to religious life. The gospel is at once the supreme norm and judgment upon religious life. Whatever forms of religious life antedated Christianity, and they are multiple and varied, what makes religious life today and gives it form and meaning in the church is the gospel of Jesus, the ultimate foundation of every religious community. Beyond and above every rule of life, every constitution, every norm and directive of the Holy See, every practice and custom of my community, stands the gospel of Jesus. Many of our great leaders and founders resisted the appeals of their followers for rules and regulations pointing to the gospel. "This alone matters," they declared. "Here is your Rule." (St. Francis, St. Vincent de Paul, Catherine McAuley and Mother Mary of the Passion come to mind at once.)

THE OPENING: SCRIPTURAL SCHOLARSHIP

The acceptance of the centrality of the word of God in the life of the religious and the new and vigorous return to scripture studies account in large measure for the radical renewal of church and religious life. The clouds of obfuscation that besieged religious life for centuries have their origin in the counter-reformation decision of the church prompted by fear and animosity to refuse the vernacular, cling to the Latin, forbid any translation of the liturgy, and establish a Roman watchdog commission to alone interpret or explain the meaning of the word of God. Not that a commission was not a good thing. It was, and is. The problem was in the manner of acting and the lack of developed scholarship. This effectively took the scriptures out of the hands of the people. The Bible became a closed book.

The consequences for religious life were very harmful and perduring. We became supremely canonical and legal. From what was to be a simple guide book reflecting the gospels, our rules and constitutions tended to supersede the scriptures. The Holy Rule became the *supreme* norm! Canonically exact, technically perfect, this legal document scrupulously observed would lead you from here to eternity. And in most institutes it was to be read every day.

The renewed scholarship and biblical research of our day reopened the scriptures: the primary source of the renewal of the church. Once the door opened, religious women and men entered in haste and rediscovered there, in God's word, the true origins and the fullness of meaning of the evangelical life.

FLORA AND FAUNA OR LIGHT FROM THE CENACLE

For centuries an erroneous teaching about the temporal origin of religious life was allowed to continue in the church unchallenged. Theological textbooks explained the origin in terms of witness. The blood of martyrs is the seed of Christians, as Tertullian proclaimed. But once the Constantinian peace was achieved, who would witness to the profound truths of Christianity? Enter the "dry" martyrs—not by blood but by testimony of their total lives. Religious became the new witnesses. For centuries masters of novices so indoctrinated the questioning aspirant like myself. Religious life began, so the instruction went, with the work of Pachomius in the desert immediately after the ending of the age of classical martyrs. And so it was piously believed, erroneously of course.

The challenge came at the council. If the church got along very well without religious up until the fourth century, are religious necessary to the church in the twentieth? Cannot the church get on quite well, thank you, without the hassle and bustle so often caused by religious? Moreover with the dawning of the age of the laity, are religious needed? Proponents of reform shouted "yea," "yea" at the waning and demise of religious life. But too eager and too soon. For the facts, the existential truths, historically and doctrinally point to the contrary.

Far from beginning amid the flora and fauna in a remote hermitage in the Pachomian deserts of Egypt, religious life is as young and as ancient as the church itself. Not in imitation of the martyrs but in imitation of Christ, religious life is due to that immediate post-Pentecostal experience of the people of God, that dynamic outpouring of the Spirit of God prompting men and women from earliest times until this very day to seek no other task in life than to proclaim Jesus as Lord, placing themselves at the service of the gospel for the good of the church. It is no accident of history that the earliest and the only authentic liturgical text remaining to us from the very first century is a parchment-fragment containing a portion of the text for the preface of the mass for the consecration of virgins. From the very first days of Christianity the church recognized the gift given to certain ones. In the most solemn and public manner known to it, in the midst of the people of God at eucharist, the church consecrates those so gifted and so called. There never has been a time nor can we foresee a time when the vivifying Spirit should cease to raise up from among the people of God lifelong witnesses to the fullness of gospel discipleship with Jesus.

It is for these reasons that the council in its most significant statement on religious in Chapter VI of the Dogmatic Constitution of the Church, *Lumen Gentium,* would declare that religious life "is a divine gift which the church received from its Lord and which it always safeguards with the help of his grace." The statements that follow are even more explicit historically and doctrinally. Acknowledging that religious life "undeniably belongs to its life and holiness," the council makes this belonging very explicit: "Religious should carefully keep before their minds the fact that the church presents Christ to believers and non-believers alike in a striking manner daily through them. The church thus portrays Christ in contemplation on the mountain, in his proclamation of the kingdom of God to the multitudes, in his healing of the sick and maimed, in his work of converting sinners to a better life, in his solicitude for youth and his goodness to all men, always obedient to the will of the Father who sent him."

Some theologians, among them no less a defender of religious life than Karl Rahner, would have preferred to have seen an even more explicit acknowledgement of the necessary and, indeed, essential relatedness of church and religious life. For Rahner rightly argues that it is *essential* to the life of the church that there exist continually among the people of God certain ones who desire and who own with conviction and enthusiasm no other place in life than at the side of Jesus, no other role in life than to proclaim Jesus as Lord, who ask nothing of this world but give all; who would walk to its ends to heal a broken heart, calm a distressed spirit, mend a broken body, seeking no other credit or reward but to know Jesus and the power of his cross and resurrection.

PATHOLOGIES OF THE PAST, OR SO WE HOPE

As you can see, it is not that religious do not love the church or do not esteem and respect the hierarchy; to the contrary, they may have loved too much. For whatever reason, fear of oppression and reprimand, seeking privileged position and favors, hurting for lack of recognition, religious have allowed themselves to become, in the words of one theologian and critic, "domesticated," "tamed," a lovely puppy, a lap-dog without bark or bite— surely a confusion of nature, role and function.

Religious are not above the church. They are not simply alongside the church but neither are they below the church. All of these have been pathologies hopefully of the past. Religious were not consulted, they did not count or counted for little. They were merely tolerated when not excluded at meetings of clergy and hierarchy. They were second class. They needed to be controlled—above all, women religious. Not only were they reduced to silence but they were not so much as to be seen, not even in the very local parochial church to which they belonged and which they sustained by their arduous and woefully unrecompensed service. And, more sadly still, for most bishops and priests this was a very happy and acceptable situation. In fact, many would declare it was God's will. So it was, is now and forever should be! Amen. Alleluia. No wonder such consternation and opposition to renewal from on high. And why not keep them in their habits? As one superior general, in a public press interview, so callously and shamefully reported, "Once you let the beagles out of their boxes how will you ever get them back in again?"

Well out they are! And not by any human fiat but by the provident activity of the Holy Spirit through the voice of the church in solemn ecumenical assembly. Proclaim they will.

The movement among religious to rediscover the meaning of their lives and to distinguish their rightful role in the church was different in approach from continent to continent but identical in intent and purpose. Some approaches, as, for the most part, in western Europe, were slow, fearful and hesitant. Others were surprising. The greatest surprise came from the southern hemisphere, in particular South America.

For centuries the religious life seemed completely dormant. In our own day just prior to the council the church in South America was facing collapse. Religious vocations were at a standstill. The church seemed comfortably tucked away in the pockets of the wealthy and under the sweet patronage of the great land-owners. Pope John XXIII stood up and made his great appeal to every religious community in the church to send as many religious as possible but at least a minimum percent to that ailing church even at the cost of great sacrifice and the abandonment of other worthy causes. The religious across the world responded with courage and generosity. The rest is history.

From out of that hitherto practically unknown land there came first a whisper, then a clear voice which rapidly increased in strength, in conviction and power until the entire world could not be still. The prophets arose, the martyrs followed. A church and people were reborn. Despite initial difficulties which became clarified by the pope himself, today liberation theology is affirmed from one end of the earth to the other. Moreover the basic ecclesial community, first developed in Brazil, has become a key instrument for the renewal of life and faith throughout the world. New hope for a downtrodden, deprived and hurting people dawned. Religious everywhere rediscovered an essential element of their calling: the prophetic.

Prophecy is not fortune telling. It is not guess work or forecast. It is not apocalyptic doomdom. It is kingdom. Its concern is not the future but the present. Its dynamism is the face of God looked upon in an unforgettable way by the prophet. Its power is the Holy Spirit. The prophet is one who must speak of what he or she knows. Prophets must witness what they see. Their life is their message. From a profound and shattering experience of God comes the voice that speaks the word of God, the two-edged sword.

The church by definition in its oneness with Christ is and remains prophetic. While prophecy may be given to anyone and may come from whatever source, still nowhere in the church throughout the centuries has it been so constant, so congenial and so co-natural as in the religious life. Both history and theology teach us that if anything is of an essence to the religious life enterprise, it is prophetic. To religious, prophecy is endemic and intrinsic. Religious life is born in the church of the Spirit to proclaim what the Spirit wills to say to the churches, young and old. Religious life born in the church, of the church and by the church lives for the church—especially when the church and churchmen are unhappy and disturbed by its prophetic message. I believe there are no more certain signs of authentic renewal of any congregation than the *perception* and the *experience* of contemplation, community and prophecy. All three are profoundly doctrinal. All three have been completely reinterpreted since the council. Of the three the most significant is the prophetic.

A further remarkable benefit of the Second Vatican Council is the renewed awareness in the entire church of that frequently misunderstood and always frightening dimension of its life and mission, the prophetic. The institutional church will always be in danger of exaggerating and misinterpreting the power that Christ, as king bequeaths to his church. The equally necessary and important gift of prophecy not only puts parameters to leadership and the exercise of authority but it also dyamizes both.

In the revivifying of religious life, it is to the resurgence of the prophetic element that we must attribute the major role. By its very nature religious life is intrinsically prophetic, as we have said. The point raised in chapter after renewal chapter needs to be addressed by all of us. We can no longer be content with a lip service to prophecy, an empty patronizing attitude. Prophets are nice people as long as you keep them in their place. We fail to see that it is precisely their "out-of-placeness" that makes them prophetic.

Pressed as I have been in these twenty-five years to address the issue, I have more recently proposed a norm for the prophetic. Unless a community or an individual can answer four questions, I do not believe there is any room for the prophetic.

Question No. 1: Have you heard the cry of the poor?

The prophet will always speak from within reality. No vague denunciation. No exaggerated, disproportioned declamation. The prophet has done the hard work of social analysis. The prophet knows wherein he or she speaks. The prophet takes side. That side is with God on the side of the poor. The prophet hears all too clearly the pitiful cry of the poor, the oppressed, the marginalized. And the prophet must know and identify the oppressors and the oppressing agencies and causes.

Question No. 2: Can you read the signs of the time?

The words of the psalmist continually stir the prophet, "If today you hear his voice...." God does not suddenly and sporadically intervene in human history. God is in continual interaction with all creation. This interaction attains its highest point of meaning and relevance in the life of the prophet and the prophetic community. God speaks through the events of life, the events of history. In these we discern the voice of God. We respond to the harsh realities that contradict or compromise gospel values. We shall never understand properly what the cry of the poor means unless we interpret that cry in our reading of the events, the signs of our time.

Question No. 3: Have you encountered Christ as liberator?

Is your Christ only to be found among the lilies of the field? Is your Christ only the meek and gentle shepherd boy watching tenderly his sweet little lambs? If that is the limit of your image of Christ, you can never be a prophet.

The prophet sees the anger in the eyes of Jesus, feels the tightness in his throat, touches the tension in his muscles as he beats the whip over the money changers and kicks over their pots of gold. The prophet hears the harsh and mean words, "You brood of vipers! You hypocrites" (Mt 23:13-28)—outside so seemingly clean and pure but inside a stinking tomb filled with dead-men's rotting bones.

The prophet must see the nail through the hand of Jesus, must feel his blood splash against the prophet's face.

Jesus, anointed in the Spirit, came "to set the captive free" and to liberate mankind from every form of evil and oppression. The prophet walks the same path.

Question No. 4: Can you drink of the chalice?

Ultimately to be a prophet means to know no other fear than the fear of not being a prophet. The prophet cannot shut up or be shut up: threats, beatings, loss of friends, especially the comfortable and wealthier ones, torture, imprisonment and death await the prophet. When James and John wanted top billing in the kingdom, Jesus simply said, "Can you drink of the chalice?" (Mt 20:22-23).

Oscar Romero said yes. Jean Donavan and the Maryknoll and Ursuline Sisters said yes. The six Jesuits said yes and their gentle housekeeper and her daughter paid the price with them.

In our answers to these four questions we will find the measure and validity of our stance as a prophetic community of disciples.

A PROFOUND MYSTICAL EXPERIENCE

The council itself was startled by the Spirit. Tracing the laborious efforts of the council through the generous release of the day-books, the conversion taking place within the council becomes clear. That conversion is marked by an increasing awareness and recognition of the power and the presence of the Holy Spirit. The confusions and bitter antagonisms, the opposition and seriously harmful divisions of the opening days of the council, yield to a near unanimity of intent, a conviction of purpose and an irresolute stance at the close of the council regarding the total renewal of church and people. The achievements of the council far exceeded even the grandest expectations of the conciliar fathers themselves. It is indeed the exhilarating work of the Spirit.

The most evident work of the Spirit has become a key document for the renewal of the church and society. It is one of the major documents of our time and one of the most important in the history of the church.

Gaudium et Spes is a monument to patience, to perseverance, to dialogue and to openness to the Spirit of God. Nothing prior to the council gave any hint of such a work. It did not seem even remotely possible. There was no previous preparatory commission, no previous drafts, no selected points, no prolegomena or lineamenta. It is entirely the work of the council, through the council and within the council. It is the work of the Spirit. It is unlike any previous document of the church in its scope and content: addressing for the first time in solemn ecumenical gathering the most confused and perplexing, complex and entangled problems of our time. It is a key document for the renewal of religious life. It addresses the prophetic.

But something even more resulted for religious through the obedience of the council to the Spirit. It may well be the most significant influence of the council on religious life. Nothing in the council reveals more clearly the nature, purpose and functioning of religious in the church.

The council affirmed as never affirmed hitherto in the church that the Spirit of the church is the Holy Spirit and that the first obedience of every baptized person from pope to peasant is to the Holy Spirit. It is the Spirit that directs the entire church. The manner of that direction gives us at once the foundation for the doctrine on the church as the people of God, the basis for the equality of membership in the church and the fountainhead from which springs the marvelous but unifying diversity of function within the one body of Christ, his church. The key is charism. The directive power and active presence of the Holy Spirit in the church is through charism. Charism is the manner in which the Spirit of God directs *all* people of God from the highest to the lowliest toward the fulfillment of the gospel life and mission of Jesus by bestowing on all—not just the pope or bishops or priests or "superiors" but upon *all*—a great variety of powers, ordinary and extraordinary. The Spirit breathes where the Spirit wills, but what the Spirit wills is for the benefit of all, for the increased achievement and the movement toward realization of the mission of Jesus. This mission is the only mission of the church. There is none other. Neither pope nor bishop nor pastor assigns mission to the church; Christ alone does.

Charism, then, is at the root of the foundation of every new community in the church. Nowhere do we see the meaning, the power and the consequence of charism better revealed than we do when we study the origin of a religious family in the church.

Every congregation is born of the Spirit. The origins of each religious institute must be placed in the profound mystical experience of the foundress or founder and founding community. In this and in nothing other do we find the origin of our distinctive gospel path—one Benedictine, another

Franciscan, a third Mercy, and a fourth Dominican, Passionist, Teresian in an almost endless variety of gift and power.

So strong, so convincing, so overpowering is the experience of the Spirit that, come what may, despite hardship, contradiction, even calumny and contempt from whatever quarter inside or beyond the church, the founder or foundress must and will obey the Spirit, fulfill destiny until the congregation lives. A new life is begotten in the church.

Wisely, then, did the council direct religious to give a priority to the rediscovery of their origin in the charismal gifting of the Spirit to whom belongs the original inspiration. That same Spirit continues to sustain and enliven the original impulse through the ages by reincarnating it, by enfleshing it afresh, again and again in the aggregation of new members to rejoice in and fully share the original inspiration. But that sharing must not be a dull, static mimicry of the past. It must be a vital life-giving reinterpretation of the profundity of meaning and the immediacy of application of that founding vision, that imperishable dream. The basic task of all religious for our day is reinterpretation.

Research and study of the founding charism has proved to be one of the most fruitful exercises of renewal. Some studies have continued for fifteen years; most are an ongoing process. And this is necessarily so because:

- in the founding charism we find the full meaning of our particular call;
- In the founding charism we rediscover our identity;
- in the charism we touch the bond of unity;
- from the charism we derive our mission;
- from the charism our spiritual physiognomy takes shape, our distinctive spirituality unfolds.

We are faced here with an amazing truth about religious life, with greater repercussions on church and world than we at first realized. Founders and foundresses are women and men of providence. They are handcrafts of the Spirit. They are shaped and formed, made stronger than granite, fresher than an ageless bubbling spring. They have an abiding, warm presence in their communities. In significance and impact among the figures of history they surpass statesmen and scientists, princes and kings, even bishops and popes. Their life goes on with renewed enthusiasm from age to age.

That is why each new member entering an established community in some way experiences something of the profound mystical experience which gave meaning and shape, function and purpose to the group's existence. It is also why no greater gift can be given a community than the re-enfleshment of its life in a new face.

A DYNAMIC, LIFE-GIVING MOVEMENT

Two other realities about religious life have been rediscovered for our day in the study of the founding charism of a community. We will treat them in order.

The first is that religious life by its very nature is a dynamic, vital, pulsating movement. It is not a static, fixed, immobile, once-for-all formulated organization. It does not stand still. It refuses to be boxed. We cannot put it in the deep freeze. That is why there was such a furor over the document—or rather the non-document, since it was unsigned—on the so-called essential elements. There are indeed, necessarily, basic elements that have a perduring value and quality. But these elements themselves are very flexible in mode, in manner, in interpretation. We rightly speak of the primacy of love and openness to the Spirit. But the religious life enterprise, as such, is very flexible, very adaptive, capable of an endless variety of expressions. The Spirit gives life. The Spirit breathes where the Spirit wills. Such is "the" essential.

From the very origin of Christianity this amazing and awesome phenomenon has unendingly manifested itself among every people, in every climate spanning the ages and attracting young and old in a continuing allegiance even until death. And everywhere it has the marks of a vital movement. It is not rigid. It is adapting and accepting. It is inviting and welcoming. It sings and dances. It cries and weeps. Always it is life-giving, life-sharing and life-sustaining. It has been natively, inherently incultural long before those wise theologians of inculturation began to unfold its meaning to us. No element in Christianity—and we dare make so broad and sweeping an assertion—*no element in Christianity* has proved to be as innovative, creative, dynamic, as challenging and attractive as has religious life down through the ages. No problem was too great, no obstacle too foreboding, no situation too complex for some small, courageous group of religious to take hold of and in the light of the gospel and the power of the Spirit work toward a solution or at least cover and care for gaping and unattended wounds.

"YES–FOREVER"—"FOREVER–YES"

The second reality rediscovered about religious life in post-Vatican II theology closely relates to the previous. It rebuts those who may, in their foolishness, have thought religious life was a passing phenomenon of Christianity. The second reality is perpetuity of commitment. It is essential to the religious life movement that certain ones from among the many who are called will vow the fullness of their lives forever. The religious life would have died out long ago if there were not members who would breathe its full meaning with their last breath, yielding *their lives* to the Spirit that anointed them in their mothers' womb.

Again we confront history and theology. Historically the record is clear. In every age despite parental objection, the dissuasion of peers, the entice-ment of fortune and inheritance, the call to society status, mobility and opportunity, women and men have declared themselves unhesitatingly con-vinced and forever committed to this extraordinary and foolish way of life. Our bookshelves are filled with the biographies of outstanding people who forsook all for a career in Christ. Thomas Merton and the newly beatified Simone Weil are a recent vintage. Nor could anyone explain why this was so or what happened, until we look at our theology.

For centuries the theologians have been telling us that the power to say with conviction and commitment, "yes–forever"—"forever–yes," is in itself a particular and specific grace, unmerited and unpredictable, the free gift of the Spirit. By it a first vow member or (for want of a better term, albeit unsatisfactory) a temporary professed member makes the transition to the core community. It is here that the charism is shared with its deepest intent. It is here that the life has its fullest meaning and from here exerts its lasting impact. The success of any congregation depends not upon the enthusiasm of its younger members but upon commitment. Success is in proportion to the commitment and enthusiasm of its core members.

In another place I have written on the "Radicalization of Membership in the Religious Life." Here I wish to refer to its central point. We must modify considerably our understanding of membership. First, we must admit that many, many more are called to the religious life than we assume. We have inhibited many because of a false notion of belonging. Second, we need to allow many, many more to experience religious life even if for a shorter time. Of the many who are called to novitiate and first vows not all will be called to perpetuity of commitment. That is no fault of theirs. But unduly insisting on final profession as the only way to experience religious life, by a treatment, unintentional perhaps, of those in first vows as somehow not truly religious, or not able to understand the religious life movement in the church, we may be limiting both the giftedness of our community to the church and the enrichment of our proper charism.

Encouragement must be given and ready room prepared for the temporary but genuine participation in religious life and the experience of our founding charism. Many more would accept the invitation "Come and see" (Jn 1:39) if the cloud of uncertainty would lift from over their heads and the pressure of final commitment were not constantly thrust before them. However long they stay—one, five, nine years—we and they are enriched. The free gift of the Spirit in a "forever–yes" is not ours either to give or to threaten.

Nonetheless, the "forever" core group is the key. From them there is a twofold movement: inward in an increasing attraction toward the center and outward in an increasing sharing and impact of the gift we have freely received. The levels both of attraction and of sharing are very many and diversified in mode, manner and content but taken altogether they comprise the one great enterprise, the dynamic movement within Christianity which we identify as the religious life, flowing from and returning to that core group of members committed in perpetuity to know nothing among you but Jesus and him crucified.

The Mission Journey:
People Church or Cement Churches?

Loretta Harriman, MM

As you know, each of us has been asked to speak about the present moment in our journey as religious in the Catholic Church, so that we may see more clearly the direction for our journey into the future. As I belong to Maryknoll, it is my task to say something about the present moment in the journey of those religious who traditionally have been called "missioners." The implication here is that we left our homelands and traveled "over the seas" to preach the gospel where it had not yet been preached or where the church was not well established.

Since the 1950s there has been a significant broadening of the understanding of mission and of who is a missioner. We now believe that the church exists for the sake of mission and that for every member of the church, by reason of baptism, "mission is a way of life." We speak of mission instead of missions. The missioner is no longer a member of a corps of specialists within the church. Also, we know that there is no place in our world where the church is not present in some form and that the idea of a "well-established" church is a matter of discussion based on one's theology of church and one's understanding of culture, God, religion. To carry this one step further, we now understand that one need not be a member of the church to be saved! And what is salvation? And so, who are we?

In preparation for our 1990 General Assembly, the members of our congregation in every world section asked the delegates to come up with a "clear statement of our identity as religious and as missioners in this last decade of the twentieth century." And as the delegates tried to do this, they "became aware of the conflicts within our understandings and the manner in which we live out some of our core values.... Tensions within these areas are to be expected and can be both positive and creative. Nevertheless, because conflicts can limit the possibility for new vision and life, we realized anew the importance for us, to name and clarify our points of unity within these values." We have realized that one historical moment in our life as women religious missioners is coming to a close and the future is not so clear.

Like so many others, we are talking of a paradigm shift. If a paradigm is a model or interpretation of a particular reality, we need to consider the elements of that reality which must be there for it to be what it is. The point here is: How much shifting is possible, still allowing the reality to be what it is? In the video *Discovering the Future: Paradigms*, they talk about paradigm shifts in watches, cars and bicycle seats. But a watch is meant to tell time no matter the mechanism used so that it can tell time. So, for us, what are the essentials of religious life and mission which must be preserved in order that we may be true to who we say we are? What are the beliefs, values, way of life which we must hold on to? What is negotiable and what is non-negotiable?

Presently, we are in the process of looking at the contours of successive paradigms of religious life and mission in the history of our church to bring these into dialogue with our own experience, and hopefully we will find the points of unity among ourselves and with our tradition, and from this dialogue we can fashion our vision for the future. We have only just begun this process! As many of the speakers will be talking about religious life per se I will focus more on the concept of mission. I will try to explain a bit how we got where are now, speak about some of the realities we are grappling with now, and then offer some broad theological ideas, the significance of which might help us in shaping the particulars of our future.

Based on my experience, I find myself agreeing with those scholars who hold that the basic contours of mission theology in the Catholic Church up until Vatican II were shaped by the theology of St. Augustine in the fifth century. During the Second Vatican Council, basic elements of this theology were given a new shape. However, I also believe that we are only now becoming aware of the significance of these shifts and their implications for us as missioners.

Since salvation is such a key concept in Christianity, it might be good to start with this—in a generic sort of way. The goal of any religion is the goal of life itself, and this goal is named salvation. The English word "salvation" comes from the Latin *salus*, meaning health, wholeness, well-being. If one receives salvation the implication is that one has moved from a state of sickness, brokenness, incompleteness to a state of health, wholeness and well-being. It is religion which embodies within it what one must do in order to experience/achieve salvation. In every religion, understandings of human health and imperfection and what one must do in order to move from one state to another are very much shaped by a particular historical context—both personal and communal. In Christianity, we believe that salvation is union with God and that the way to salvation is in and through and with Jesus Christ. From this basic foundational belief comes mission, church, religious life. What do we mean by union with God and the role of Jesus Christ in all of this? Answers to these questions have varied over the years, and we are still searching today!

Earlier I said that Catholic mission theology was shaped by the theology of St. Augustine up until Vatican II. So, it might be helpful to say something about the significant aspects of his theology which were still in place when we began mission and which some of us have had to relearn. What I will say is a very simplistic narration, and I understand that these aspects of his theology showed themselves in varying degrees in different parts of our church's history.

Because of his own experience of coming to life, Augustine sincerely believed that membership in the church through the sacrament of baptism was the only way to salvation. A little phrase from Luke's gospel (14:23) became the principle for all missionary activity: "Go out into the roads and lanes and *compel people to come in*, so that my house [church] may be filled." Thus it was the responsibility of the missioner to bring non-Christians to the baptismal font as soon as possible, for their own good. Once baptized, the new Christian became the object of ecclesiastical discipline, and by means of prayer and penitential practices performed within the church he or she would eventually be conformed to the Christian way of life. After death, the person who had endured in doing good would be rewarded with a life of eternal happiness with God in heaven.

As the shape of Europe developed, by the ninth century church and state were united in the Holy Roman Empire, and it was now the responsibility of the Christian emperor to help the growth and development of the church, even using methods of coercion to *compel people to come in* for their own good and for the good of the state. From the sixteenth to the middle of the twentieth century, the right to colonize carried with it the responsibility to evangelize, and to evangelize meant to European-ize. This historical reality affects our mission efforts until today.

Although this mentality dominated missionary thinking for centuries, it was challenged by some prophetic religious. The Benedictine monks whose method of "compelling" was by example and love; living with and working among the peasants of Europe, teaching them by example how to live in community and also how to be better farmers. The writings of Bartolome Las Casas, the Dominican friar who believed that one "compels" by persuasion and not by force, had a great influence on the mission methods of the early missioners in the Philippines, the Dominicans and the Franciscans. Two famous Jesuits, Roberto de Nobili in India and Matteo Ricci in China, believed that one "compelled" by immersing oneself in the culture in a radical way, thus witnessing that Christianity was not intrinsically "foreign." In Maryknoll we have lived with the inspiration of Fathers Vincent Lebbe and Anthony Cotta, both Vincentians, who did battle with Rome so that the

Chinese clergy could be ordained bishops; to be Christian is not to be European. Even though these religious were more creative and gentle in their mission methods, they still believed that membership in the Roman Catholic Church was necessary for salvation.

The word "mission" was first used by Ignatius of Loyola. It implied a magisterial commissioning. The established church, as a legal institution, entrusts its mission task to a corps of specially trained religious who are then commissioned to act in the name of the church and confer salvation on those who accept the tenets of faith and the authority of the bishop of Rome. A mission situation existed where the church and hierarchy had not been constituted. From the sixteenth until the twentieth century, missioners were religious, and the focus of mission was the establishment of the church in a particular geographical location, and from this church the gospel would be preached and people would be brought to membership in the church and, following the practices of the church, would be enabled to achieve salvation. This understanding of mission still applies today as can be seen in the discourse of Cardinal Josef Tomko to the General Assembly of the Pontifical Missionary Societies on May 11, 1992.

I think you can see that in this paradigm of mission, salvation is union with God, in heaven, after life on this earth. God dwells outside of the earth. The way to salvation is to follow the teachings and practices of the church. Although we preached to and baptize people, we save souls. That which was material, physical, earthly was not as important as that which was spiritual and heavenly. Relationship with God was established on a merit system; as one did good, one received grace and vice versa. And one's place in heaven was determined by the good one had done and one's state of grace. And good was determined chiefly by one's faithfulness to the teachings and practices of the church, which in all fairness did include love of neighbor. The church is now the kingdom of God. Soteriology was divorced from Christology and was subordinated to ecclesiology.

A number of things could be said about this paradigm of mission. First, it really could not have been otherwise, given the world view that prevailed in those times. The idea of separation of church and state is an American invention and Rome is still not at ease with it. Second, it could not have been otherwise, as long as we believed that there was no salvation outside formal membership in the Roman Catholic Church, as long as we believed that all other ecclesial communities were in error and error had no right to exist. The full implications of this were brought home to us in the case of Fr. Leonard Feeney. In the 1940s Fr. Feeney preached a literal interpretation of statements made by medieval popes and councils. Next, I believe it is quite true to say that most of the missioners were dedicated, holy people who sincerely believed that what they were doing was for the good of the people they were trying to evangelize. And, a lot of good was done. When I saw the movies *The Mission* and *Black Robe*, I was quite impressed by the dedication of those missioners. I no longer believe many of the tenets of faith which shaped their lives, but I did have to pause and question my own strength of commitment and clarity of purpose.

Those of us who entered missionary congregations in the 1940s and 1950s were not especially aware of all this history. However, we still believed that membership in the church was the surest way to salvation, and we wanted to tell people about it and convince them to join us. We would never have compelled people to join the church as our ancestors did in the seventeenth and eighteenth centuries, but we did use a lot of persuasion, particularly in the form of material goods and professional expertise from the affluent west. Many of us were very much influenced by mission stories and wanted to "go over to Macedonia" to help the poor pagans. It might not be going too far to say that somehow, in our minds, not being Christian and being poor were somehow connected. We can all remember all the nickels we gave to Sambo to save the poor pagan babies! For myself, when I was assigned to teach in our school in Quezon City, I was shocked by the economic wealth of the young women in the school. I had never seen such wealth in all my life and I had serious questions about being a missionary in such a setting. When I was later assigned to a rural community in southeastern Mindanao, I felt like a real missioner! Having grown in experience and wisdom, I have come to understand that the students in Maryknoll College in Quezon City were poorer in many ways than the students I taught in Mindanao.

Another less noble motive for becoming a missioner might have been that in the American Catholic Church at that time, the missioner was the "marine." There was a sense of doing something really great for God! In fact, in our congregation, we had unusually high numbers of women entering during the war years. One of our novice mistresses used to say, "They couldn't go to war, so they entered the convent!" Constrained by the love of Christ for the poor, concerned about their salvation and our own, convinced that we were "going all the way" for God, we set out with a sense of confidence and optimism in the rightness of what we were doing and in the western way of life. We were determined and enthusiastic in our willingness to offer a cure for the ills of these "poor people" through the spread of either knowledge and technology or the gospel.

In the years immediately after World War II, and preceding Vatican II, there was tremendous activity among American missioners: building, establishing, organizing. We were going to "light up the jungle." We had plenty of personnel, and thanks to the generosity of American Catholics, we had material resources. Our works were called pre-evangelization or indirect evangelization. The desired end was that those we helped would be attracted to

Christianity and then we could do real evangelization—teaching religion and baptizing. People were impressed by the dedication and hard work of the outrageous foreigners, and they did become Christians and the church was established. We made great efforts to reflect in every detail of the local church the Roman custom of the moment, even if it was meaningless to the people of the local church. In our parish the pastor took out all the heavy baroque statues, and the people complained that the church was very lonely; their friends were gone. To replace the statues, he commissioned a Maryknoll Sister artist to do a mosaic for the wall of the sanctuary. As the main occupation of the people of the parish was fishing, she created a huge mural depicting a fishnet in which were all kinds of fish—a "modern" image of the church. The mural was proudly shown to any visitor who came to the village as a sign that they were "modern." However, among themselves they called it *sancta kinilaw*, kinilaw being a raw, pickled fish which is eaten while drinking some form of alcohol!

Mission for us was the preaching of the message of Christ as believed in the Roman Catholic Church. The stress was on verbal expressions of the truth, and faith was an intellectual assent to these truths. And we hoped that the wisdom of our lifestyle and technology would convince people of the truth of our religion.

However, the more we did, the more the poor seemed to multiply, and we did not seem to be making much progress in creating a new world. With the liberating atmosphere inspired by Vatican II, we felt free to pursue what we had long suspected to be true. If we were going to make any progress in changing the quality of people's lives, we, the church, had to work for a just society. We were convinced that we had to work to change the structures of society. This was confirmed in 1971, when the Synod of Bishops on Justice declared that "action on behalf of justice and participation in the transformation of the world fully appear to us as a constitutive dimension of the preaching of the gospel." *Evangelii Nuntiandi* confirmed this, saying that evangelization must "deliver a message, especially relevant and important in our age, about liberation." It also spoke of the need to evangelize "human culture and cultures." Now we would no longer focus on charitable services, but we would work with people to awaken in them a consciousness of their dignity and their rights as human beings and help them to understand why they never seemed to enjoy a fully human life. We would work to support them in their efforts to help themselves.

The way to this new social order was through the use of reason and objective scientific knowledge whereby we could come to understand all aspects of our world—physical, social, economic and religious. Then with the power of knowledge which had come through analysis, we were free to make unlimited progress in creating a better world. This belief in progress expressed itself pre-eminently in the development programs so popular in the 1960s and 1970s. The main focus in all these projects was that of the use of western technology, applied to all areas of life, so that the poor of our earth could live more humanly. (We took little notice of the poor earth.) It was as if what was "real" was only now beginning to manifest itself. Optimism was in the air! In the church, our novitiates were full!

The peoples of Latin America, Africa, and Asia organized themselves into small communities and worked together in myriad ways to try to make a better life for themselves and their children. They read the scriptures, they prayed together and they gained strength and confidence in themselves and in their way of life. In this process of working for their own lives, they threatened the life and power of others who enjoyed more of the material goods of this world. They were a threat, and there was opposition which eventually became diabolical and violent. There was much suffering and dying. The missioners walked with the sorrowing and buried their dead, sharing their pain and even their death.

As we became involved in this mission paradigm, we experienced changes in our understanding and practice of religion. Somehow the "old" practices of piety and devotion just were not meaningful or relevant. We were not too comfortable with a form of prayer that relied on God's power when we were trying to encourage "people power." Now we could understand and control many of the powers of nature so we didn't need to pray to a distant-hacienda-God who needed to be kept happy so that he would be beneficent toward us. Of course, this affected the age-old spiritual practices of the people in the local church. We read the scriptures and began to see discrepancies between what we read and what we had been taught to be God's teaching. We no longer "found" God in the liturgy/sacraments. Instead, the power and giftedness of grace were experienced much more strongly in the community when we gathered to pray and reflect and share life in dialogue with the scriptures. More and more our ideas of church were changing. The church was not only the hierarchy, we also were the church. That our church leaders did not support us in our ministries which gave priority to the needs of the poor was something that was very discouraging and painful. We had become religious missioners to be active in working for the mission of the church, and now we were finding ourselves rejected and even denounced by the leaders of our church. It caused many of us to ask what we were about and why we should continue working within the structures of the church. For me, this question was answered when I heard a story related to the pope's visit to Nicaragua in 1981. Shortly before the pope arrived in Nicaragua, a number of men had been arrested and "disappeared." The families asked help from the government, and of course they received no satisfaction. During the pope's mass, the mothers, wives and sisters stood before the pope with a banner and pictures telling of their plight. The pope made no reference to their sorrow at the mass and was disturbed by their silent demonstration. In 1984 I was talking with a sister from Detroit who had been in Nicaragua at the time. She was introduced to an old woman whose husband and sons had "disappeared." The sister asked the woman if she would leave the church because of what the pope had done. The woman looked very puzzled, and so the sister thought she had not understood her *gringo* Spanish. She then repeated the question, "Will you leave the church now?" Again, she got the same puzzled look. Convinced that the problem was her Spanish, the sister asked her companion, a resident of Nicaragua, to ask the woman the question in real Spanish. After the question was asked, the old woman answered, "How can I leave the church? We are the church." Reflect on the wisdom of this and it will give a whole new dimension to one's spirituality.

Now, where are we? We are holding a number of pieces in our hands, looking at them carefully, and hopefully, with prayer, the wisdom of God and the combined experience of all of us, we will move into the future—well. What are we looking at? Our evaluation of our recent past; changes in the world and in our church vis-à-vis the missioner; most importantly, we are looking carefully at the theology of mission.

As we look at our past, we see that it was eminently good. But a return to the past is not the way to the future. We still have a dream of a world where all will enjoy the blessings of peace with justice, but we realize that we must find another way to work for the fulfillment of this dream. We who had placed great faith in the liberating grace of the resurrection have to come to grips with the reality of the crucifixion still at work in our world. Where is the justice of God? Where is the love of God? Why do the good continue to suffer because of the sins of others? What is the sin that continues to crucify the brothers and sisters of Jesus? And what is our position and our strength in the face of this evil?

Development is good, but what kind of development and how to go about it? The application of technology is not merely a technical matter, but it is deeply influenced by the social and religious dispositions behind it. Science and religion are not necessarily inimical yet the two cannot always live together in perfect harmony. Authentic religion imperils the popular world view and comes into conflict with the anti-gods. Authentic Christian faith has always designated as evil whatever destroys life and concerned itself with the victims. Therefore, it is to be expected that we will meet opposition from the perpetrators of injustice.

From where we stand now, we can see that unlimited objectification of people, of nature, of societies has had disastrous consequences on our ecology, our cultures, our people. Progress, instead of liberating us, has enslaved us. Production, material progress, social prestige, intellectual power have become the signs by which we determine humanness. As a society we have lost touch with the deep, life-giving human values. Where they are alive, people are struggling to hold on to them at great effort and at great risk. Is it because human values are no longer desired, or is it because we have become so caught up in the concept of progress that we no longer take time to nurture what is truly human and, therefore, accept easy substitutes? Have we, religious missioners, become so caught up in the modern (enlightenment) world view that we have lost sight of what is truly and essentially Christian/human?

A distinctive characteristic of our world is that people are looking for new meaning in life. We see that interest in religion and spirituality is on the rise. It might be true to say that a lot of this interest has to be judged somewhat negatively as evidence of an inability to cope with the pressures of society or the insecurity of living in a time of significant transition. Still, I do believe that there is more to it than this. Is this not a human response to the intellectual dryness of religion in the last thirty years? Is this not a human response to an undue emphasis on the individual, the material and the factual?

All purposeful and human activity needs to be inspired, nourished and critiqued by purpose. What is the goal of life itself? We seem to know that we need to get in touch with spiritual values, but these have to be known, named and nourished. We are looking more carefully at the reality of contingency and unpredictability and process. We are relooking at our ideas of God, grace, sin, prayer and church. This has brought us in touch with the reality of mystery, wonder, trust and inner freedom in the face of uncertainties and the rough edges of life. We are looking at the role of metaphor, myth, symbol and ritual. There is an upsurge of interest in theology as story. These forms touch the mind and its thoughts, evoke action with a purpose and compel the heart. These are valid ways of expressing the deeper realities of life, but they also require that we become more involved with them. They can no longer exist just on the surface of our lives. They require that we be more quiet, more sensitive, more thoughtful, more insightful, more creative, more present to our reality and the reality of God in our midst.

After Vatican II, we moved out of the mission paradigm which focused on saving souls through membership in the Catholic Church. We moved into the modern or enlightenment/modern mission paradigm where we focused on saving the human life of the person by improving his/her material life by means of knowledge and technology. In the medieval paradigm we looked upon salvation as something which was achieved in the afterlife, in heaven. In the modern paradigm salvation was something to be tasted in this life, here on earth. Does the answer for tomorrow lie somewhere in between these two poles? Is the challenge of tomorrow to be able to hold the both/and in equilibrium?

What are some of the changes that we are experiencing in our own lives as missioners?

Our name has changed and we are still not certain what it is! Previously we were called missionaries. Now every Christian is called to be in mission. In *Evangelii Nuntiandi* and *Redemptoris Missio* we are called missioners *ad gentes*. *Gentes* here refers to the nations/Gentiles. Gentiles has such a negative connotation—nobody wants to be called a Gentile or to call another a Gentile. It is especially unpleasant for those of us who have lived and worked with non-Christians. The Christian stereotype of the Gentile just isn't true. Others are suggesting that we are missioners *ad extra*—meaning that we go beyond or outside of our own culture. Sometimes this is referred to as cross-cultural or trans-cultural. And then we need to ask what exactly constitutes trans-cultural. If I were to return to reach into the high school from which I graduated thirty-five years ago, I would most certainly be in a trans-cultural situation!

Like so many religious, our age is increasing and our numbers are decreasing and the work expectations are increasing. The greater the challenge!

Previously all missioners were religious. Today we work and live with religious from non-missionary congregations (!) and diocesan priests who want to have an experience of church in another culture. Most significantly, many lay people have joined us in cross-cultural mission. We are most heartened, inspired and challenged by their interest and enthusiastic commitment. However, this reality causes us to pause and ask: What distinctive gift do we bring to the church as religious whose specific charism is mission *ad extra?* If mission is a way of life for all Christians, then why be a religious?

If we were drawn to be missioners because of the oppression of poverty and unjust social structures in third world countries, we can find exactly the same situation in the United States. So often we would say, "There is so much work to be done *there*." But, in truth, we know that there is so much work to be done *here*. So, why go *there*?

If we were committed to the establishment of the church in another place, we now know that the church is more truly established in some third world countries than it is in the first world. Those countries which first sent out so many missioners are badly in need of evangelization today. So, why go *there?*

For those of us who work in local churches which are somewhat established as far as structure is concerned, we know we are wanted if we take the back seat! As missioners coming from the sending church, this is very hard, because we think that we have been sent to bring something to the receiving church. We are there to give something which they do not have, or which we believe they do not have. Father Horatio de la Costa, S.J., a Filipino historian, once told us, "Stay with us, but in the background. Help us with your experience and moral support. And when we make mistakes, help us to pick up the pieces and start over again." When I was teaching in a college seminary and was the only American and only woman on the faculty, I tried very hard to be sensitive to this instruction of Fr. de la Costa. One day one of the young Filipino priests on the faculty told me that it was good for me to be there with them. When I asked why, he told me that it was good for them to have old religious around to witness to them that it was possible to be faithful for a lifetime. It was not my reason for being there, but it was okay!

Another aspect of our reality is the anomaly of our mode of mission sending. Theoretically we are sent from one local church to another local church. Yet, for the most part, Catholic missioners, both lay and religious, are sent by religious orders. At this point there is little structural relationship between the local bishop and the missioners from his diocese. A few dioceses and parishes do wish missioners well, encourage them in their work and receive them when they return. However, these are the exception and not the rule. Do we belong to the church? Which church?

Yet, few of us are prepared to give up the mission-ary idea and ideal. We believe that Christianity is by nature mission-ary. We believe that the Christian faith experience is too precious and meaningful to just walk away from it. It is a way of life which has been significantly meaningful for us; we have been enriched beyond our wildest dreams by the mutual evangelization we have experienced as missioners *ad extra*. It is a way of life which enables us to share our own life in God and to be continually amazed at the many ways in which our God is manifested and known in our world.

We know that we no longer go on mission for the primary purpose of establishing the church or saving souls by bringing them into church membership through baptism. We have also learned that we do not go on mission so we can bring the "good life" of the west to the "poor" of the third world. We know that there is no intrinsic relationship between the technological progress of the west and Christianity. But I do believe that we still go on mission to "preach" the good news of the reign of God as preached by Jesus of Nazareth, whom we believe to be the Christ of Yahweh.

If we believe that the goal of any religion is the goal of life itself, or salvation; if we believe that Yahweh is a God who is essentially person-al, relational, *hesed*; if we believe that the purpose of our life is union with God, then it must follow that Yahweh/God wills salvation for all peoples. To say that life with God is possible only within the sacramental system of the Christian church is not even fair, much less loving, when we consider the thousands of peoples who have never even had the chance to accept or reject the gospel, together with all those who could not accept it because of the inadequate way it was communicated.

More than any other theologian of our time, Karl Rahner struggled with the question whether God's salvation is available only through explicit faith in Jesus Christ or whether it is available to all men and women. He has answered with a resounding yes. And his theology of grace has influenced the shape of many church documents. In *Lumen Gentium, Gaudium et Spes, Nostra Aetate* and most recently in *Redemptoris Missio* it is made quite clear to us that there is salvation outside the Catholic Church. The Holy Spirit is present and at work in the hearts of people in ways which we cannot know or predict. We respect non-Catholic and non-Christian religious as true and valid mediators of God's grace.

What is prominent in these writings is that God's Spirit is present and operative both inside and outside the church. God's Spirit—the life of God in God—is grace, the Spirit of God, the life of God, in us: a tremendous mystery! The life of God, the power of God, is love. The power, the perfection, the wisdom, the omnipresence of God is his ability to love *all*—the good and the bad. The perfection of God is found in the power to make the sun and rain available to the good and the bad, the just and the unjust.

The divine power, the power to know, receive and give love, is a gift which God offers to all peoples in which all are free to accept or reject. And we know from experience that love freely given for the good of the other is a universal phenomenon. When another reaches out to us in love, God is offering us the gift of himself, and when we accept this gift of live in freedom, then salvation has taken hold of us through justifying grace. This positive response takes place in the option to accept a demand of our conscience as binding. The request that is made to us is to go beyond ourselves, to reach out to the other for the good of the other, and, in so doing, find our own life. Love of neighbor *is* love of God—offered, accepted, given, received. When we see love in action, there is grace, there is God, because love is the divine power, and it is only in receiving this power that one is able to give it. And the more one receives, the more one gives, and the more one receives and gives, the more we are in relation with God, the source of life and the fulfillment of our life. (The challenge here is to know the distinction between what the "world" calls love and God's love—love which reaches out to the other for my own good as compared to love which reaches out to the other for the good of the other. And then there is the challenge to honestly try to discern what is "the good" in this situation for this person.)

Wherever human history is lived, there the history of salvation or its rejection takes place. Salvation is not something that is received only after physical death; it is something that begins here on earth as we live in relation with each other and thus with God. Salvation does not necessarily have to be mediated by religious words or rites. God is experienced in the heart of human existence in the world, and in our rituals we recall, remember, name and celebrate this mystery, and once again God is present among us in our minds and hearts. And in remembering and celebrating, we renew our commitment to *live* what we have known through experience.

If union with God, salvation, is possible outside the church, what then is the purpose of the church? The church as the community of those committed to discipleship of Jesus Christ takes its purpose from the mission of Jesus, which was the *missio Dei*, i.e. God's plan to make himself known to all peoples as an overflow of love. Jesus and the Father have given their Spirit to the disciples of Jesus, so that they may continue the mission of Jesus. While the Spirit of God is not limited to the disciples of Jesus, it is the mission of this community to witness to the presence and life-giving activity of the Spirit in a definite and deliberate way. The mission of the church is to be at the service of the mission of God: where there is love/Spirit to give testimony to it and, where love is lacking or absent, to enable it/God to be present. As members of the church, made up of many different parts, all working for the good of the whole, we are called to membership for the sake of mission. Baptism is a call to mission; it is a call to a specific task in God's plan for the salvation of the whole earth.

Lumen Gentium says that the church is to be the sacrament/sign of the mystery of God's love. As the church is community and love is relational in a personal way, it is in the way that we live together that we are sign. By our lives together, we are called to be a witness-people, to be a sign of what it means to live the "good life" as a people at peace with one another.

The theological paradigm that Jesus used to speak the message of God's love was the reign of God—a paradigm well-known to his listeners. But it is only in recent times that we have come to understand the fullness of meaning in this paradigm.

The central motif of Jesus' ministry was "the coming of the reign of God" (Mk 1:14-15). Yet at no point in the New Testament are we given a definition of the reign of God. What Jesus meant by this metaphor has been arrived at by comparing its meaning in the Hebrew scriptures with the message and lifestyle of Jesus.

The reign of God motif was thoroughly Jewish, having evolved from Israel's experience of itself as a people and its relationship with Yahweh. At its deepest level, this metaphor referred to the "saving [life-giving] relationship between Yahweh and his people." Once they were only a band of wandering Aramaeans, but Yahweh chose them, made a covenant with them, made of them a people and brought them into a land of their own.

The metaphor, reign of God, is best translated as the kingly rule of Yahweh. According to the biblical ideal, the function of the king was to defend the weak against the strong. Yahweh, therefore, revealed himself as king when he chose Israel to be his special people and defended them from the strong nations of their world. Throughout the Bible, it can be seen that

God has a special preference for the youngest, the small, the weak, the oppressed, because it is with these people that God's power is most clearly seen. And God's power is his unconditional love which frees from personal bondage and societal constraints, which enables one to reach out to the neighbor to do good for the neighbor. The experience of God's love changes hearts and structures and enables a people to live together in peace and harmony, to enjoy the fullness of life. Yahweh entered into a covenant relationship with Israel, not because Israel was so worthy or great, but because Israel was the smallest and most insignificant among the nations of the world.

Israel, for its part, was asked to worship *only* Yahweh. As Yahweh cared for them, they were to care for one another, showing special care for the widow, the orphan and the refugee (Dt 10:17f). They were called to be a community of equals. They were not to lord it over each other as the Gentiles did. They were called to be advocates of mercy and justice in all areas of life. In this way, as a community living in peace and harmony, they would be a witness-people among the nations. The nations would see them and wonder how *such* a people could live together so peacefully. Surely their God must be very powerful and wonderful!

Yahweh entered into a covenant relationship with the *people* of Israel. For the individual Israelite, the greatest evil was to be cut off from the community because, outside of the community, there could be no relationship with Yahweh. Outside of the community, one could not worship Yahweh and be assured of Yahweh's life-giving love. By the time of Jesus, Judaism had become a religion of many sects. The Jews were known to be a factious people and their God was not honored among the gods of their neighbors. Each sect believed that its understanding of the law and the prophets constituted true worship of Yahweh. One who was not a member of our sect was not a true Israelite.

Jesus, inspired by his own relationship with Yahweh, understood that his mission was to restore Israel to its true vocation, to be a witness-people for Yahweh. The reign of God that Jesus preached by word and action is most beautifully described in Isaiah 11. Among this people, the poor shall be judged with righteousness, the meek shall be judged with equity and the wicked shall not have a chance to succeed. Among this people, there shall be no "insiders" and "outsiders"; those who are considered to be social enemies shall live together in harmony.

The God of Jesus, Yahweh/Abba, is generous to a fault in his compassion, in his forgiveness. This experience of God as overwhelmingly compassionate calls for a response on the part of those who experience it. The gospels present Jesus as provocatively associating with those members of Jewish society considered to be outside the law and therefore excluded from participation in the religious and social community of Israel. Jesus shared table fellowship with outcast public sinners and with acknowledged religious leaders, showed sympathy for the defenseless, sided against the exploiters, had an open attitude toward Samaritans, women and the foreigner. Jesus seemed to be able to detect goodness in those people his society presumed to be beyond salvation.

These provocative associations of Jesus are not incidental to his mission. The extension of compassion, loyalty and friendship across well-defined boundaries of exclusion was a parable in action. The compelling mercy of the God of Jesus overcomes all forms of alienation, and because this is happening, "the reign of God is in your midst" (Lk 17:20-21). Jesus had experienced and then made the heart of his mission a renewed appreciation of the free and gracious nature of the God of Israel. This God could not be controlled or limited by any boundaries constructed by society or religion. This prophetic insight of Jesus becomes a crucial link to the ultimately universal mission of the church.

The disciples of Jesus believed that Jesus was anointed and commissioned by God to re-establish a righteous *people* of God, within which levels of status would be overcome and the humble and poor would be fully integrated into the life of the community. Within this community, the reign of God would grow gradually as people slowly learned to love, to forgive and to serve one another.

The early Christian communities took the teachings of Jesus seriously and lived in communities which were revolutionary because of the new relationships that came into being in the community. Jews and Romans, Greeks and barbarians, free and slave, rich and poor, men and women—all lived together as equals. This was a sociological impossibility.

The early Christian communities were noted for their practice of love and service to all. There is evidence of a remarkable picture of early Christian involvement with the poor, orphans, widows, the sick, mine workers, prisoners, slaves and travelers. The action of love and hospitality was a social gospel, practiced not as a way to lure people into the church, but simply as a natural expression of their own faith in Jesus Christ. Christians did not attempt to usher in a utopia. They were called to erect signs of God's incipient reign, not to try to destroy all the evil in the world. They ministered in weakness, under a shadow of suspicion and scorn, and they were persecuted. They witnessed from a position of weakness. Yet, in the final analysis, it was the exemplary lives of ordinary Christians which impressed the peoples of the Roman empire. What kind of a God is their God, that they are able to be so caring of each other and of the outsider?

Each time I think of this historical data, I am reminded of the story told by Fr. Bob McCahill, M.M., who lives as a "holy man" in a village in Bangladesh. For his "ministry" he cares for their sick. One day a Moslem man asked him why he did this for them. "You are not one of us."

And now we come to the most challenging part! How does all of this relate to us as religious missioners today and in the near future?

We know that we cannot describe our future journey as well as we describe where we have come from. Yet I do believe that we do have a good map to guide us into the future. Certain fundamental Christian truths and characteristics of religious life in all faith communities will tell us why we go, how we go and what we do along the way. Of course, the basic belief underlying all of this is our desire to be about God's work.

We believe that the church is a community of believers called into being for the purpose of participating in and continuing the mission of Jesus Christ, namely, to preach the reign of God, in the power of the Spirit of Jesus, with all of our life. The peaceable kingdom in Isaiah 11:6-9 and the wedding banquet in Luke 14 are especially good images of the reign of God for us. The reign of God is a time in history in which all peoples will live together in peace and harmony because all will have accepted God's self-offer, made real in the love offered, accepted, given, received within the community. The reign of God is for all peoples; it is universal, inclusive and collegial. It cannot be controlled or limited by any boundaries constructed by society or religion. The church, called into being to be in mission to the reign of God, is thereby called to be universal, inclusive and collegial in all aspects of its life. And all members of the church, by reason of baptism, are called to be in mission to the reign of God in some way consistent with their personal and historical reality. For every Christian, "mission is to be a way of life."

What does this say to us today when we experience economic, cultural, religious, racial, ethnic and gender boundaries which create exclusive and/or hierarchical groups which reinforce the "us *versus* them" mentality? We know that these boundaries and exclusive groups exist within our church and within every nation and/or cultural group on our earth. And we know the "sin of power" that is committed in the name of preserving our exclusivity. We all have a very hard time realizing that differences do exist on a horizontal line and not on a vertical plane. And yet we hold that the church is to be a sacrament/sign of the mystery of God's universal and salvific love. As the church is essentially a community of believers/disciples and love is essentially relational in a personal way, it is in the way that we live together and in the way that we reach out to include the "outsider" in our circle of love that we are a witness-people who give glory and honor to our God by our lives.

Religion is a social-institutional expression of a people's response to the presence and action of God in their midst. Within religions, there usually exist a small group of people called "religious" who are involved in the religion in a more organized and visible way. They exist *within* a faith community and *for* a faith community as a sacrament/sign which embodies for the larger group its relationship with the divine and the values which the faith community holds sacred. Therefore, they take their meaning from the faith community, exist to be in service to the community and have no meaning apart from the faith community.

There groups live within a liminal space in the communities, witnessing to the faith of the community in a prophetic way. They serve as a mirror in which the larger community can see more clearly the values it cherishes and, as such, challenge, critique, inspire the larger community and are themselves strengthened, inspired and challenged by the faith community they serve. While religious do not have the monopoly on the prophetic ministry, they are meant to be the primary bearers of this vocation within the faith community.

The church is called to be the sacrament of God's love—a love which is universal, inclusive and collegial. Yet we know that there are countless places among countless peoples where people are excluded from the banquet table because of religious and/or social boundaries, where the lamb still lives in fear of the lion. The mission of the church to preach the universal, inclusive character of the reign of God is still valid and urgent, and every Christian is challenged to be faithful to their baptismal vocation: to be a sign of God's incipient reign in their own world. But in order to be a sacrament/sign, the church must be credible, must be seen to be living the truth of what it preaches.

Based on what we know of our world and of our church, I believe we will all agree that there is still a valid mission for religious within our church—to be signs for the church, calling the church to be faithful to its mission. But we also must be credible signs.

As religious, we are called to be signs for the church, calling the church to be faithful to its original mission. Yet, as signs, we must be seen and our message must be understandable. The institutional expressions of our church and religious are meant to be complementary, to exist in tension with each other and not to be absorbed within each other. Yet, in some instances, we have become so involved in the activities of the institutional church that we have lost our prophetic voice. In other instances, we have become so much a part of the values of secular society or have moved so far to the edge of society that we have no visibility and/or relevance. In such situations, religious no longer serve the purpose for which they exist, and other groups come forth, fulfilling society's need for liminal and prophetic groups in its midst, but who do not necessarily witness to the values of the reign of God.

Because we exist in the church as signs for the church, I do not believe that we need to have as many religious as we had in the 1950s. I believe that today we are challenged to become *quality* signs. As the church is called to be salt, light on a mountain, yeast, we are called to be "small but terrible!" By our living, we will call and empower others to live. If we get too involved in the numbers game, maybe we have absorbed the values of the "world"—quantity vs. quality!

I would like to offer that religious who are missioners *ad extra* are called to live in such a way as to call the Christian community, in every culture, to be faithful to its vocation to be inclusive, universal and collegial. We must reach out and cross the boundaries and limitations established by society and/or religion. There is no boundary which allows me to withhold love from the "other," no boundary which allows me to ignore the "other," no boundary which allows me to take advantage of the "other" or to abuse the "other." There is no boundary which prevents me from sitting at table with you. And when we sit at table together, we will learn not to fear each other; we will learn how much we have in common; we will come to appreciate the beauty of our differences. As I am strengthened by what we share in common and enriched by your difference, so will you be strengthened and enriched. Try it and see!

As we go beyond boundaries, we come to know God and to experience the myriad expressions of God's love—more numerous or varied than we could ever have imagined had we stayed in our own place. My own experiences of being church in Boston in the time of Cardinal Cushing were wonderful—energizing, life-giving, and even triumphant! And it was this experience of church that I was going to bring to the Philippines! Yet they had church long before we had it in Boston, and I learned a way of being church that I could never have known in Boston, and I am the richer for my life with people in the Philippines. My experiences with the parochial school system in Boston were A+. School was fun and stimulating, and we learned well. It was this wonderful experience that I tried to bring to a situation which had unpleasant experiences of "religious schools." The alumni tell me that their high school years were good!

In the early days of our church, Christians were concerned with the idea of *communio*. They were concerned that members of a local church be in unity with each other and with their bishop and they were concerned that each local church be in unity with other local churches. And they had a number of ways of expressing this unity with each other; besides hospitality given to all, they would often send the consecrated bread from the eucharist to another community. In this sharing they enriched, strengthened and challenged each other. I believe that missioners *ad extra* are in a position to do the same thing in our church today. We can foster unity present in so many seemingly diverse ways.

Because of our unique position as members of two local churches, I believe we are in a very good position to serve as bridges between the two communities. If we have entered into a new culture and formed friends there, we know and are known; this people has become my people. Then people from the original community can come and be with us and we can be the ones who introduce one to the other. We can enable members of one community to experience life and God in another community; we can help both to appreciate the differences and also to see beyond the differences to the common humanity we share. When people look into each other's eyes, they cannot fight! If we take on this mind set, I believe that many of us will change our project-oriented concept of mission and will focus on living gentle, humble lives among people in witness to God's love present among us. This is not to say that we will not have a specific ministry where we live, but the "why" of the ministry will change.

We are called to become ever more deeply steeped in the mystery of the reign of God so that we may see that the Spirit of God has been given to Cornelius (Acts 10:46) and this we must announce to the community in Jerusalem, thereby enabling them to cross the boundaries they have established between themselves and the "Gentiles"—so that they also may know the manifest ways in which God is known and worshiped. We must help Jerusalem to become universal, inclusive and collegial, as it was intended to be from the start.

This requires that we enter into an ever closer relationship with God, so we may be open to know God present in a myriad of different ways. We need to slow down, become quiet, sensitive and perceptive so that we may see beyond external differences to the beauty of the person in front of us. We need to be free to enter into relationships with the "other." Building a cement church is so much easier than building a "people church." We need to be so peaceful and free that the lambs will not be afraid of us and will be willing to invite us to join them at their banquet table.

Mission that goes to bring something and is not sensitive to the mystery of God already present among peoples of many cultures is oppressive. We will find ourselves limiting the goodness of God and setting up our own images (idols) of God. More serious, we will not be aware that God was there before our arrival and we are the losers! Shoes off! This is holy ground!

Sources

Bosch, David J. *Transforming Mission: Paradigm Shifts in Theology of Mission*: Maryknoll: Orbis Books, 1991.

O'Murchu, Diarmuid, MSC. *Religious Life: A Prophetic Vision*. Notre Dame: Ave Maria Press, 1991.

Senior, Donald and Carroll Stuhlmueller. *The Biblical Foundations for Mission*. Maryknoll: Orbis Books, 1983.

Sullivan, Francis A. *Salvation Outside the Church?* Mahwah: Paulist Press, 1992.

Editor's Postscript: Ten Statements

My own reflections upon reading these excellent papers were contained in a series of jottings all over the place. Upon rereading, I saw how they may be formulated into a succinct summary of my conclusions. None of the contributors has reviewed them. Therefore, I take full responsibility for whatever inaccuracy or ineptness they may contain. Any good they may proffer is due to the fine work of the scholars who made this work possible.

Statement One:

Religious life is a unique phenomenon in human history. It belongs to all peoples. It belongs to all times. It is at home and sought after in every culture and clime. When you touch religious life you are at the center of the mystery of human life in the unfolding mystery, the continuing revelation of God. For in its essence religious life is a seeing through and seeing beyond appearances, to glimpse and to share life's deepest values and life's fullest meaning. Every age has searched for and found such visionaries of the absolute.

Statement Two:

The coming of Christ gives definitive expression and an absolute fullness of meaning to religious life which existed thousands of years before his coming. The Christian religious life is distinct from all other forms (which continue to exist) inasmuch as the source and center of Christian religious life is Jesus himself: the incarnate Lord. This total fascination with Jesus in a profound and dramatic act of faith gives substance to religious life in the church and is at the same time its sustenance. The foundation of Christian religious life is the full self-revelation of God in Jesus.

Statement Three:

By its very nature religious life, in the Christian dispensation, demands a certain wild abandon—a flying in the face of what to the generalate of people is accepted as normal, natural and expected human behavior. The religious life will pluck out the eye and cut off the arm in a radical and immovable opposition to naked evil, to any deed or act that denies the primacy of God. Therefore, there is a certain exclusivity to religious life. It forbids lukewarmness and insipid mediocrity in favor of the clear and radical yeah and nay of gospel imperatives. While not above or better than the multiple expressions of the gospel way, it is distinct—it claims its own uniqueness.

208

Statement Four:

The church did not create religious life. Religious life is not a tool of the church. It may not be manipulated or autocratically controlled or directed. The church cannot suppress religious life. Canonicity has a very limited function but a very positive function to foster, preserve and develop religious life. As the council so firmly and straightforwardly declared, "Religious life is a gift that the Church lovingly receives from its Lord and Master" (*Lumen Gentium*, Ch. VI).

Statement Five:

Perpetuity of commitment is required for religious life no matter where it is found. By its very nature as a constant pursuit of the ultimate in life, the continuous search for the fullness of life's meaning and purpose, it may never be a passing phenomenon, a turning on and turning off, a temporary excitement.

For Christian religious life there is a further and stronger testimony to the necessity of perpetuity of commitment: it has to do with the urgency for authentic, eschatological witnessing to the truth that Jesus is Lord. True to his gospel promises he will return again in the time appointed to put a definitive end to this world and inaugurate the unending, eternal and perpetual reign of God. Religious life breathes and celebrates that end-time even now.

Statement Six:

Within the Christian experience and hence within the church in the fullness of its Catholic expression, no element has proved to be as daring, as courageous, as innovative, creative and prophetic, yes, and even as abrasive and troublesome as has the religious life through its amazing two thousand year history.

Statement Seven:

Consequent upon this amazing testimony of its historical evolution is the concomitant truth that religious life has been a primary agent of change in the church. All the major transitions in the church over the centuries have been either preceded by a major transition in religious life or the immediate accompaniment of that transition.

Statement Eight:

Religious life refuses boundaries. It defies strict definition or the naming of fixed essential elements. It will not accept determined limits. You cannot nail it down. It is not static. It is a dynamic, life-giving and life-sustaining movement. Nothing has been as harmful to religious life as has been the post-reformation effort to reduce it to a manageable, pre-determined form and expression in which uniformity in expression and conformity to norm became the hallmark of the "good, humble and ever obedient" religious, head bowed and hidden hands folded.

Statement Nine:

No one form, no particular expression, no fixed manner can ever express adequately the fullness of meaning of the religious life. There will always be as many expressions and forms of religious life as there are diverse peoples and cultures and needs. The effort to categorize religious life into five or six major expressions which may have some validity for educative purposes is but witness to its transformatory nature and a scholastic attempt to better manage and describe the truly complex, free-flowing phenomenon the religious life movement really is—from apostolic, to desert, to classical monastic, to mendicant, to regular, to congregational, to modern and to post-modern.

Statement Ten:

At the moment as we come to the end of the second millennium we are witnessing the death not of religious life but rather of religious life as we have come to know it: the persistence of a medieval tradition that was found to be the most effective response to the destruction of Christendom at the beginning of the modern age and the revolution against papacy and hierarchy we have falsely named "the Protestant reformation." This form of religious life was fatally flawed from its beginning and was destined to expire. It was born out of the fear and violence, the agony and treachery, the havoc and bloodshed of those turbulent times. But all that has changed.

Contributors

Sister Sandra M. Schneiders, IHM, a member of Sister Servants of the Immaculate Heart of Mary, received the S.T.D. from the Gregorian University in Rome in 1975. She is Professor of New Testament and Spirituality at the Jesuit School of Theology and Graduate Theological Union in Berkeley, California. She is the author of *New Wineskins* and *Women and the Word,* as well as numerous articles in such journals as *Catholic Biblical Quarterly, Theological Studies, Horizons, The Way,* and *Spirituality Today.* She lectures widely in the United States and abroad. Her latest work, *Beyond Patching,* is clearly the best statement to date on the role of women in the church and the need for an immediate and daring response.

Sister Barbara Fiand, SND de N, is in great demand as a lecturer and consultant for religious communities. She is an associate professor of philosophical theology at the Athenaeum of Ohio. Her recent works have attracted wide attention and have won great commendation and approval: *Releasement: Spirituality for Ministry* and *Living the Vision: Religious Vows in an Age of Change.*

Father Benjamin Tonna STD, Ph.D., is a diocesan priest of Malta. From the time of the council he has worked to advance the teachings of the council throughout the church. For thirteen years he directed SEDOS, the International Research and Documentation Center for Mission-sending Institutes of Religious. He is a long-time associate of Brian Hall and with him developed the well-known Tonna-Hall Indicator of Values. He has lectured widely in Europe and the United States. His major area of concentrating has been in spiritual discernment. Together with Fr. Cassian J. Yuhaus he is preparing a new publication on the meaning, value and use of spiritual discernment for the church of our day. He has recently established a new research center in Malta at the service of the entire church to enable dioceses, parishes and communities of religious to engage more fully in discernment as the normative mode of decision-making in a faith community.

Sister Joan Chittister, OSB, Ph.D., was the Prioress of the Benedictine Sisters of Erie, Pennsylvania. She was President of the Conference of American Benedictine Prioresses, a U.S. delegate to the International Union of Superiors General (in Rome) and a past President of the Leadership

Conference of Women Religious. She served as Chairperson of the LCWR National Taskforce on Peacemaking and directed a research project on Contemporary Christianity for the Institute of Ecumenical and Cultural Research at St. John's, Collegeville, Minnesota. She holds a Doctorate in Social Psychology from Penn State University. She is author of *Climb Along the Cutting Edge: An Analysis of Change in Religious Life* (Paulist), *Women, Ministry and Church* (Paulist), and *Winds of Change* (Sheed and Ward) as well as other books and articles about religious life and contemporary issues. She is very active in Pax Christi USA. Her work concentrates on religious life, peace and justice, and Christian feminism.

Sister Margaret Brennan, IHM, is former President of the Leadership Conference for Women Religious. Sr. Margaret quickly became an acknowledged leader of renewal immediately following Vatican II. She filled the office of Superior General for twelve years. She is a highly respected theologian and taught for a number of years as professor of pastoral theology and director of continuing education at St. Michael's School of Theology at the University of Toronto. Sr. Margaret has given special attention to the problems of ministry in religious life today.

Father Austin Smith, CP, Ph.D, is a professor, lecturer, and the author of numerous articles and books including *Passion for the Inner City, Journeying with God,* and *Paradigms of Power and Powerlessness.* Fr. Smith, a pioneer in inner city ministry, lives in a one room flat in the lowest slum area of Liverpool, England. In solidarity with the poor he has effectively addressed the major issues of our day.

Sister Marie Augusta Neal, SND de N, Ph.D, Professor of Sociology for Research and Teaching at Emmanuel College, is in constant demand as lecturer, consultant and facilitator. No one inside or outside the church has studied North American religious life as thoroughly and competently as Sr. Neal. She was also a member of the sub-committee of the bishops' committee for the study of religious life in the United States. Her numerous articles and books include *The Just Demands of the Poor, Values and Interest in Social Change, Catholic Sisters in Transition from the 1960s to the 1980s,* and *From Nuns to Sisters.*

Father John Manuel Lozano, CMF, a Claretian, has written extensively on the renewal of religious life from the close of the council until our own day. His research and writings have given special attention to charism, community, founders and foundresses, the vows, discipleship and the historical evolution of religious life. He has been a consultant to a large number of institutes throughout the world. He is a founder of the *Claret Center for Resources in Spirituality* with centers in Chicago, Los Angeles and Manila. He also was a central figure in establishing the advanced studies program on religious life at the Claretian Institute in Rome.

Fr. Thomas Berry, CP, author, teacher, geologian, is one of the most acclaimed and renowned scholars of our day. Founder of the Riverdale Religious Research Center, he is known throughout the world for his understanding and promotion of the new cosmology: a theology of the sacred earth, an exploration of the global brain. He has done outstanding research into patriarchy and hierarchy—the two dominant-support theories of the defunct Paradigm I. Among his voluminous writings are *The Riverdale Papers,* a collection of volumes of published and unpublished essays; *The Dream of the Earth,* a Sierra Club publication; and more recently with Thomas Clarke, SJ, *Befriending the Earth,* a theology of reconciliation between humans and the earth.

The Reverend Cassian J. Yuhaus, CP, HED, former President of CARA (Center for Applied Research in the Apostolate) of Washington, DC, has been engaged with religious communities in the process of renewal since the close of Vatican II. Previous to his position as President, Father Cassian coordinated the Religious Life Program at CARA. While there, his efforts were constantly directed toward expanding the research services CARA renders to the church. He was Co-Founder and Executive Director of the Institute for World Concerns at Duquesne University, an institute sponsored by the Congregation of the Holy Spirit to explore the survival issues of our day. Father Cassian is also the founder and director of the International Institute for Religious now in its twenty-fifth year.

Sister Loretta Harriman, MM, is from the Boston archdiocese. Most of her missionary career has been spent in the Davao area of Mindanao in the Philippines in two almost equal assignments of eleven years. In between these assignments she attained her Master's in theology, majoring in Systematic Theology at Boston College. She taught at the Major Seminary and at the Ateneo de Davao. Sr. Loretta developed a graduate studies program in theology for religious, clergy and laity. She also participated in formation programs. Currently Sister Loretta is secretary to the President of Maryknoll, sister Claudette Laverdiere, and a member of the Renewal Program Team for Maryknoll.